Male Suicide and Masculinity in 19th-century Britain

History of Crime, Deviance and Punishment

Academic interest in the history of crime and punishment has never been greater and the *History of Crime, Deviance and Punishment* series provides a home for the wealth of new research being produced. Individual volumes within the series cover topics related to the history of crime and punishment, from the later medieval to modern period and in both Europe and North America, and seek to demonstrate the importance of this subject in furthering understanding of the way in which various societies and cultures operate. When taken together, the works in the series will show the evolution of the nature of illegality and attitudes towards its perpetration over time and will offer their readers a rounded and coherent history of crime and punishment through the centuries. The series' broad chronological and geographical coverage encourages comparative historical analysis of crime history between countries and cultures.

Published:

Policing the Factory, Barry Godfrey
Crime and Poverty in 19th-Century England, Adrian Ager
Print Culture, Crime and Justice in Eighteenth-Century London, Richard Ward
Rehabilitation and Probation in England and Wales, 1900–1950, Raymond Gard
The Policing of Belfast 1870–1914, Mark Radford
Crime, Regulation and Control during the Blitz, Peter Adey, David J. Cox and Barry Godfrey
A History of Private Policing in the United States, Wilbur Miller
Italian Prisons in the Age of Positivism, 1861–1914, Mary Gibson
Life Courses of Young Convicts Transported to Van Diemen's Land, Emma D. Watkins
Photographing Crime Scenes in Twentieth-Century London, Alexa Neale
Combating London's Criminal Class, Matthew Bach
Probation and the Policing of the Private Sphere in Britain, 1907–1962, Louise Settle

Forthcoming:

The Forefathers of Terrorism, Johannes Dillinger
Feminist Campaigns against Child Sexual Abuse, Daniel Grey
Deviance, Disorder and Music in Modern Britain and America, Cliff Williamson
Prison and Workhouse Reform in 19th-Century England, Lewis Darwen and David Orr
Crime and Criminal Justice in Early Modern Ireland, Coleman A. Dennehy
Motor Bandits in Interwar England, Alyson Brown
Prosecuting London's Fraudsters 1760–1820, Cerian Griffiths
Sex and Violence in 1920s Scotland, Louise Heren
Mothers, Criminal Insanity and the Asylum in Victorian England, Alison Pedley

Male Suicide and Masculinity in 19th-century Britain

Stories of Self-Destruction

Lyndsay Galpin

BLOOMSBURY ACADEMIC
LONDON • NEW YORK • OXFORD • NEW DELHI • SYDNEY

BLOOMSBURY ACADEMIC
Bloomsbury Publishing Plc
50 Bedford Square, London, WC1B 3DP, UK
1385 Broadway, New York, NY 10018, USA
29 Earlsfort Terrace, Dublin 2, Ireland

BLOOMSBURY, BLOOMSBURY ACADEMIC and the Diana logo are
trademarks of Bloomsbury Publishing Plc

First published in Great Britain 2022

Cover image: Shocking suicide at the Crystal Palace, Illustrated Police News 25 May 1867
© British Library Board (shelfmark: NEWS2824)

A catalogue record for this book is available from the British Library.

Library of Congress Cataloging-in-Publication Data
Names: Galpin, Lyndsay, author.
Title: Male suicide and masculinity in 19th-century Britain : stories of
self-destruction / Lyndsay Galpin.
Description: 1 Edition. | New York, NY : Bloomsbury Academic, 2022. |
Series: History of crime, deviance and punishment |
Includes bibliographical references and index.
Identifiers: LCCN 2021054349 (print) | LCCN 2021054350 (ebook) |
ISBN 9781350264892 (hardback) | ISBN 9781350264922 (paperback) |
ISBN 9781350264908 (pdf) | ISBN 9781350264915 (epub)
Subjects: LCSH: Suicide–Great Britain–History–19th century. |
Men–Great Britain–Psychology. | Masculinity–Great Britain–History–19th century.
Classification: LCC HV6548.G7 G35 2022 (print) | LCC HV6548.G7 (ebook) |
DDC 362.280941–dc23/eng/20211217
LC record available at https://lccn.loc.gov/2021054349
LC ebook record available at https://lccn.loc.gov/2021054350

ISBN: HB: 978-1-3502-6489-2
         ePDF: 978-1-3502-6490-8
         eBook: 978-1-3502-6491-5

Series: History of Crime, Deviance and Punishment

Typeset by Integra Software Services Pvt. Ltd.

To find out more about our authors and books visit www.bloomsbury.com
and sign up for our newsletters.

Contents

Acknowledgements

I owe a debt of gratitude to many people who have helped me on the road to this publication. I am deeply grateful to Alex Windscheffel and Ruth Livesey, who supervised this project when it was a PhD thesis. Their honest advice, guidance and ideas have been invaluable to this work. In addition, thanks must be given to Stella Moss and Jane Hamlett for the encouragement they gave when the idea for this research first came to me, and for the feedback they have provided along the way.

I am indebted also to the Friendly Hand, who funded the PhD and allowed me to develop this research beyond just an idea. Without this financial aid, this project would not have been possible.

Completing this work would have been considerably harder without the support of friends and colleagues. Thanks to the members of the Royal Holloway Postgraduate History Seminar, particularly Michaela Jones and Benjamin Bland, who have become close friends and provided an invaluable network of support. A special thanks to Lara Thorpe who has continually been there for me through the anxieties and triumphs of this work in all its forms, especially in the final few months. Joe Salisbury also deserves a special mention, for the endless moral support he has given even when he just wanted to sleep, and for pretending to listen to me talk about dead men for the last six years. In more recent years, I have also been deeply grateful to the support of Julia Biggane, who has gone above and beyond in her support of this project, and whose unwavering belief in me has helped keep me going.

Last, but by no means least, thanks go to Mum and Dad who have never placed limits on what I thought I could achieve.

Introduction

Over the last decade, increasing attention has been drawn to the male suicide rate. In 2013, suicides amongst men hit their highest in just over a decade, and in 2020 they hit their highest in thirty years. Whilst the most recent statistical bulletin from the Office of National Statistics for 2020 indicates that male suicides are once again decreasing, men are still three times more likely to die by their own hand than women.[1] This trend has sparked a public discussion on the state of modern masculinity. The discourse around male suicide has blamed a rigid model of masculinity, which has put pressure on men to perform, succeed and remain emotionally reticent, for damaging men's mental health and pushing them to the very edge. Many feel that this emphasis on male success and strength has left little space for men to open up about personal and emotional struggles for fear of being branded as weak, and campaigns such as the Campaign Against Living Miserably (CALM) have attempted to 'challenge male stereotypes and encourage positive behavioural change and help-seeking behaviour'.[2]

Whilst this recent rise in male suicide rates has caused alarm today, such high rates are nothing new. Kyla Thomas and David Gunnell's time-series analysis of suicide statistics in England and Wales from 1861–2007 shows that, with the exception of a closing gap between approximately 1930 and 1970, the male suicide rate has consistently been significantly higher than that of women. It also reveals that, whilst the twentieth century saw a dramatic drop in male suicide rates overall (with the exception of peaks during the Great Depression, the 1950s and 1980s), the current male suicide rate is not far below that of the nineteenth century.[3] Then, as now, men killed themselves three to four times more frequently than women. Given this relatively persistent trend, it begs the question of whether what has been branded a 'crisis' of masculinity today can be called a crisis at all. Historians of masculinity have been making this point for some time. John Tosh and Michael Roper have suggested that the concept of the 'crisis of masculinity' was born out of the historicization of masculinity in the 1980s, and argue that masculinity has always been 'tenuous' because it is bound up 'with negotiations about power'.[4] Opening his monograph dedicated to 'anxious masculinity', Mark Breitenberg argues along the same lines, that the assumptions of patriarchal culture create an inherent anxiety around masculinity.[5] Michèle Cohen has similarly argued that historians should ask how anxieties of masculinity were 'articulated at any particular historical moment', rather than what caused these anxieties in the first place.[6]

The nineteenth century provides fertile ground for a discussion of male suicide and masculinity. It was a formative period in the history of both issues. Suicide occupied a prominent place in what Ian Hacking has described as the 'massive enumerations of the 1820s and 1830s' across Europe, which brought the regularity of suicide (amongst other behaviours and social patterns) into sharp relief – particularly in the second half of the century for Britain, when suicide statistics were published with regularity.[7] With these 'massive enumerations', and the proliferation of newspapers, whose pages were littered with reports of suicide, suicide was more visible than ever. This new visibility brought increasing alarm at the rising suicide rates across the century and heightened discourse around the causes of suicide. By the end of the century, Europe saw numerous works dealing solely with the issue of suicide, and the 'massive enumerations' became the basis of two key texts: Henry Morselli's *Suicide: A Study in Comparative Moral Statistics* (1882) and Emile Durkheim's *Suicide: A Study in Sociology* (1897), arguably the defining text in suicidology. But I am not concerned with statistics here. Instead, this work looks at the narratives that surrounded male suicide (and to some extent still do) and what they can reveal about expectations of masculinity during the long nineteenth century. These narratives are found not only in novels, but in the evidence given by witnesses at coroners' inquests as friends, relatives, acquaintances and medical professionals attempted to assign motives to, provide explanations for and understand suicidal actions. Narratives were also constructed in medical writings on suicide, in attempting to identify causes of suicide, and in newspaper reports in choosing what information to report from inquests.

Whilst many blame twenty-first-century masculinity for the current perceived crisis of male suicides, it was arguably during the nineteenth century that this model of masculinity took shape. Cohen has highlighted how the concept of the stiff upper lip that has come to define British, and particularly English, masculinity was born out of English efforts to distance themselves from the French. The refined manners, politeness and the ability to engage in polite conversation that had characterized eighteenth-century masculinity gave way to taciturnity, and what was perceived as a more natural, rugged and manly character.[8] As the century progressed, this evolved into a masculinity typified by the Evangelical stoicism, morality and self-restraint of the mid-nineteenth century, that historians such as John Tosh and James Eli Adams have discussed.[9] This was a masculinity typically defined as being particularly middle class, rejecting the leisure of the upper classes in favour of a punishing work ethic that came to define Victorian masculine morality.[10] Eventually, this gave way to the Christian manliness – or muscular Christianity – of Charles Kingsley and Thomas Arnold, which has been labelled as a reaction to the perceived effeminacy of the Oxford movement and Tractarianism of John Henry Newman and Edward Pusey.[11] By the end of the century, this masculinity was characterized by a new imperialism that valued bravado and presented more externalized shows of strength, competition and honour, as detailed by Bradley Deane.[12] But this trajectory, focused as it is on what R. W. Connell describes as hegemonic masculinity, obscures the picture. These shifts in ideals have, perhaps, been overstated, and while I find some evidence that supports these changes, they often co-existed.

This hegemonic masculinity, Connell points out, is usually a fantasy; one which is largely inaccessible to most and is therefore not representative of masculine experience for the majority of men. Since Connell coined the term hegemonic masculinity in 1987, scholars across disciplines have made efforts to challenge the idea of this dominant, hegemonic ideal of masculinity and began to consider other 'types' of masculine experience. Works by historians such as John Tosh, Linda Dowling and James Eli Adams, on the multiplicity of masculinities throughout Victorian Britain, highlight the 'contradiction within Victorian patriarchy' in that the same system which 'underwrote male dominance' also questioned the manliness of other men, such as writers and intellectual workers.[13] This is what Connell describes, in the ground-breaking *Masculinities* (1995), as the gender politics that is at work as much *within* masculinity as between masculinity and femininity.[14] It is this understanding of masculinity that underpins my work here. The narratives of male suicide discussed throughout this work show that masculinity was multifaceted. Although the commentary provided by inquest witnesses and the press demonstrate that hegemonic ideals were powerful, they also show that men who were unable to meet the standards of these ideals were not simply feminized for their failure to measure up.

What histories of masculinity have illustrated is the complex nature of gender, highlighting the problems of talking about 'hegemonic' ideals, when even these ideals ebb and flow with the pace of history. The idea of a single hegemonic masculinity, whether achievable or simply an ideal standard, is misleading. Society's ideals are never fixed but are fluid, changing over time and adapting to the developments in the cultures within which they are embodied. One of the most marked changes in the history of masculinity across the nineteenth century was the shift from 'gentry masculinity' to industrial or urban masculinity,[15] in which middle-class men had to negotiate their position between the physically focused, rough, working-class masculinity, and a leisurely upper-class masculinity that was categorized as 'effeminate'.[16] A further shift in industry from an industrial society to a technological one has meant similar reconfigurations of masculinity in that men are no longer more likely to work in manual labour, but in relatively sedentary jobs with computers, what used to be considered women's work.[17] 'Hegemonic' masculinity has again had to be renegotiated to accommodate these changes in labour division. As Carlyle wrote in *The Edinburgh Review* in 1831, 'The old ideal of Manhood has grown obsolete ... Werterism, Byronism, even Brummelism, each has its day'.[18] That is to say, masculinity was not (and is not) monolithic. Instead, ideals of masculinity co-existed and competed with one another, in a constant state of negotiation that was dependent on a variety of factors including time, place, class, race, religion and many others.

Why suicide?

When Olive Anderson published *Suicide in Victorian and Edwardian England* in 1987, she stated that her aim was not to write a history *of* suicide in the nineteenth and early twentieth centuries, but rather to use suicide as a means by which to study Victorian and Edwardian society in England.[19] What about suicide makes it a valuable entry point in understanding cultures past? In the novel *Suicide* (2008), written as a letter to a friend who recently died by suicide, Edouard Levé ruminated on how a suicide's life comes to be defined by their death. Suicide, he writes to his friend,

> rewrote the story of your life in a negative form. Those who knew you reread each of your acts in light of your last ... When you are spoken of, it begins with recounting your death, before going back to explain it.[20]

In searching the lives of suicides for explanations of these, sometimes unfathomable, deaths, the narratives constructed around motives shed light on the attitudes and beliefs of those who lived through the nineteenth century.

Particularly, they demonstrate the gendered scripts available to make meaning of a self-inflicted death. Suicide, then, offers a more personal insight into the lives of everyday people and provides alternative examples to those in the canon of histories of nineteenth-century masculinity, such as Thomas Carlyle, Charles Kingsley, Oscar Wilde, Thomas Arnold and John Henry Newman. The narratives of suicide were in many places – in the press, literature, medical discourses, religious sermons and in the testimony of friends, family and acquaintances at inquests. These latter, personal narratives, as told by those close to the suicide in the coroners' courts, and repeated on the pages of the press, document the pressures of being a man in nineteenth-century Britain, giving some insight into the experience of those who often go undocumented on the historical record. The act of suicide contravened the laws of man, God and self-preservation, and so the commentaries of suicides' lives show how people negotiated, explained and reacted to such behaviours. In focusing on the individual narratives of a suicide's life and behaviour, as constructed in the coroner's court and the press, this work offers some insight into the experiences of men, what was expected of them, what behaviours were deemed appropriate and how people explained behaviour that was not.

Histories of suicide

This individualized approach diverges from some of the major contributions to the history of suicide, such as those made by Olive Anderson and Victor Bailey, which have taken a more Durkheimian approach.[21] Durkheim's *Suicide* had a lasting impact on the way suicide was studied. One of the most important contributions it made was in establishing suicide as a social fact, showing that suicide rates were consistent each year, and that when rates did increase, they did so in consistent increments.[22] He concluded, then, that suicide was influenced not by individual circumstances but by larger social forces, and in doing so divided suicide into three types; egoistic, altruistic and anomic suicides.[23] Whilst I agree that larger social patterns can be useful in understanding suicide, this approach has elided the individual experiences of suicidal people and the specific contexts in which they take place. Moving away from Durkheimian categories of analysis, this work is aligned with Jack Douglas' post-modernist suggestion that suicide can only be understood on an individual basis through the individual's own construction of their actions.[24] The works of Anderson and Bailey are not without their merits. Both have shown just how multifaceted the experience of suicide was; the frequency of suicide depended not only on sex, but age, geographical location, marital status and occupation. They also make some attempt to grapple with the social and cultural understandings of suicide, but their social-scientific focus on larger-scale trends affords little room for the deep cultural readings of suicide narratives that I believe offer a richer understanding of the cultural construction of the pressures people face, their apparent motives to suicide and society's understanding of the act of taking one's own life.

It is incredibly difficult to access an individual's construction of their own suicide. Suicide notes and interviews with those who have made near-fatal attempts to end their lives provide some insight, but these are rarely accessible to historians.[25] Suicide notes were occasionally printed in the press, but there is no way to confirm their authenticity, and we have no way of interviewing survivors of suicide for obvious reasons. In the absence of such sources I turn to the press, which reported accounts of coroners' inquests with varying degrees of detail, providing access to how contemporaries constructed the meaning and narratives of male suicide in individual cases. This makes my approach slightly different than that which Douglas called for, but it nonetheless focuses on approaching suicide at a much more individual level than a Durkheimian approach, whilst also contextualizing them in a broader cultural environment.

This is not the first cultural history of suicide. Since the works of Anderson and Bailey, historians have grappled with questions such as what it meant to die by suicide in Victorian England, the assumptions made about those who chose to end their own lives, the perceived reasons for suicide and the implications of the different verdicts of insanity or *felo de se*.[26] These cultural histories of suicide have made impactful moves to look beyond statistics and Durkheimian categories of analysis to consider the complex ways in which suicide was experienced, understood and embedded within cultural and social contexts.[27] In particular, work on press representations of suicide has challenged claims that newspapers reproduced bland factual accounts that normalized suicide, suggesting instead that these accounts of suicide located the act in a 'specific social and ethical context, conveying moral truth rather than merely literal facts'.[28] I pick up this theme throughout this work, examining how newspaper accounts of suicide inquests divulge more than just the factual circumstances surrounding a self-inflicted death, but show how assumptions about why men killed themselves are guided by gendered cultural scripts and reproduce gendered narratives of suicide.

However, despite the inroads made by these histories in looking at suicide from a social and cultural perspective, few have focused on the way gendered assumptions have informed cultural understandings of suicide. This is all the more surprising when we consider that statistics suggest men and women experience suicide in different ways. Both Anderson and Bailey made an attempt to wade into the gendered patterns of suicidal behaviour and motive. Anderson notes how women's suicide, especially when committed through drowning, were perceived as an escape from sexual dishonour, whilst male suicides were seen to be a result of worldly dishonour.[29] Discussing suicides of those aged twenty-four to forty-four, Bailey suggests that his statistics support this gendered dichotomy of 'She died for love and he for glory', but encourages readers to resist the temptation to endorse this as an unproblematic conclusion. Bailey argues that conventional attitudes towards suicide could have influenced the witnesses and juries in what they might reveal about the circumstances leading to suicide and how these depositions were interpreted.[30] Work by Margaret Higonnet and Barbara Gates placed the image of the lovesick or fallen woman at the heart of Victorian suicide, claiming that suicide's cultural image was inherently feminine and, as a result, suicidal men were feminized in the eyes of society.[31] Although Gates does acknowledge a more nuanced concept of 'otherness' than such a strict gender dichotomy would allow, the work offers little acknowledgement of the implications that this might have for our understanding of gender, and masculinity in particular. Others, such as Katrina Jaworski and Howard Kushner, have suggested, instead, that suicide was (and still is) conceived as an inherently masculine act. Suggesting that its association with modernity and the city, in which men were perceived to be subsumed, and the way it is treated as a type of death rather than a method of dying, results in an understanding of suicide as a masculine act.[32]

Whilst I find it unhelpful to label suicide as inherently masculine or feminine, I agree that gender is integral to how we understand suicide.[33] Undoubtedly, suicide was (and still is) a gendered experience. This is borne out by gendered patterns of suicidal behavior that have persisted for as long as we have kept statistical records on suicide. This is evinced in the fact that men's attempts at suicide are more likely to end in death than women's, that men were more likely to choose more 'violent' methods such as firearms while women choose poison and drowning, and the gendered assumptions that surround suicidal motive.[34] It would, therefore be disingenuous to suggest gender does not impact understandings of suicide. However, whilst those such as Jaworski uses this to argue that suicide is understood as inherently masculine, I look at how expectations of masculinity are enshrined in the way narratives of male suicide are constructed. I also build on Jaworski's use of Judith Butler's theory of performativity, and suggest that this can also be applied to discussions of suicidal motive. In the same way that Butler described gender as a series of acts, in which 'expectation ends up producing the very phenomenon that it anticipates' and meaning is made through repetition and ritual, the suicide narratives identified here perpetuate themselves on the pages of the press.[35] In seeking to find meaning in the suicides of their loved ones, witnesses construct narratives that conform to familiar and inherently gendered expectations of behaviour, such as the gendered assumptions made about suicidal motives.[36] Looking back through a suicide's life in the search for events that might explain why they chose to kill themselves, those tasked with identifying motive and cause could draw on cultural perceptions of why men took their own lives, the kind of worries that weigh heavily on men based on expectations of their roles as providers, the kind of behaviour that was expected of them, as well as the myriad reports of suicide published in newspapers throughout the nineteenth century which have attempted to do the same, in order to inform their conclusions. In turn these narratives become points of reference for others who find themselves in the same circumstances, trying to understand and explain the suicides of friends and family.[37] In this way, also, gender is integral to how suicidal motive is understood and ascribed.

Suicide in the press and other methodological challenges

The conclusions around gendered suicidal behaviour have largely been based on statistics but motives, which I am interested in here, prove trickier to study statistically. Whilst we can know that more deaths by suicide are registered amongst men than women, and that more women choose to die by poisoning, knowledge about suicidal motives is almost always interpretive and is usually left out of statistics. The purpose of the coroner's inquest was, ultimately, to determine cause of any suspicious death, and not, in the case of suicide, the reasons why the person in question chose to take their own life. Whilst the certificate of death produced by the coroner lists the state of mind of a suicide and the means by which they came to their death, no motive was present. Instead, possible motives can be found in depositions, interpreted and negotiated by those left behind, often not explicitly given but rather hinted at through recollections of past events that constitute the suicide narratives identified in this work. These depositions can be found amongst coroners' papers with varying degrees of legibility, but surviving records are patchy. Having been considered the personal property of the coroner, many records might not be kept or may have been destroyed on the death of a coroner. In lieu of these documents, newspapers have been an invaluable source. They offer up details of a suicide's name, occupation, age, method, inquest verdicts, and sometimes they provide detailed accounts of inquest proceedings, including possible motives.

But these are not perfect sources. At the inquests, witnesses may have misremembered and misrepresented details, forgotten or chose them selectively, and likely made assumptions about why the man they knew had taken his own life based on their own subjective experiences and understandings of suicide. On top of this, newspaper reports of inquest proceedings were often summarized or paraphrased, details might have been selectively included whilst others are left out, words of witnesses might be misconstrued or even made up. In others, there is a layer of journalistic and editorial discretion, on top of the possible inaccuracies, embellishments or elisions of the witnesses, which affect not only which suicides were worthy of reporting, but the way the suicide might be framed. Whilst I had hoped to be able to cross reference a sample of coroners' reports with newspaper coverage of the same inquests, in order to provide some indication of how accurate newspaper reports of inquests might be, this proved trickier than I expected. The London Metropolitan Archives have an impressive run of coroners' records from the nineteenth century, but I found the majority of deposition notes to be illegible, and the cases I was able to decipher proved hard to find in newspapers. As such, it is hard to know how true these reports are as to what happened at the coroner's inquest, what details were left out and what made some suicides worthy of reporting beyond the obviously sensational cases. In many cases, they are the best source available for studying the narratives constructed around suicide, for shedding light on suicidal motives and assumptions about why people killed themselves, and possibly the closest we can get to contemporary understandings of and reactions to the act of self-destruction. Given the wider audience of newspapers compared to the inquests themselves, they prove to be a useful source for examining the narratives of suicide and masculinity that were circulating in the larger cultural imagination. So, whilst some claim that these reports of inquests are unreliable because they, as Bailey described, 'embodied, not to say molded, contemporary perceptions of suicide', it is for this same reason that I consider them a valuable resource.[38]

Newspapers produced and perpetuated discourses around both suicide and masculinity. Drawing on Michele Foucault's work on power, Nicola Goc has shown how newspapers, acting as 'influential communicator[s] of news, information and knowledge', offered models of acceptable and unacceptable behaviour. Specifically, Goc argues that court reports were used as 'ideological morality tales … warning people of the consequences of behaving badly', particularly when capital punishment was a possible outcome.[39] I take this same approach in interpreting newspaper reports of suicide. The stakes might have been much lower for verdicts on a suicide but, as a powerful channel of communication, the press had the potential to influence people's understanding of why men killed themselves and what kind of behaviour was appropriate for a man. Although 'insanity' was overwhelmingly the most common verdict for suicides by the nineteenth century I suggest that *felo de se* or 'medium' verdicts were occasionally meted out as a punishment of a suicide's past (mis)behaviour.[40] A message that is further amplified by the reach of the press to a wider local and sometimes national audience, occasionally with additional moralizing commentary. In this way, the press helped perpetuate notions of acceptable gendered behaviour.

These reports also offered cultural scripts for understanding, and opining on, what might lead a man to take his own life, which others could draw upon to contextualize the suicide of their friend or family member. Contrary to criticism of newspaper reports of suicide as 'emphasizing the exceptional in motivation and execution', the narratives identified here from such reports reflect some of the most commonly cited motives for suicide.[41] When comparing suicide statistics compiled in medical texts on suicide to the narratives found in the press, we find that the narratives reflect many of the motives commonly identified in the statistics as the main reason for suicides – poverty, heartbreak, financial ruin, dishonour. That is not to say that nineteenth-century newspapers did not have a penchant for the sensational, certainly many of the main cases that appear in this work are sensational and provide a level of detail that less sensationalized cases simply do not. But in presenting the public with explanations of suicidal motive as a reaction to common life events and experiences, I suggest that they provided gendered narratives through which others were able to contextualize suicidal actions and as such they contributed to and perpetuated narratives surrounding suicide. Those involved in this process, and engaging with these narratives, are drawn from all levels of society. Witnesses and juries who recounted the events that might have led to suicide and delivered verdicts; novelists like Charles Dickens and Anthony Trollope who wrote plausible suicides into their works for audiences to consume; medical men who sought to explain the causes of suicide; and the press who decided which suicides were newsworthy. Many of these engaged with one another. Whilst inquest witnesses were generating narratives of individual suicides, they also likely encountered suicide narratives in newspapers and novels, as did coroners and their juries, which could influence their understanding of why men took their own lives. In turn, novelists drew on the suicides they encountered in the press in shaping their narratives of suicide – a subject that I will expand upon in chapter 3.

Whilst I suggest that these reports of suicide inquests offered up narratives for others to use and interpret, it is hard to say with any certainty how consumers of these reports engaged with these narratives and to what extent they incorporated them into their own understandings of suicidal behaviour. This is a problem for many a cultural historian. Cultural historians have access to a vast landscape of culture and cultural documents, but we have little way of knowing how historical actors engaged with that culture. Christine Grandy has offered up a possible avenue for accessing this knowledge through the use of public opinion surveys from the twentieth century, but, as she acknowledges, those of us researching earlier periods are left with little in the way of evidence for the reception of culture by ordinary people.[42] Surviving diaries and letters might show some engagement with our subject of interest, but blindly reading through such archives in the hope of finding a mention of (in my case) suicide would be impossible. Occasionally, a letter to an editor appears in a newspaper in response to a particular case that goes some way in showing how readers engaged with narratives of suicide (some of which I have been able to use here), but these cannot be taken as representative of a whole population and in some cases were written by the editors themselves.[43] We can, however, acknowledge that, with the growth in circulation of newspapers following the repeal of 'taxes on knowledge', the representations of events found within newspapers became, as Joanne Jones acknowledges, 'extremely powerful'.[44] Given the use of newspapers as the primary source-base, my work here is more in the realm of what Grandy describes as concept-oriented cultural history rooted in 'a sort of thick description of a period in which [my] subject operates'.[45]

This research has benefited from the massive expansion of digital archives over the last decade. Without these developments, a work of this scope would not have been possible, and the common themes much harder to identify. During the early years of these digitization efforts, whilst many praised the practicalities of keyword searching, concerns were also being raised surrounding editorial discretion in selecting newspaper titles for digital publication and the effect this would have on the histories being written. Andrew Hobbs raised concerns about the 'over-generalized conclusions' being made as a result of an overreliance on *The Times* and other London papers, which were largely unrepresentative of the majority of nineteenth-century papers.[46] Whilst the digitization of newspapers offered the possibility of moving away from the disproportionate use of unrepresentative papers, the data Hobbs collected on the type of newspapers cited in articles from nine journals between 1980–9 and 2003–12 found instead that citations of *The Times* and other London papers had only increased in the wake of digitization.[47] But now, over a decade since the first digital archives were launched, we have access to a wider variety of papers than ever before and problems of editorial and commercial priorities have been somewhat lessened. Hobbs rightly complained of the lack of searchable provincial papers available through the *19th Century British Library Newspapers* in 2013, but although this database is no longer updated with new material, those able to access the commercialized *British Newspaper Archive* (BNA) are able to search over forty million pages of national, metropolitan and provincial papers. These archives have allowed me to draw on cases from across Britain rather than limiting my study to a smaller, more defined geography, and as a result I have been able to understand the perceived troubles that men across Britain faced, the expectations placed on them and reasons people thought that men killed themselves. The sources I use here suggest that narratives of male suicide did not vary from place to place, because these were issues faced by men across the country. Neither did attitudes towards men who died by suicide appear to differ much between regions in these cases. Variations in attitude towards these men appear to be more dependent on their individual character. For example, in chapter 2 I discuss how two cases from the same city within only a few years of each other were framed very differently in reports by the same paper. In chapter 4 we see how Hector MacDonald's Scottish background possibly influenced the framing of his masculinity in the context of the martial races ideology surrounding the Scottish Highlanders. But in chapter 3 nothing is made of John Sadleir's Irish background despite widespread anti-Irish sentiment during the period.

The 'digital turn' has also brought forward calls for historians to be more transparent about their methodologies.[48] Whilst these calls have been heeded by those engaging more explicitly in digital histories and utilizing innovative, often computational, methods of analysis, more open discussions about methodologies from those using digital archives to access content alone seem to have been less forthcoming. This is despite the fact that, as Zoe Alker and Christopher Donaldson acknowledge, tools such as keyword searches are an 'essential first step' for the majority of academic research, including my own.[49] The majority of the case studies used in this work have been found in this way. Keyword searches began with broad search terms like 'suicide' and the various alternatives, such as 'self-murder', 'self-killing', and *'felo de se'*. By casting such a wide net initially, I was able to pick up on the recurring narratives in these reports of suicides (of which I have chosen four), allowing the sources to shape the themes and structure of the research. As a result, this work is driven, primarily, by a select few cases of suicide, supported by brief encounters with others, which provide detailed accounts of the circumstances surrounding the suicides and their social context. In turn, they offer some insight into societal expectations placed on men during the nineteenth century.

The intention with this approach was to start from the bottom, with the stories of mostly 'ordinary' (although sometimes extraordinary) lives, in an effort to move away from both the grand-scale observations found in earlier histories of suicide and the traditional canons of Victorian masculinity. As a result, it goes some way towards a microhistorical approach to researching suicide, following the likes of Giovani Levi, Carlo Ginzburg, Natalie Zemon Davis and Robert Darnton (to name only a few), who sought to challenge a preoccupation with grand historical narratives and structures which had defined social history in the twentieth century.[50] This approach, however, has been dogged by questions. Brad Gregory highlights the contradiction in attempts to recapture the experiences of past actors on their own terms whilst using modern social-scientific frameworks to explain their behaviours;[51] others, such as Gareth Stedman-Jones, criticize how the microhistorical focus on individual agency prevents a consideration of wider processes that necessarily require a broad analysis.[52] This latter point is true of my own work. Although I cover the whole of the nineteenth century, I am not trying to recount a chronological change in attitudes towards suicide, common narratives of suicidal motive or expectations of masculinity. Punitive laws against suicide may have steadily been removed throughout the century but, for the most part, there appears to be little concrete evidence of clear change in attitudes towards suicide in the sources I examine here. According to the reports of inquests, most witnesses appear to have recounted the same kind of details about a suicide's life throughout the century – any personal worries, disagreements, their disposition and any changes in behaviour. Most verdicts were of insanity, and the occasional verdicts of *felo de se* appear to be contextual reactions to specific cases, rather than indicative of any systematic change in attitudes towards suicide.

Questions are also raised around how far the individuals, villages and episodes of microhistory can be considered representative, and Edoardo Grendi's notion of the 'exceptional "normal"' is particularly relevant to my work here.[53] At a macro level, suicide is both an unusual death and also, as Durkheim elucidated, one that occurs with some regularity. At the micro level, for the majority of the men we meet in this work, suicide is an exceptional incident in otherwise ordinary lives, and, drawing on Levé's observation on reading a suicides life 'in reverse', the lives of many of the suicides in this work are made extraordinary by virtue of their self-inflicted death. They are exceptional enough to leave a mark on the historical record, but that is not to say that they are entirely unrepresentative. The trials and tribulations these men faced – heartbreak, unemployment, financial losses, exposure, dishonour – were not unique to these men alone. In this way, it is perhaps not a traditional microhistory, but throughout I draw on the principles that underlie the microhistorical approach and believe in the richness that the detailed narration of these, sometimes obscure, stories add to the historical record.

Throughout, I give ample room to narrating the stories of individual suicides. By telling the individual stories of men, my aim has been to reconstruct their lived experience and reveal something about the society they inhabited – what people thought about suicide, and, particularly, men who committed it, about what was expected of men and about the myriad issues that can be extracted from these stories, such as insanity, poverty, bankruptcy, crime, honour, shame and love. Few histories of suicide have taken this approach. The closest is Kelly McGuire's work on the role that gendered suicide narratives played in the formation of national identity, but this work does not concern itself with narratives of motive. To some extent, Victor Bailey has also taken a similar approach, looking at how constructions of suicidal motive are embedded within the social contexts in which they are constructed. He has not, however, used this approach to look explicitly at masculinity.[54] The value of looking at suicide by perceived motive or narrative type is in what these narratives tell us about the pressures and expectations of being a man in nineteenth-century Britain because, as Kali Israel notes, '[p]eople enact as well as write the stories they inherit, learn, are imprisoned by, recast, and renew'.[55] Coroners' inquests, witness depositions and the press reports on suicides tell stories about lives. Throughout this work I give ample room to these stories, telling them in full where my sources allow, because as Kali Israel has recognized, historical subjects cannot be 'reconstructed separate from the stories [they] inhabited'.[56] This work follows in the footsteps of Israel, as well as others such as Carolyn Steedman and, more recently, Matt Houlbrook, in approaching narratives as a site of historical analysis. In telling stories, these inquests are more than just a window into the past, they 'do' history, they *are* history, 'they organize perception and delineate possible ways of thinking, acting and being'.[57] The narratives witnesses told were constructed to make a suicide's life intelligible in light of their action, both drawing on and producing gendered conventions. More to the point, considering the frequency with which suicides and inquests were reported we need to consider the possibility that these stories have been told with a broader audience in mind, with the knowledge that they might end up on the pages of local, or even national, newspapers.

The narrative method is not completely novel in the study of suicide. It has been used in psychological research for some time through 'Psychological autopsies', which gather information about the lives and events leading up to a suicide since the 1950s.[58] The psychological autopsy involves lengthy face-to-face interviews with close relatives of a suicide victim, usually the next of kin, with the aim of reconstructing an individual's life and establishing the causes of suicide.[59] It is in this same way that I use the details of coroner's inquests and the narratives of the press, to conduct a 'historical autopsy' of suicide. Whilst the aim of the coroner's inquest was to examine the suicide's mental state in the time leading up to the death, the witness depositions also reveal perceived motives for the act. In this way, the depositions of witnesses and the press narratives are not dissimilar to psychological autopsy interviews. The details of the inquests and depositions printed in newspapers, then, can be used in the same way that modern psychological autopsies are, in conducting a qualitative study of suicide in the nineteenth century. The reconstructions of a suicide by relatives produce narratives that provide a forum for meaning-making, and offer insight into lay understandings of what leads someone to take their own life.

Of the various narratives I identified in reports of suicide, I choose to focus on the four which seemed to appear most frequently and constituted the richest research material – the heartbroken and the jealous; the unemployed; the exposed fraudster and the bankrupt; and the dishonoured soldier. It is around these four narratives that this work is structured. In the first chapter I explore the narratives of male suicide associated with love – particularly heartbreak and jealousy. Here I show the various ways in which suicidal men might be othered. I begin with a discussion of Goethe's *The Sorrows of Young Werther* (1774) as the archetypal love-suicide, and the controversies surrounding the book in England. Here I show how criticisms of 'Wertherism' in England focused not on feminizing these lovesick, suicidal men, but instead othered them in different ways. Particularly, they reveal a Europhobic discourse that branded early-nineteenth-century romanticism as antithetical to a specifically English masculinity. In doing so it challenges assumptions of the feminized male suicide and instead builds on the work of Kelly McGuire to show that men who failed to live up to hegemonic standards of masculinity were othered in a more general sense, such as through nationality. The chapter then turns to look at suicides motivated by the jealousy of a lover, many of which were cases of murder-suicides. The focus here is on three main case studies, which also provide a platform to discuss notions of male insanity, centred around the jealous character. To be heartbroken or to be branded as insane did not necessarily mean that men were feminized, even though it might mean that their masculinity was not up to the hegemonic standard. I use these narratives of love-suicides to demonstrate that masculinity did not operate in a simple binary dichotomy of masculine/feminine, in which unmanliness was equated with femininity, but instead show how it operated within a hierarchy of multiple masculinities akin to that described by R. W. Connell.[60]

In chapter 2 I turn to discuss one of the most common narratives of suicide: unemployment and poverty. It engages with the traditional standard of masculinity that placed men as independent breadwinners able to support their entire families, and shows how despite Davidoff and Hall's conception of 'separate spheres'[61] being unrepresentative of the working-class experience, the male breadwinner was still a powerful masculine ideal amongst the working classes. It also explores how the conflation of morality and productive labour induced feelings of shame and failure amongst working-class men. I begin by outlining how Thomas Malthus' views on population, which underpinned the Poor Laws, heightened individualism of the nineteenth century and the language of burden used in discussions of poverty created an environment where suicide became a rational response to unemployment. It is within this context that I look at these narratives of poverty and suicide, using it as a framework to interpret these stories. In doing so I suggest that work was a central concept in the construction of masculinity and show how the ideals of 'separate spheres' and domesticity were not simply middle-class ideals, but incorporated into working-class rhetoric. It goes on to look at how, through the use of melodramatic narratives when reporting these suicides, newspapers that were sympathetic to the working-class cause went some way in highlighting systemic suffering and attempting to alleviate these feelings of shame and burden. In concluding the chapter, I look at how shame was a central experience of poverty and an underlying theme in the narratives of these suicides. For example, many men chose to die by their own hand rather than entering the workhouse, which was part of a ritual of public shaming designed to encourage conformity to social expectations. Here I suggest that shame played a key role in the policing of masculinity for these men.

The exposed fraudster and issues of financial failure are the focus of chapter 3. These narratives evince the anxieties that participation in a seemingly immoral marketplace could threaten the moral integrity that underpinned distinctly middle-class notions of masculinity. Drawing on Max Weber's conception of the Protestant work ethic, I begin with a discussion of the contradictory attitudes towards money during the nineteenth century, that saw the accumulation of wealth through hard work as moral triumph whilst simultaneously decrying the pursuit of wealth for its own sake as morally suspect. I then highlight how these concerns were reflected in popular literature through the trope of financial ruin and suicide in works such as Anthony Trollope's *The Way We Live Now* (1875) and Dickens' *Little Dorrit* (1857). I argue that this was not simply a literary trope, but that real life suicides, such as that of John Sadleir, were used to comment on the moralities of the market.

The final chapter turns to narratives of the suicides of military men, addressing two key themes – trauma and honour. It begins by addressing the history of post-traumatic stress and symptoms of trauma in nineteenth-century soldiers. Whilst some have argued that symptoms of post-traumatic stress disorder (PTSD) can be found in historical sources, the chapter argues that this ignores historical contexts and understandings of war-related trauma. Whilst some medical observations on the stresses of war, and the occasional anecdote at inquests on soldier suicides did display some level of understanding about the negative effects of war on soldiers' mental health, few made the same connections between service and suicide that we see today. As such it would be ahistorical to attempt to retroactively diagnose soldier suicides as manifestations of what some argue is a peculiarly modern disease. Instead, the narrative type identified in this chapter is embedded in masculine codes of honour. The chapter shows how, despite some subtle changes in concepts of masculine honour across the century, honour was central to military masculinity throughout. In doing so it draws on the work on military masculinity, new imperialism, colonialism and concepts of honour.

In organizing this work according to these narratives, I have paid less attention to chronological details. There are, however, some general trends that are worthy of note. The reports of lovesick suicides that proved to be most fruitful for this research are primarily drawn from the beginning of the nineteenth century, when Romanticism was at its peak. Similarly, the issue of unemployment became a particular concern in the latter half of the nineteenth century and, again, it is reports from this period that have offered the best insight into narratives of suicide constructed as reactions to poverty and unemployment. The scandal of John Sadleir's suicide was obviously determined by the extent of his fraudulence, but it is also symptomatic of anxieties surrounding money and value in a period of regular financial crises and similar exposés. When it comes to the narratives of military suicides, it is clear that honour was a persistent part of masculine identity throughout the nineteenth century, despite the nuanced changes it underwent. The construction of masculinity seen in reports of Hector

MacDonald's suicide are also emblematic of the New Imperialism of the late nineteenth century. In this way, it becomes clear that the narratives of suicide, constructed by both witnesses and newspapers, are contextually located in, and are informed by, wider societal and cultural issues. It is this that makes suicide a valuable avenue of historical inquiry for understanding not only how people viewed suicide, but also the concerns of society.

It is also worth pointing out that these narratives types are not necessarily inherent in the sources themselves. I, as a researcher, have imposed these narrative types onto these sources, and grouped them together accordingly. Many of these narratives might be classed in other ways – the murderer who takes his own life could be incorporated into a narrative of the criminal evading punishment similar to those seen in the suicides of swindlers; and the suicide of embezzlers or bankrupts could be conceptualized within a narrative of honour not too dissimilar to those of military men. In making these decisions, I acknowledge that I myself am partaking in this narrative meaning-making through which 'the past' becomes 'history'.[62] In taking this approach I have 'emplotted' these suicides according to my own interpretation of the speculative motives provided. Suicide is, of course, a complex issue that cannot be reduced entirely to these singular motives. But it is also not so complex and unfathomable as to be completely removed from personal and social contexts in which they occur, and through which they are understood.

Notes

1   'Statistical Bulletin: Suicides in England and Wales: 2020 Registrations' (Office for National Statistics, 7 September 2021), https://www.ons.gov.uk/peoplepopulationandcommunity/birthsdeathsandmarriages/deaths/bulletins/suicidesintheunitedkingdom/2020registrations (accessed 19 November 2021); similar trends can be seen in Scotland, 'Probable Suicides 2020' (Edinburgh: National Records of Scotland, 17 August 2021), 6; the most recent report for Northern Ireland does not specify suicide rates by gender. It does, however, note that 83.2 per cent of self-inflicted injuries were by men, 'Registrar General Northern Ireland Annual Report 2019' (Belfast: Northern Ireland Statistics and Research Agency, 16 December 2020), 14.

2   'What Is CALM?', Campaign Against Living Miserably, https://www.thecalmzone.net/about-calm/what-is-calm/ (accessed 9 May 2019); David Lester, John F. Gunn III and Paul Quinnett, eds, *Suicide in Men: How Men Differ from Women*

in Expressing Their Distress (Springfield, IL: Charles C Thomas Publisher, Ltd, 2014); Daniel Coleman, Mark S. Kaplan and John T. Casey, 'The Social Nature of Male Suicide: A New Analytic Model', *International Journal of Men's Health* 10, no. 3 (1 October 2011): 240–52; 'Men, Suicide and Society: Why Disadvantaged Men in Mid-Life Die by Suicide' (Samaritans, September 2012), 4; Owen Jones, 'Suicide and Silence: Why Depressed Men Are Dying for Somebody to Talk To', *The Guardian*, 15 August 2014; Telegraph Men, '"A Crisis of Masculinity": Men Are Struggling to Cope with Life', *The Telegraph*, 19 November 2014.

3 Thomas and Gunnell have noted a correlation between a significant increase in the use of gas poisoning in women during the same period that the male to female ratio of suicide declined and reached its lowest; Kyla Thomas and David Gunnell, 'Suicide in England and Wales 1861–2007: A Time-Trends Analysis', *International Journal of Epidemiology* 39, no. 6 (2 June 2010): 1467, 1474.

4 Michael Roper and John Tosh, 'Introduction', in *Manful Assertions: Masculinities in Britain since 1800*, ed. Michael Roper and John Tosh (London; New York, NY: Routledge, 1991), 18.

5 Mark Breitenberg, *Anxious Masculinity in Early Modern England*, Cambridge Studies in Renaissance Literature and Culture 10 (Cambridge; New York, NY: Cambridge University Press, 1996), 1.

6 Michèle Cohen, *Fashioning Masculinity: National Identity and Language in the Eighteenth Century* (London; New York, NY: Routledge, 1996), 8–9.

7 On suicide's place in the collection of statistics about human behaviours during the nineteenth century, see Ian Hacking, *The Taming of Chance*, Ideas in Context (Cambridge; New York, NY: Cambridge University Press, 1990), chaps 7–8, quote on 67; Olive Anderson, *Suicide in Victorian and Edwardian England* (Oxford: Clarendon Press, 1987), 10.

8 Michèle Cohen, 'Manliness, Effeminacy and the French: Gender and the Construction of National Character in Eighteenth-Century England', in *English Masculinities, 1660–1800*, ed. Tim Hitchcock and Michèle Cohen, *Women and Men in History* (New York, NY: Addison Wesley, 1999), 46–56.

9 John Tosh, *A Man's Place: Masculinity and the Middle-Class Home in Victorian England* (New Haven, CT, and London: Yale University Press, 1999); John Tosh, 'Domesticity and Manliness in the Victorian Middle Class: The Family of Edward White Benson', in *Manful Assertions: Masculinities in Britain since 1800*, ed. Michael Roper and John Tosh (London; New York, NY: Routledge, 1991); James Eli Adams, *Dandies and Desert Saints: Styles of Victorian Masculinity* (Ithaca, NY: Cornell University Press, 1995).

10 Martin A. Danahay, *Gender at Work in Victorian Culture: Literature, Art and Masculinity*, The Nineteenth Century Series (Aldershot, Hants, England; Burlington, VT, 2005), 7–8, see also chapter 1 in this book; John Tosh,

'Masculinities in an Industrializing Society: Britain, 1800–1914', *Journal of British Studies* 44, no. 2 (2005): 331; Tosh, 'Domesticity and Manliness in the Victorian Middle Class: The Family of Edward White Benson', 46.

11 For detailed discussions on the muscular Christianity movement, see Norman Vance, *The Sinews of the Spirit: The Ideal of Christian Manliness in Victorian Literature and Religious Thought* (Cambridge; New York, NY: Cambridge University Press, 1985); Donald E. Hall, ed., *Muscular Christianity: Embodying the Victorian Age*, Cambridge Studies in Nineteenth-Century Literature and Culture 2 (Cambridge; New York, NY: Cambridge University Press, 1994); Andrew Bradstock et al., eds, *Masculinity and Spirituality in Victorian Culture* (Basingstoke: Macmillan, 2000).

12 Bradley Deane, *Masculinity and the New Imperialism: Rewriting Manhood in British Popular Literature, 1870–1914* (New York, NY: Cambridge University Press, 2017).

13 Quote from Adams, *Dandies and Desert Saints*, 51; Linda Dowling, *Hellenism and Homosexuality in Victorian Oxford* (Ithaca, NY: Cornell University Press, 1994); Tosh, *A Man's Place: Masculinity and the Middle-Class Home in Victorian England*; John Tosh, *Manliness and Masculinities in Nineteenth-Century Britain: Essays on Gender, Family, and Empire*, 1st edn, Women and Men in History (Harlow, England; New York, NY: Pearson Longman, 2005).

14 R. W. Connell, *Masculinities* (Cambridge: Polity Press, 1995), 37.

15 Connell, quoted in Martin A. Danahay, *Gender at Work in Victorian Culture: Literature, Art and Masculinity*, The Nineteenth Century Series (Aldershot, Hants, England; Burlington, VT: Ashgate, 2005), 2.

16 Adams highlights Kinsgley's attack on the Oxford Movement focus on elitism, which can be seen 'in his letter of 1851 expressing the wounded sense of social exclusion that dogs his entire career: "In all that school, there is an element of foppery, even in dress and manners; a fastidious, maundering, die-away effeminacy, which is mistaken for purity and refinement; and I confess myself unable to cope with it, so alluring it is to the minds of an effeminate and luxurious aristocracy".' Adams, *Dandies and Desert Saints*, 98.

17 Roper and Tosh, 'Introduction', 19.

18 Thomas Carlyle, quoted in Adams, *Dandies and Desert Saints*, 1.

19 Anderson, *Suicide in Victorian and Edwardian England*, 1.

20 Edouard Levé, *Suicide*, trans. Jan H. Steyn, 1st edn (Champaign, IL: Dalkey Archive Press, 2011), 29.

21 Anderson, *Suicide in Victorian and Edwardian England*; Victor Bailey, *This Rash Act: Suicide Across the Life Cycle in the Victorian City* (Stanford, CA: Stanford University Press, 1998).

22 Émile Durkheim, *On Suicide*, trans. Robin Buss, Penguin Classics (London: Penguin, 2006), 24–7; Jack Daniel Douglas, *The Social Meanings of Suicide*, 2nd edn, Princeton Paperbacks (Princeton, NJ: Princeton University Press, 1973), 9.

23 A fourth category, fatalistic suicide, was also identified, but consigned to a footnote. Durkheim, *On Suicide*, 305.

24 Douglas, *The Social Meanings of Suicide*.

25 Anne Cleary has conducted a valuable study of suicide and masculinity through interviews with men who made near-fatal attempts on their lives. See Anne Cleary, *The Gendered Landscape of Suicide: Masculinities, Emotions, and Culture* (Houndmills, Basingstoke, Hampshire; New York, NY: Palgrave Macmillan, 2019).

26 Barbara T. Gates, *Victorian Suicide: Mad Crimes and Sad Histories* (Princeton, NJ: Princeton University Press, 1988); R. A. Houston, *Punishing the Dead?: Suicide, Lordship, and Community in Britain, 1500–1830* (Oxford; New York, NY: Oxford University Press, 2010); R. A. Houston, 'Explanations for Death by Suicide in Northern Britain during the Long Eighteenth Century', *History of Psychiatry* 23, no. 1 (1 March 2012): 52–64; Kelly McGuire, *Dying to Be English: Suicide Narratives and National Identity, 1721–1814*, Gender and Genre 8 (London; Brookfield, VT: Pickering & Chatto, 2012); Ian Miller, 'Representations of Suicide in Urban North-West England c.1870–1910: The Formative Role of Respectability, Class, Gender and Morality', *Mortality* 15, no. 3 (August 2010): 191–204.

27 Other important works include Christian Goeschel, *Suicide in Nazi Germany* (Oxford; New York, NY: Oxford University Press, 2009); Diane Miller Sommerville, *Aberration of Mind: Suicide and Suffering in the Civil War-Era South* (Chapel Hill, NC: University of North Carolina Press, 2018); David Silkenat, *Moments of Despair: Suicide, Divorce, & Debt in Civil War Era North Carolina* (Chapel Hill, NC: University of North Carolina Press, 2011); Irina Paperno, *Suicide as a Cultural Institution in Dostoevsky's Russia* (Ithaca, NY: Cornell University Press, 1997); Susan K. Morrissey, *Suicide and the Body Politic in Imperial Russia*, Cambridge Social and Cultural Histories 9 (Cambridge; New York, NY: Cambridge University Press, 2006); John C. Weaver, *A Sadly Troubled History: The Meanings of Suicide in the Modern Age*, 33 (Montréal; Ithaca, NY: McGill-Queen's University Press, 2009); Alexander Murray, *Suicide in the Middle Ages: The Violent against Themselves* (Oxford; New York, NY: Oxford University Press, 1998).

28 R. A. Houston, 'Fact, Truth, and the Limits of Sympathy: Newspaper Reporting of Suicide in the North of England, circa 1750–1830', *Studies in the Literary Imagination* 44, no. 2 (2011): 101.

29 Anderson, *Suicide in Victorian and Edwardian England*, 196.

30 Bailey, *This Rash Act*, 208–9.

31 Margaret Higonnet, 'Speaking Silences: Women's Suicide', in *The Female Body in Western Culture: Contemporary Perspectives*, ed. Susan Rubin Suleiman (Cambridge, MA: Harvard University Press, 1986), 71; Gates, *Victorian Suicide*, chap. 7.

32 Howard I. Kushner, 'Women and Suicide in Historical Perspective', *Signs* 10, no. 3 (Spring 1985): 537–52; Tony Kushner, 'Oral History at the Extremes of Human Experience: Holocaust Testimony in a Museum Setting', *Oral History* 29, no. 2

(2001): 83–94; Katrina Jaworski, *The Gender of Suicide: Knowledge Production, Theory and Suicidology* (Farnham, Surrey: Ashgate, 2014).

33 Jaworski, *The Gender of Suicide*, 3.

34 Enrico Agostino Morselli, *Suicide: An Essay on Comparative Moral Statistics* (New York, NY: D. Appleton and Company, 1882), 189–226, 335–49; Anderson, *Suicide in Victorian and Edwardian England*, 19–20, and chap. 2; Silvia Sara Canetto, 'She Died for Love and He For Glory: Gender Myths of Suicidal Behaviour', *Omega: Journal of Death and Dying* 26, no. 1 (1993): 1–17.

35 Judith Butler, *Gender Trouble: Feminism and the Subversion of Identity*, Routledge Classics (New York, NY: Routledge, 2006), xv.

36 Cleary, *The Gendered Landscape of Suicide*, 12; Canetto, 'She Died for Love and He For Glory: Gender Myths of Suicidal Behaviour'; Anderson, *Suicide in Victorian and Edwardian England*, 196; Bailey, *This Rash Act*, 208–9; Jaworski, *The Gender of Suicide*, 25.

37 Anne Cleary has also acknowledged this in relation to suicide. Cleary, *The Gendered Landscape of Suicide*, 12.

38 Bailey, *This Rash Act*, 31.

39 Nicolá Goc, *Women, Infanticide, and the Press, 1822–1922: News Narratives in England and Australia* (London: Routledge, 2016), 11–14, quotes on 11; on the role of the press in policing behaviour, see also David G. Barrie, 'Naming and Shaming: Trial by Media in Nineteenth-Century Scotland', *Journal of British Studies* 54, no. 2 (2015): 349–76.

40 By the 1790s, the verdict of insanity was given in 90 per cent of cases. Michael MacDonald, 'The Medicalization of Suicide in England: Laymen, Physicians, and Cultural Change, 1500–1870', *The Milbank Quarterly* 67 (1989): 75.

41 Barrie M. Ratcliffe, 'Suicides in the City: Perceptions and Realities of Self-Destruction in Paris in the First Half of the Nineteenth Century', *Historical Reflections/Réflexions Historiques* 18, no. 1 (1992): 25–6.

42 Christine Grandy, 'Cultural History's Absent Audience', *Cultural and Social History* 16, no. 5 (20 October 2019): 643–63.

43 Laurel Brake et al., eds, *Dictionary of Nineteenth-Century Journalism in Great Britain and Ireland* (Gent: Academia Press, 2009), 359.

44 Ibid., 454; Joel H. Wiener, 'The Nineteenth Century and the Emergence of a Mass Circulation Press', in *The Routledge Companion to British Media History*, ed. Martin Conboy and John Steel (London: Routledge, 2015), 208; Joanne Jones, '"She Resisted with All Her Might": Sexual Violence against Women in Late Nineteenth-Century Manchester Press', in *Everyday Violence in Britain, 1850–1950: Gender and Class*, ed. Shani D'Cruze, Women and Men in History (Harlow, England; New York, NY: Longman, 2000), 107.

45 Grandy, 'Cultural History's Absent Audience', 647.

46 Andrew Hobbs, 'The Deleterious Dominance of *The Times* in Nineteenth-Century Scholarship', *Journal of Victorian Culture* 18, no. 4 (December 2013): 472.

47 Ibid., 479–81.

48 Katrina Navickas and Adam Crymble, 'From Chartist Newspaper to Digital Map of Grass-Roots Meetings, 1841–44: Documenting Workflows', *Journal of Victorian Culture* 22, no. 2 (1 June 2017): 234.

49 Zoe Alker and Christopher Donaldson, 'Workflow', *Journal of Victorian Culture* 22, no. 2 (1 June 2017): 222.

50 Richard D. Brown, 'Microhistory and the Post-Modern Challenge', *Journal of the Early Republic* 23, no. 1 (2003): 10; David A. Bell, 'Total History and Microhistory: The French and Italian Paradigms', in *A Companion to Western Historical Thought*, ed. Lloyd Kramer and Sarah Maza (Malden, MA: Blackwell Publishers: 2002), 262–9; Ginzburg traces the development of microhistory back even further, arguably to the nineteenth-century novel, and notes how his own interest in this micro-scale approach was inspired by Tolstoy's *War and Peace*. Carlo Ginzburg, 'Microhistory: Two or Three Things That I Know about It', trans. John Tedeschi and Anne C. Tedeschi, *Critical Inquiry* 20, no. 1 (1993): 10–35.

51 Brad S. Gregory, 'Is Small Beautiful? Microhistory and the History of Everyday Life', ed. Alf Lüdtke, William Templer and Jacques Revel, *History and Theory* 38, no. 1 (1999): 107–8.

52 Bell, 'Total History and Microhistory: The French and Italian Paradigms', 273.

53 Ginzburg, 'Microhistory: Two or Three Things That I Know about It', 33; Bell, 'Total History and Microhistory: The French and Italian Paradigms', 271.

54 McGuire, *Dying to Be English*; Bailey, *This Rash Act*; Ian Miller has also looked into the representations of working-class suicides, however, this work takes more of a survey approach than deep analysis of narratives. Miller, 'Representations of Suicide in Urban North-West England c.1870–1910'.

55 Kali Israel, *Names and Stories: Emilia Dilke and Victorian Culture* (New York, NY: Oxford University Press, 1999), 14.

56 Ibid., 13.

57 Ibid., 14.

58 Christabel Owens and Helen Lambert, 'Mad, Bad or Heroic? Gender, Identity and Accountability in Lay Portrayals of Suicide in Late Twentieth-Century England', *Culture, Medicine, and Psychiatry* 36, no. 2 (June 2012): 349; Anne Cleary has also undertaken a similar approach thorugh interviews with survivors of near-fatal attempts at suicide. Cleary, *The Gendered Landscape of Suicide*.

59 Mike Gavin and Anne Rogers, 'Narratives of Suicide in Psychological Autopsy: Bringing Lay Knowledge Back In', *Journal of Mental Health* 15, no. 2 (January 2006): 137.

60 Connell, *Masculinities*, 78–9.

61 See Leonore Davidoff and Catherine Hall, *Family Fortunes*, rev. edn (London; New York, NY: Routledge, 2002).

62 In doing so, I have been influenced by the likes of Matt Houlbrook, Alun Munslow and Hayden White. Matt Houlbrook, *Prince of Tricksters: The Incredible True Story of Netley Lucas, Gentleman Crook* (Chicago, IL; London: University of Chicago Press, 2016); Alun Munslow, 'Genre and History/Historying', *Rethinking History* 19, no. 2 (3 April 2015): 158–76; Hayden White, 'The Value of Narrativity in the Representation of Reality', *Critical Inquiry* 7, no. 1 (1980): 5–27; Hayden White, 'The Question of Narrative in Contemporary Historical Theory', *History and Theory* 23, no. 1 (1984): 1–33.

1

Love and jealousy

It is admitted, by almost universal consent, that there is no affection of the mind that exerts so tremendous and influence over the human race as that of love.
– Forbes Winslow, *The Anatomy of Suicide*[1]

On 15 July 1825 a young man named Sydney Walsh shot himself through the chest with a rifle pistol. The inmates of 11 East-street, where he was living, heard the report of a pistol and rushed to his apartment to find him lying on his bed in a pool of blood, the pistol lying next to him. The shot had pierced his lung and the ball was lodged in his body, and despite his best efforts the surgeon, Mr Swift, was unable to remove the ball or save the young man's life. He lingered for a while and when his friends asked him what his motives were for 'so rash an attempt upon his own life', Walsh directed them to a letter in his pocket. The letter was from a young girl, Mary Keep, to whom, with the approval of her mother, he had proposed. In it, she stated that she 'had taken a sudden dislike to him' which she could not account for, and that 'she could never marry any body unless she loved him'. In concluding the letter she thanked him for the kindness he had showed her and begged him 'not to suffer foolish despondency to operate too much upon his mind' and he would always be her friend.[2] Sydney Walsh was not the only man who decided that his disappointment in love was too much for him to bear, and it was by no means an uncommon narrative of male suicide. Nineteenth-century newspaper reports of suicides attributed to love appear to bear out Forbes Winslow's observation above, and it would appear that men were particularly affected. The popular refrain 'She died for love and he for glory' was inaccurate.[3] Whether it was romantic rejection, jealousy, the breakdown of a relationship or the death of a loved one, love was a frequently attributed motive to suicide throughout the nineteenth century.

Whilst some early cultural histories of suicide in the nineteenth century have identified the love-suicide as one of the most well-established narratives of suicide, the primary focus here has been on the fallen or lovesick *woman*.[4] The love-madness of men has largely been ignored. These assertions that the love-suicide of women embodied Victorian conceptions of the tragic act are not without cause. Arguably the most potent image of suicide during this century was that of Ophelia, and by 1850, no less than fifteen paintings depicting Ophelia had been exhibited at the Royal Academy.[5] Thomas Hood's 'Bridge of Sighs' offers another popular depiction of suicide in the shape of the 'fallen woman', who plunges herself into the river after being seduced and betrayed. There can be little doubt that the lovesick woman was a popular trope throughout the late eighteenth and nineteenth centuries, but the frequency of reports in which men's suicides were attributed to romantic difficulties warrants discussion. As Margaret Higgonet acknowledges in her work on the feminine representation of suicide, 'the most famous literary suicide of the pivotal period' was not, in fact, a woman, but Goethe's Werther. Describing him as 'a Man of Sensibility whose virtues turn out to be symptomatic of his fatally feminine susceptibility', Higgonet suggests that a man who killed himself for love was characterized by stereotypically feminine weaknesses, 'hypersensitive … unable to control his feelings or to consider the pragmatic situation in shaping his behaviour'.[6] In what follows I argue that, contrary to Higonnet's interpretation, the representation of Wertherism embodies a more complex and nuanced debate about nineteenth-century masculinity.

Historians such as James Eli Adams, Linda Dowling, Andrew Dowling and John Tosh have demonstrated how, throughout the century, masculinity was nuanced and complex, often dependent on factors such as nationality, class, religion and sexuality. Rather than being defined along a masculine/feminine binary, masculinity was measured against other men. In this more nuanced framework, descriptors such as unmanly and effeminate did not necessarily equate to feminine. As historians have noted, the meaning of 'effeminate' was traditionally associated with inactivity and luxury, rather than being a signifier of being feminized. In this way, effeminacy did not signal a binary opposite femininity but acted as a more nuanced 'other' to traditional forms of masculinity.[7] Although Werther's masculinity certainly came under fire, nineteenth-century discussions of 'Wertherism' focused more on his 'un-English' qualities than on his supposedly feminine ones.

The reports of love-suicides used throughout this chapter reveal a variety of ways in which a man's masculinity might be found lacking. Beginning with a discussion of romantic suicide narratives, I draw on the work of Kelly McGuire and Michèle Cohen to highlight the implications that these men failed to live up to an idealized English manliness, and associated them with an effeminate European masculinity akin to Goethe's Werther. Moving onto the narratives of jealous murder-suicides, discussions around state of mind often served to 'other' these men in reaching a verdict. Symptoms of psychological troubles could portray a man as unmanly through their inability to carry out typical masculine tasks such as attending to business, whilst a frenzied loss of control was equally damaging to masculine character. In these cases, I suggest that, although insanity verdicts were returned mostly as a matter of course, the masculinity of these men was brought into question through evidence given to support this verdict. On the other hand, I show how a *felo de se* verdict might be used as a punitive measure when the inquest revealed behaviour that did not live up to expected standards of masculinity at the time. Ultimately, I suggest that the reports of suicide inquests reveal complicated, sometimes conflicting and usually highly contextualized attitudes around masculinity and the kind of behaviour that was acceptable for men.

The romantic character

In looking at nineteenth-century representations of male love-suicides, it is important to acknowledge the role of the eighteenth-century cult of sensibility, which found a hero in the 'man of feeling'. This 'man of feeling' was exquisitely in tune with his feelings, overtly emotional and, as Inger Sigrun Brodey describes him, 'valued the moment over future plans, the unspoken over the spoken, the felt over the reasoned, and process over product', all of which stood in opposition to the normative 'man of the world' model of masculinity.[8] The figure was famously embodied by the protagonist of Goethe's *The Sorrows of Young Werther* (1774), who, after falling in love with the already-engaged Lotte, goes on to commit suicide at the end of the novel in order to resolve the pain of unrequited love. Werther fit 'comfortably' into what Robyn Schiffman describes as a 'taxonomy of men of feeling' in England, with Henry Mackenzie's novel *The Man of Feeling* having been published in 1771, and Werther became a popular character for the English. The popularity of Goethe's novel is evidenced not only through continued reprints into the late nineteenth century, but also through the adoption of Werther himself into British literary tradition.[9] With the novel's popularity, Werther became a 'cult hero', and his suicide became the ultimate symbol of sensibility. The novel's popularity also became a growing concern for many who saw the novel as an apology for suicide, particularly in England.[10]

As a Werther mania erupted across Europe, fear was sparked over the novel's potential to influence others to follow the example of Werther's suicide.[11] In November 1784, the *Gentleman's Magazine* published a report of a young girl who had died suddenly, a copy of *Werther* was found under her pillow, which, the magazine added, was 'a circumstance which deserves to be known in order, if possible to defeat the evil tendency of that pernicious work'.[12] As Kelly McGuire has noted, whilst there was no substantive evidence to support what is now termed the 'Werther-effect', Goethe's novel gave rise to fears of social, and textual, contagion.[13]

Charles Moore's *A Full Inquiry into the Subject of Suicide* (1790), raised these concerns in a chapter devoted to criticizing *Werther*, describing the effects of the novel as 'highly mischievous', confounded by the fact that 'many a wretched victim to his passions' had been found with copies of the book on their person at the time of their suicide. Moore's concern was the way in which Werther is presented as an object of pity and sympathy. He believed that 'the more distinguished the character of Werter is described to be for taste, abilities, and improvements, and the more innocent his previous life, the more dangerous and fatal is the example of his death'.[14] These concerns surrounding *Werther*'s potential for contagion persisted well into the nineteenth century, and discussions could still be found at the *fin de siècle*. In Forbes Winslow's *Anatomy of Suicide* (1840), he lamented how works such as *Werther* had 'unhinged the minds of thousands, before they were aware of its impoisoned and insidious tendency'.[15] As late as 1893 the *Birmingham Daily Post* ran an article about 'Wertherism in England', which complained of 'sentimental suicides', branding them as cowardly and criticizing the attempts to make suicide stagey as hiding 'cowardice under an aesthetic veil'.[16]

As Brodey has argued, these eighteenth-century men of feeling did not present a 'revolution in the concept of masculinity', but an alternative and conflicting model, which hovered 'on the edge of illness, madness, impotence, inactivity, silence, and death'.[17] Charles Moore's critique of *Werther* went beyond derision of the novel itself and lambasted Werther's character for the way in which he indulged his passions, describing them as 'unlawful and uncontrolled'.[18] For Moore, the 'ungovernable' passions were, more often than not, passions that had gone on 'ungoverned', with the blame falling on the man who, like Werther, allowed himself to indulge them.[19] Wertherism, like melancholia or hysteria, was a disease that needed to be cured. The most effective ways to curb this 'exquisite sensibility', according to the physician Dr William Rowley, was 'a masculine habit of body and mind'.[20] Medical discussions of Wertherism clearly placed the man of feeling at odds with normative masculinity, and evidence of this attitude can be found well into the nineteenth century. The press placed Wertherism in opposition to traditionally masculine habits of work and rationality. Benjamin Disraeli, whose 'heroic courage' and 'example of fortitude' were laudable, and Thomas Carlyle were both held up as examples of traditional English masculinity, both having 'supplied a powerful counteraction to the Wertherism which threatened to become an overwhelming force in the early part of this century'.[21] In 1878 *The Times* ran an article about a recent volume on the life of Baron Von Stein, describing him thus:

> When half of his friends were bitten with Wertherism, and a great many of the other moiety were mooning about in philosophy, he kept to the world of facts as firmly as an English statesman who had been to Eton and played cricket and rowed in his youth could have done …[22]

The contrast drawn between Von Stein and his friends places Wertherism in opposition to 'facts', rationality and the values of normative English masculinity inculcated in public schools. And as late as 1895, the *Illustrated London News* commented how the 'practical duties … that Goethe had to perform as an administrator at Weimar … cured him of Wertherism. The lesson thus learned was embodied in the career of Wilhelm Meister, reconciled as he becomes, after many illusions, to effort and action in this workaday world'.[23] Work, then, was the cure for Wertherism. This placed Werther outside of traditional masculine characteristics; hard-working, practical and rational. The persistent interest in Wertherism a century later can be contextualized against the rise of aestheticism at the *fin de siècle*, bringing with it another model of masculinity that ran counter to hegemonic models and echoed the sensibility of the previous century. With it came a renewed debate about the diverse forms of masculinity and disrupted fixed ideas of gender norms and a renewed interest in Werther. Massenet's operatic adaptation of Goethe's novel premiered in England in 1894 and depicted Werther as an infantile 'crybaby', a characterization that emasculated the sentimental hero.[24]

Werther is a prime example of how a more general 'otherness' operated to define masculinity. Others have noted how Werther's emasculation, through his heightened sensibility, should be seen as feminization, but what we see in contemporary discussions of Werther is that he occupied a pivotal space in the British imaginary at the intersection of gender and national identity, and in concerns about social contagion. Kelly McGuire's work on suicide narratives and national identity has questioned why *Werther* inspired such a watershed of criticism when suicide had been a preoccupation of English novels throughout the eighteenth century, highlighting how prototypes of 'tragic sensibility' could be found in the works of Frances Sheridan and Henry Mackenzie.[25] As McGuire argues, derision of Werther as a symbol of everything that was wrong in English and European society was a product of the anti-Jacobin and Europhobic sentiments that lay at the heart of British conservatism. Werther's European origins – both in his German birth and his transmission to Britain through translation into English from the French version – saw Werther pathologized as a symbol of foreign social contagion, whose danger could be seen in the 'Werther effect' despite England's already-notorious reputation as a suicidal nation.[26]

This Europhobic discourse around Werther continued into the nineteenth century and is carried over into issues of gender. Condemnations of Werther by British critics vehemently placed him in opposition not just to a general type of manliness, but to a specifically an *English* manliness. *Bell's Life in London* stressed how 'Englishmen had a healthy contempt for anything in the form of Wertherism' and, commenting on a poem submitted to their 'Literary Olympic' that had been inspired by Werther, the *Young Folks Paper* lamented the influence of this 'most foolishly sentimental' book, again emphasizing that 'There is nothing in common between the love of a young Englishman and the sickly sentimentality of Werther.'[27] It is easy to simply read Werther's unmanliness as femininity, his intense sensibility of feeling as a feminine disposition, but in discussions of male love-suicides that were compared to Werther, gender does not operate in a simple dichotomy of masculine and feminine, but in a more nuanced 'otherness' that incorporates, among other things, national identity. National character played an important part in defining masculinity in Britain at the beginning of the nineteenth century, as would sexuality by its end.

The narratives and meanings surrounding suicides are often left to be constructed by others, because the only person who is able to reveal the true motive of a suicide is also the victim. Friends, family, acquaintances, medical professionals, coroners and coroners' juries had to look back at the suicide's behaviour – their words, events in their life and their relationships – and attribute a cause based on what the deceased had said and done. In some cases, letters might have been written to relatives or friends that provided clues, or, less frequently, a suicide note might be left divulging the reasoning behind the desperate decision. Or, as with Sydney Walsh's case, the scene of the incident itself could also provide clues as to the suicidal motive. Similarly, when a 22-year-old surgeon's assistant, Joseph William Jones, poisoned himself, no clear motive could be discerned 'beyond conjecturing that it was a love affair'. This conjecturing appears to be on account of a number of love letters found torn up at the foot of the bed, and a photograph of a girl to whom he was engaged found broken amongst them. However, Harriet Ranson, Jones' fiancé, deposed that they had 'parted as friendly as ever' and he had promised to see her again that month.[28] Nothing in his manner had made her, or anyone else, suspect that he might commit suicide. Without enough evidence to support a verdict of insanity in light of Jones' consistently 'cool and collected' conduct, but reluctant to condemn him as *felo de se*, the jury returned the verdict of suicide, but leaving the state of his mind an open question.[29]

Despite Harriet's assurances that nothing unpleasant had passed between them, the press fixated on the link between love and suicide. The incident was explicitly framed as 'Love and Suicide' in the press, with emphasis placed on the torn love letters at the scene and Harriet's intense emotion at the inquest; as a letter from the deceased addressed to her was read out she 'became much agitated, and swooned away', then after being 'restored to consciousness' she finished her deposition 'amidst continued emotion'.[30] Some shorter articles give only passing mention to other witnesses, or ignored them completely, focusing only on Harriet's intense emotion.[31]

The case presented by the reports of Jones' suicide was laden with romantic imagery and a sense of tragedy. Readers were left with the dramatic image of a broken-hearted Jones, found prostrate on the floor, next to a pile of torn love letters. This was a familiar scene to many. The imagery of Jones' body surrounded by torn love letters echoed the Romantic suicide of Thomas Chatterton in 1770, who had poisoned himself after failing as a writer and struggling to sustain himself, and was found with his writings scattered around him on the floor. Although, unlike Jones, Chatterton's suicide was not motivated by a broken heart, he had become a symbol of romantic suicide.[32] Matthew MacDonald has suggested that Chatterton became almost inextricably linked to Werther in the public imagination, as it was with the publication of *Werther* four years later, and its translation into English in 1779, that his death 'became the stuff of legend'.[33] Not only this, but Herbert Croft's *Love and Madness*, published only a year later in 1780, portrayed Chatterton 'as the victim of Wertherian passions' and 'more than any other single work established him as a romantic hero'.[34] *Love and Madness* was a story of the murder of singer Martha Ray, and the subsequent attempted suicide of her murderer, James Hackman. Chatterton, then, became tied up in Romantic suicide, both in the sense of being associated with the Romantic Movement and with the romantic suicides of lovelorn men. Despite the reassurances from Harriet Ranson that she and Jones had been 'friendly as ever' before his death, the press used the stagey drama of his suicide, which invoked the imagery of Chatterton, to appeal to the romanticism of the suicide. In framing the suicide as a romantic tragedy, Jones was identified as being outside the normative masculine character of the period through association with the refined feelings of a past era and a foreign nation.

In some cases, allusions to the romantic genre and sensibility were made overtly by those reporting the suicides. As the first decade of the nineteenth century was coming to a close, an unhappy young man named Barr, apparently 'of the most promising hopes', shot himself. He had formed an attachment to a young girl and their intimacy had 'threatened to produce a *living witness of their loves!*' (emphasis in original). *The Portsmouth Telegraph*, in an article that was dramatically titled 'Love and Duty. —Suicide', reported that, being 'bound by the strongest ties of honour, feeling, and humanity', and 'independent of his own inherent sense of moral rectitude', Barr asked his father for permission to marry the girl. The father, guided 'by those considerations which the world deem imprudent', treated his son's request as 'romantic', and refused to give his consent. In consequence, 'the unhappy youth' left his home in Birmingham and travelled to London where he was received by friends of his father, under the pretence of wishing to work as a shopman before going abroad. He was reported to have displayed a 'great lowness of spirits' and declined many parties 'in which most young men occasionally indulge'. One afternoon, he left the shop at two o'clock and retired to his room, where he shot himself. Being wanted at about three, 'his room door was bust open' where 'the unhappy young man was found on his back, with a pistol in his hand, weltering in his blood!'. At the inquest the jury returned a verdict of lunacy and the article's concluding remark draws an explicit parallel between Barr's suicide and 'modern Novels and Romances':

> We by no means stand forth as defenders of the wild and enervating principles inculcated by modern Novels and Romances; but we are not so totally devoid of feeling, or such strict votaries of prudence, as not strongly to sympathize in the sensibility of this victim to 'love and duty.'[35]

Whilst the direct motive for the suicide was never explicitly revealed, the story told about his death is an excellent example of how narratives were constructed in the reports of suicide. The explicit link to modern novels and romances does this with great force. The suicide is framed as the tale of a young boy whose father refused to allow him to marry the woman he loves, and so, 'bound by love and duty' left for the city in order to earn money to provide for the girl carrying his illegitimate child.

As with Chatterton and Werther before him, Barr is portrayed as being unable to bear the difficulties he faced. He was presented as melancholy and even brooding, indicated by his refusal to partake in the 'pleasurable parties' that his peers were attending. In so doing, the press set Barr against normative models of masculinity and aligned him instead with those characteristics of the sentimental heroes of sensibility. This was also done through reference to Barr's father. Whilst the father's considerations in refusing to consent to the marriage were 'prudent' and sensible, Barr's were deemed as 'romantic' and lacking serious thought. But although many have argued that the heroes of sensibility, like Werther and Chatterton, were charged with effeminacy and feminine sensibilities, this is not the case with Barr. His masculine character might have been brought under question, but it was in contrast to other men, such as his peers and his father, that these questions of masculinity were being raised.

As late as the 1890s there was still a belief that few men would kill themselves over romantic rejection. *The Ladies' Journal* published an essay on the issue of 'Women and Suicide' in January 1896, in which the author asserted that 'The only suicides for love among men are either double suicides of both man and woman or those of the Werther character where the passion engenders such rare spiritual exaltation that suicide seems the only natural solace for disappointment.' It was, however, conceded that 'While love causes more suicides among women than among men, marriage on the other hand, causes four times as many suicides among men as women; and most of these are due to man's inability to reconcile himself to the loss of his wife by death.'[36] This view had been given some weight by statistics on motives for suicide earlier in the century. In his *Anatomy of Suicide*, Winslow presented statistics on the causes of suicides committed in London, broken down by sex, between 1770 and 1830. Whilst 'grief from love' accounted for 157 suicides out of 2,853 amongst women, it was the motive in only 97 out of 4,337 suicides amongst men.[37] Later, however, when addressing the psychical causes of suicide and the 'peculiarities of the French people, particularly their indifference to human life', Winslow draws on the example of a love-suicide to illustrate his point. 'We can be romantic', he states, 'without blowing out our brains', and argues that when the course of love is uneasy, we do not 'retire to some sequestered spot, and rush into the next world by a brace of pistols tied with cherry-coloured ribbons. When we do shoot ourselves, it is done with true English gravity.'[38] The point here is the same as those made in discussions of Wertherism in the British press, and which highlight a critique of masculinity in reports of romantic suicides; that the sensibility and romanticism of these love-suicides went against the normative English masculine character. But despite such apparent distaste for the romantic masculine character, love was nonetheless an established narrative for suicide amongst men which many were willing to accept.

The jealous character

Whilst the statistics show that love was a less frequent cause of suicide amongst men than women, they also show that jealousy and envy were the cause of a higher proportion of suicides amongst men than women. Winslow believed that insanity and suicides were often the result of such feelings and that there were few passions which 'tend more to distract and unsettle the mind'.[39] Jealousy was a common narrative in suicide attributed to love and was frequently preceded by the murder of a wife or lover. Throughout these narratives we see how the expectations placed on men to protect, and to keep control of their passions, were used to other these men through narratives of insanity or a failure of masculine character. One striking example was that of John Sheppard. In late November 1859, John Sheppard went to the house of Ann Smitham, in North Nibley, Gloucester, and shot her through her window before fleeing the scene and shooting himself in a nearby orchard. The cause of the incident had been assigned as 'love and jealousy'.[40] At the inquest, Ann's parents deposed how Sheppard had been harassing their daughter. According to her father, on the night of the murder Ann had noticed Sheppard lurking about the house, and her father observed that, 'It doesn't seem to matter what the weather it is, rain or wind ... he's about.' Eventually Ann returned to the table where she was sewing, but after several minutes a gunshot was heard outside, coming from near the window. The father rushed to Ann after hearing her scream, to find that she had been shot, and within ten minutes she had died.

Ann's mother recounted that her daughter had kept company with Sheppard for four years until the previous Christmas and had since been trying to part with him for some time, but 'he would never take no for an answer'. She, herself, had also attempted to intervene on several occasions when he had come to the house looking for her daughter, telling him that Ann 'should not think anything more of him, for she should have no prospect but the Union before her'. She insisted that her daughter 'would never give up her home for such a character' and described Sheppard as 'a worthless piece of humanity'. The article went on to describe how, during their acquaintance, Sheppard had 'exhibited the most ardent affection for Miss Smitham', but he had been 'idle' and 'squandered some little savings of his father, who is a most respectable man'. It was this, according to the reports, that had prompted Ann to reject him.

Further evidence at the inquest revealed that, on the night before Ann Smitham was shot, the two parties had run into each other at the local beerhouse, where 'some altercation took place between them about making friends' and Ann refused to shake Sheppard's hand. A witness, Elizabeth Frape, had told Sheppard that if he wanted to marry Ann he would need to 'get a place' and make himself 'respectable'. This he refused to do and stated that, 'before Saturday night you shall hear such a row in Pit Court (Ann's residence) as you never heard before'. Frape took this to mean that Sheppard was planning to kill Ann, but this he denied, insisting that he would 'never put the weight of my finger upon her'.[41]

Several letters from John Sheppard to Ann Smitham were presented at the inquest and printed in the press, each one becoming increasingly threatening. Despite Sheppard's insistence that he would do Ann no harm, the final of the three letters makes some allusion to what was to come:

> Do what you like, but I can tell you, Ann, there is something hangs over your head heavier than you may think for; and you will find it out before Christmas next, if you don't look out. I will look out for you more than I ever did … You may think Dan is going to have you; you will find yourself mistaken in that, I can tell you … I never knew any young girl act as you have done to me but they came to some bad end, and I shall see you the same before I die, although I love you, Ann, more than all.[42]

At the inquest held on Ann Smitham's body, the coroner's jury returned a verdict of 'Wilful murder' against Sheppard. Whilst Sheppard had been found alive in the nearby orchard on the morning after Ann's murder, the court was informed that he had succumbed to his wounds during the inquest on Ann's body. The jury were sworn in for a second inquest, this time on Sheppard's body. The coroner went over the evidence given during Ann's inquest by the attending officer, PC Ford, who had found Sheppard, and after hearing the surgeon's judgement that the cause of death was a self-inflicted gunshot wound, the jury returned a verdict of *felo de se*.[43]

A verdict of *felo de se* was uncommon by the nineteenth century. Victor Bailey has noted how historians' explanations of such verdicts have tended to the belief that they were reserved only for those who existed at the margins of society, failed to conform to expected norms, outsiders of the community or criminals. The verdict of *felo de se*, according to historians, was a form of moral judgement.[44] With this in mind, the verdicts of 'wilful murder' and *felo de se* in Sheppard's case come as no surprise; in light of his murder of Ann Smitham, it appears that Sheppard was pronounced guilty of his crime in being deemed *felo de se*. But it was rarely as simple as that. Whilst Olive Anderson observed that provincial juries were more willing to pronounce a *felo de se* verdict in cases where murder was followed by suicide, Bailey found that in all of the cases of murder and suicide recorded in Hull, verdicts of 'temporary insanity' were returned.[45] As Bailey's study shows, the factors influencing a jury's verdict were many and varied, and there was no consistent measure of which circumstances would warrant *felo de se*. Whilst Sheppard was clearly found criminally responsible for his actions, many murder-suicides were found to be temporarily insane.

One of the key things in determining a jury's verdict was the character of the individual in question. The evidence presented at the inquest on the body of Ann Smitham was a damning indictment of Sheppard's masculine character. At a time when respectable working-class manhood was based on the breadwinner ideal (regardless as to whether it was achievable or not) and underpinned by the self-help ideals of Samuel Smiles, the accusations of his idleness and his wasting of money were also accusations against his masculinity.[46] In light of this and his murder of Smitham, it is perhaps no wonder that the jury quickly returned a verdict of *felo de se*. There was also nothing to suggest that he might have been of unsound mind at the time of either the murder or suicide, but neither was the question of his state of mind raised when it came to the inquest on his body. Instead, the verdict was reached based on the same evidence given by the officer over Smitham's body, and the medical testimony as to the physical causes of Sheppard's death. It seems that the jury had little wish to enquire into whether Sheppard's actions could have been the result of a disturbed mind, and were content to base their verdict on the evidence given against his masculine character.

In contrast, a case just four years earlier provides an insight into how seriously jealousy was thought to affect the state of one's mind. On the morning of 27 April 1855, James Sproston got up at his usual early hour, made the fire and set the table for breakfast, much to the surprise of his wife Ann. At half past six Mrs Gill, his sister who lived with them along with her son, went out to take a can of barm to Sandbach for Mrs Sproston. When she returned three hours later she found the door of the back yard was locked. After entering the house through the back door she found Mrs Sproston lying in a pool of blood on the kitchen floor and

Mr Sproston in a chair with his head shattered. In her absence James Sproston had 'slaughtered his wife with a sword' and then shot himself through the head with a pistol. Help was sent for immediately but it was too late, the surgeon arrived just after Ann had breathed her last breath. *The Standard* reported that the motive 'appears to have been jealousy on the part of the husband, for which there was not the slightest foundation'.[47]

James Sproston had privately expressed suspicion of his wife six or seven years before the incident took place, but in the weeks leading up to the tragedy his conversation had become 'an almost continued manifestation of jealousy'.[48] So bad had Sproston's jealousy become, that his sister described it as having 'amounted to monomania'.[49] This was picked up on by other newspapers and the *Liverpool Mercury* described him as 'a confirmed monomaniac on that subject', but noted that, 'in all other respects his mind was quite sound'.[50] The concept that a person could be of unsound mind with regards to one subject, but be perfectly sound in all other regards was not new. In his study *On the Different Forms of Insanity, in Relation to Jurisprudence*, James Cowles Prichard stressed that in partial insanity, or monomania, 'the mind is sane and unimpaired in all particulars, beyond the sphere of one single delusion' and points to a German writer, Hoffbauer, who 'observed that, in criminal law it is necessary to pay attention to the leading idea or delusion, and to inquire how far it may have exerted influence on the mind of the insane person'.[51] For the jury, Sproston had clearly acted under the delusion of his jealousy and the jury found that he had first killed his wife and then himself, 'being at the time in a state of insanity'. The article highlighted how the couple had been considered the happiest in their village and upstanding members of the community; Mr Sproston had taught at a Sunday school and was a leading office-bearer, whilst Mrs Sproston was 'indefatigable in her visitation of the sick and needy'.[52]

The *Daily News* reported the inquest in more detail, revealing that Sproston's nephew, Mr Gill, deposed that he had frequently spoken 'in a low and desponding way' about his family, quoting from the 69th Psalm and saying 'that he had "become a stranger to his brethren and an alien to his mother's children"'. It also added that it was 'very doubtful' that Mr Sproston had premeditated the incident, unlike John Sheppard. The weapons used had been in the house for years, Mrs Gill had gone out at his wife's request, and the locked door had been satisfactorily explained by the fact that the lock was a drop latch and could have easily slipped. Sproston had, however, pointed out to his apprentice some wood out of which 'his coffins' would be made, and had chosen those he wished to carry his body to the grave, 'as if he had entertained some general idea that he would not live long'.[53] All reports of the incident emphasized how well respected the couple were throughout the village, highlighting their leading roles within their church, and all revealed how they were believed to be the happiest couple there. Apart from the inexplicable and obsessive jealousy that Mr Sproston had displayed, there was nothing out of the ordinary in his character, or anything to indicate signs of insanity; he had been a fervently pious man, was well respected and lived comfortably. It is not improbable, then, it was the respect he received from the community that encouraged a more sympathetic view of his actions, resulting in a verdict of insanity rather than *felo de se*.

Whilst most reports portrayed the events in an apparently sympathetic light, there are two reports which stand out for their unfavourable representations of Sproston. The *Cheshire Observer*, after repeating the report and inquest much the same as others, appended two further announcements at the end of the report. The first was of a sermon preached by Reverend T. G. Morgan from Deuteronomy, chapter 5, verse 17, 'Thou shalt not kill.' With reference to the events earlier that week, the Reverend 'admonished his hearers, at considerable length, upon the sin of allowing the evil passions to gain the mastery; and showing how by indulging in evil and wicked ideas, that persons were led on to the perpetrations of such horrid deeds' as Mr Sproston had. The second announcement was of 'the funerals of the murdered woman and her guilty husband'.[54] This is the first instance in which James Sproston is explicitly blamed for his actions. The Reverend Morgan's sermon, rather than excusing the actions of someone suffering from insanity, places the blame on his not adequately suppressing his passions; he 'allowed' them to 'gain the mastery' and 'indulged' his 'evil and wicked ideas'. In this way, Sproston had failed to exert the self-control expected of masculinity. In pointing this out, these reports serve a damaging blow to Sproston's manhood, and held him up as an example of where this failure might lead.

Notably, in the Sproston case there was also little moral polarity in the way in which the murder and suicide were portrayed. As Bridget Walsh has shown in her work on domestic murder, press coverage of these incidents was regularly adorned with the motifs of melodrama. In particular, the moral polarity of victim and perpetrator was a popular one in dramatizing the narratives of crime.[55] The closest we come to this is the description of the wife's countenance as bearing 'a sweet and posed expression, not at all indicative of passion' having sunk to her knees to ask for mercy, raising her hands only in an attempt to protect herself, despite being 'a tall and powerful woman'.[56] The contrast painted between the frenzied passions of Sproston's violence and the description of Mrs

Sproston as sweet, maintaining composure and not fighting back when it was implied that she could, presents an element of this melodramatic moral polarity. Going even further, *Lloyd's Weekly Newspaper* presents a much stronger tone of moral polarity than other accounts. Firstly, it suggests that, on account of Mr Sproston's accusations of his wife's infidelity the two had 'begun to have frequent bickerings'. Secondly, and most importantly, is the description of how the incident played out:

> … when the only other two inmates of the house … were absent, Sproston made a deadly attack upon his wife, with an old sword. He inflicted several wounds on the back of the neck; and, in the struggles which the poor woman seems to have made to protect herself, she received deep cuts on both arms, the bone of one being broken. On seeing that his violence had taken fatal effect, he had obviously gone direct into another room, seating himself on a chair, and discharged a pistol, the contents of which entered below the chin, and passed upwards, nearly splitting his head in two.[57]

Whereas other accounts simply described the scene after the fact, speculating on the sequence of events, this report takes on a more melodramatic narrative as if Sproston's movements were known. In this melodramatic narrative, Sproston is given a greater amount of agency in his actions, implying the timing of his attack, and the attack itself, was calculated. The portrayals of James Sproston as either the frenzied madman or the melodramatic villain place him outside the remit of acceptable masculinity. On the one hand he had failed to exert due control over his passions, on the other he had rejected the patriarchal role as protector of his family. His otherness is demonstrated in his failure to measure up to a hegemonic masculinity.

Murder and suicide in Manchester

In January 1850 'considerable gloom'[58] was cast over the city of Manchester, with news of an 'appalling domestic tragedy' in Higher Broughton, a suburb just outside the city.[59] On the morning of 21 January 1850, as the servants of the Novelli household were rising and opening up the house, one of the children was found 'rambling about the house crying for her mama' who was absent.[60] On going to the dining room to open the shutters, the servant boy found the body of his mistress, Mrs Harriet Novelli, lying on the dining room floor. Having called to the other servants, they rushed to the bedroom of Mrs Novelli's brother-in-law, Alexander Novelli, only to find him hanging from his bedpost by the cord of his dressing gown. Mrs Novelli's body was cold, and had evidently been dead some time, but both Mr Novelli's body and his bed were still warm, as if he had been lying there only half an hour before.[61] The circumstances of the incident were shrouded in mystery. The scene presented the appearance of a dramatic struggle – the tablecloth had been pulled significantly to one side, the cushions from the sofa had been disturbed and lay on the floor and the victim's brooch had been bent – yet no disturbance had been heard during the night, even by the female servant who slept above the dining room.[62]

The Novellis were a wealthy middle-class family from Manchester; the family business was known as being one of the largest shipping companies in the city, and the father, Philip, had recently retired from business in 'very affluent circumstances' and now lived in London. The eldest son, Lewis Novelli, would have been set to take over the business, but he had died suddenly sixteen months prior to the incident, leaving his wife, Harriet, and their two children 'very handsomely provided for'.[63] After the death of her husband, Harriet Novelli moved from their house in Prestwich to a residence at The Cliff, Higher Broughton, which had been purchased for them by her father-in-law, Philip Novelli.[64] After Lewis' death, his brother, and one of the executors of his will, Alexander, came to live with Harriet at the Broughton house whilst he settled his late brother's affairs.

The day before the two bodies were discovered, Sunday 20 January, Harriet and Alexander had attended church twice, at Prestwich in the morning and then at Broughton in the afternoon. Afterwards they went to tea with Mr Edmund Coston, another executor named in Lewis Novelli's will, where they remained until half past nine in the evening. At the inquest Coston deposed that, during this time he had 'observed no peculiarity about the manner of either of them'.[65] They left at half past nine that evening and walked home, where they took supper together. One of the female servants deposed to having taken some hot water and two tumbler glasses to them before she retired at half past ten, when they were left alone. This was the last time the two were seen alive and what had occurred during the night was left open to speculation and interpretation.

These speculations resulted in a variety of theories. The presence of the two tumbler glasses (only one of which appeared to have been used), brandy and signs of vomiting initially excited suspicions that poison had been involved in the incident, either against Mrs Novelli or by Alexander Novelli on himself. However, medical inspections of both bodies, and the post-mortem of Mrs Novelli provided no evidence to support this claim. Fingernail marks were found on Mrs Novelli's neck, 'which corresponded to echymosis in the muscular structure immediately beneath' but no other external marks of violence were found. The post mortem on Harriet Novelli's body revealed that,

> The great vessels about the neck were gorged with blood. There were no other external marks of violence about any part of the body. The lungs were highly congested and gorged with venous blood. The right side of the heart was also gorged with blood; there were no marks of disease about it. The contents of the stomach were examined, but nothing peculiar was found in them; nothing but what might have been found in a state of health ... The membranes of the brain were in a highly congested state. I should think that the condition of the brain, and lungs, and heart, was sufficient to account for death, without the external marks of violence. To the best of my knowledge, I should conceive that death had arisen from strangling. There was nothing else to account for death.[66]

In her work on domestic murder Shani D'Cruze discusses the reading of the body in cases such as this one. Using the Novelli case as an example D'Cruze points out how the bodies of Harriet and Alexander Novelli were treated very differently. 'As the newspaper accounts layered the evidence of the two Coroner's court hearings over the initial details gleaned by journalists in the neighbourhood, the reader came to know a fair amount about Harriet Novelli's body', yet little interest was paid to Alexander's body, with no post-mortem being held. Rather, it was his mind that had been of interest to the inquest and readers. A medical examination and post-mortem of Mrs Novelli's body was conducted in order to establish that no other marks of violence could be found, which, as D'Cruze points out, required the removal of her clothes, and questions were even raised about her sexual and moral reputation.[67] Mrs Novelli's body was found with her dress partly unfastened 'as though she had been preparing for bed'. The *Manchester Courier* remarked on the topic that 'We cannot account for the unfastening of the dress, except upon a supposition which makes the affair still more hideous; we shall not further allude to it',[68] which D'Cruze has suggested 'necessarily did all kinds of imaginary work in the minds of its readers'.[69] And in fact, at the adjourned inquest, Mr Coston highlighted that 'it had been foully insinuated' that Mrs Novelli had been in the family way, but in reply to a question of whether anything improper might have occurred Mr Harrison 'stated, in the strongest terms, his opinion as a medical man, that this was utterly impossible'.[70] Whilst D'Cruze appears to have interpreted this as being an insinuation against Mrs Novelli's character, I interpret this reading of Mrs Novelli's unfastened dress as the implication of an attempted rape. Such an act would have presented Alexander Novelli as a man with no control over his impulses, passions, and desires – acting almost as an animal.

During the investigation it came to light that rumours had been circulating suggesting that Novelli was 'passionately fond' of his sister-in-law but his feelings were not reciprocated, and it was quickly conjectured that this was the cause of the tragic incident. The *Morning Chronicle* reported that during the evening of the fatal act, he had been 'tendering his suit', was rejected by Mrs Novelli and then 'in a moment of frenzy' he had strangled her.[71] Similarly *The Hull Packet and East Riding Times* reported that Novelli had strangled his sister-in-law 'in a frenzy of disappointed love and jealousy'.[72] Although this was only speculation, this became the de facto narrative of Novelli's actions. The interpretation of his suicide was open to more debate. Whilst one paper suggested it was done out of 'remorse and horror', another framed it as a cowardly escape.[73] Noting the apparent lapse of time between the murder and his own suicide, *The Hull Packet* suggested that he had been woken by the servants and, 'dreading the speedy discovery of his crime, he must have committed the act of self-destruction'.[74] Whilst the reports of the tragedy were generally consistent, these two examples indicate the differences in how Novelli's act of suicide was represented and perceived. In one, Novelli's suicide was motivated by remorse after the realization of what he had done, in the other it was a cowardly escape from the consequences of his actions. Based on the evidence laid before them, the coroner expressed his strong belief that no other verdicts could be given apart from wilful murder against Harriet Novelli and *felo de se* regarding Alexander, but would allow the jury to adjourn if they wished.

The jury, being keen to get a better sense of Novelli's state of mind, suggested that the family doctor, Dr Radford, might be consulted. The coroner revealed that he had already consulted Radford on the matter and whilst he knew that his mother and two brothers had been afflicted with insanity, 'he could say nothing whatever on Alexander himself'. He then reiterated statements given by witnesses who had known him well. Mr Cottam, a member of the jury, had known him through business and thought Novelli had always 'conducted his affairs in a business-like manner', noting nothing that led him to suspect his mind might have been disordered. Mr Withington had known Novelli for ten years, and also knew two of his brothers and his father, and had seen nothing to 'excite his suspicions'. Whilst he was aware that 'certain things existed in the family' he insisted there had been nothing of the kind in 'this young man'. Nevertheless, the jury was keen to postpone the verdict in order that they might gather more evidence.

When the inquest readjourned, further evidence of Novelli's state of mind was given. Mr Hampson, solicitor to those executing the will of Lewis Novelli, reflected on his recent interactions with him. He remarked that Alexander Novelli had regularly complained of the work, saying 'I must give up this work; it does not suit me; it makes my head feel bad; it makes me ill, and confuses me', and that he had been advised not to exert himself by medical men, as it would make him ill. He also appeared extremely irritable and excitable, more so than he had ever seen him previously. Hampson also recalled him at school, revealing that 'he was always looked upon as a weakly soft-headed boy compared with his brothers. He was decidedly passionate and impulsive, and did not control himself'.[75] Further to this he remarked how 'he could never sit down to two or three hours' work like another man, but always gave up again after doing two or three things'.[76] A Mr Charles Bowker, who had known Novelli for six or seven years, confirmed Hampson's remarks and deposed how 'He was seized with occasional fits of melancholy: and was sometimes exceedingly excited. He was extremely violent in giving expression to his thoughts.'[77] His nerves and temperament as described appear to have affected his ability to carry on business. Alexander Novelli had given up his own business on the recommendation of his brother, a medical man, who was concerned that 'he would never be able to bear up in case of any sudden reverse' due to his temperament, he had retired and spent his time travelling in order 'to divert himself as much as possible'.[78] Through these descriptions of insanity and incapacity, witnesses undermined Novelli's ability to partake in the everyday routines of middle-class masculinity.

More evidence was also given on the family's history of insanity. Two of his brothers had committed suicide, his mother had been insane and confined 'for some years', and his sister had been 'under the supervision of two ladies'. Although several witnesses believed that there was no evidence of insanity in Alexander himself, the surgeon giving evidence at the inquest, Mr Harrison, believed that given the evidence presented as to Novelli's temperament, it was 'extremely probable that such a person as Mr. Novelli … would, under extreme excitement, be betrayed to maniacal impulses'. He went on to describe how there had been many such cases throughout history, of people who were 'capable of pursuing the usual transactions of life, without showing any external appearances of insanity' but 'from a sudden impulse, commit either great crimes or some act that would fall under the common denomination of insanity'. Alexander Novelli, he concluded, 'would be likely to be such a case'.[79]

The idea that someone who appeared outwardly healthy but might harbour a dormant insanity, which could be awoken at the slightest excitement or provocation was a source of anxiety throughout the Victorian era. Amy Milne-Smith's work on masculinity and madness highlights these anxieties by exploring Victorian ideas that the motion of rail travel could excite a dormant insanity which was invisible to the human eye: 'Doctors warned that the intense vibrations of the railway carriage, the speed of travel, and the danger of traumatic incidents could unsettle both people's physical and mental health'. She suggests that this anxiety was concerned, not with technological advancement or danger, as most railway panics were, but 'the combination of technological progress and failed masculinity'.[80] What Milne-Smith highlights in this article is how these concerns about madmen, and male madness, were part of a larger anxiety about masculinity; 'mid-Victorian sensational tales of male failure were part of a larger process to firm up new models of gendered authority. For men, the loss of their wits could represent the loss of their manhood: it entailed a loss of control over themselves, their families, and their participation in the state.'[81] The suggestion that 'the existence of railway madmen challenged the perception that Victorian masculinity embodied self-control' can also be said for the plethora of male suicides that Victorian readers encountered in the papers.[82] Whilst, for most cases, something could be found in the suicide's recent or distant past which could be used as evidence of insanity, an unprecedented change in behaviour destabilized the restraint expected of hegemonic masculinity during the nineteenth century.

Novelli's recent behaviour on its own would likely have been enough for the jury to come to a verdict of insanity, but his family history was key. As historians of science have shown, the idea that physical diseases, such as scrofula, gout and cancer, could be hereditary became popular in the nineteenth-century medical community.[83] By the mid- to late nineteenth century, this had been extended to diseases of the brain. Citing works of prominent early-nineteenth-century physicians, John Waller notes that most 'were inclined to impute some degree of heritability in cases of insanity whenever a member of the patient's close family also suffered'.[84] At the Novelli inquest, witnesses' evidence of insanity within the family played a key role in solidifying a verdict of insanity. Novelli's mother had been insane, and confined; two of his elder brothers, Hippolite, the eldest, and Edward, had both committed suicide, in 1836 and 1840 respectively; and his sister, Caroline, was confined at Hadham House (Hadham Palace) Asylum, Much Hadham, in 1850.[85] One of his nephews would also go on to commit suicide in 1905, shooting himself on the balcony of his office in view of passers-by.[86]

Hippolite Novelli had suffered from a derangement of intellect for some years before his suicide. He had been placed under the care of a Bury surgeon, Mr Goodlad, by his friends, six or seven years prior to the incident, but appeared to have recovered, and lived with an attendant in a cottage within the immediate vicinity of the surgeon's house. Recently, he had been so much better that there no longer appeared to be any reason to place him under restraint. On the morning of 29 February, on his way back from being shaved, he called in to Mr Goodlad's surgery, as was his usual habit. At that time a young man employed in the surgery was compounding medicine for a patient, but on his leaving his post for a few minutes, Novelli got up, took a bottle of Prussic Acid from a tin case and immediately drank the contents, before returning the bottle. The effect was instantaneous and despite the best efforts of Mr Goodlad, who had been called to assistance, nothing could be done to save him. Hippolite, we are told, had been of 'very promising talents' until 'seized with the mental malady' and his 'literary acquirements were of a superior order'.[87] The *Manchester Times* concluded their report by stating that 'his studious, retiring, and inoffensive habits showed, even in "the wreck of mind," the bent of his inclinations "before reason had lost her empire" over him, and left him a mournful spectacle "of human nature in ruins."' The jury returned the verdict of insanity.[88] This representation of Hippolite as a retiring, studious and literary man did not fit the typical image of hegemonic masculinity of the period and played into anxieties about the effects that overwork and excessive concentration on one subject could have on the mind.[89]

Edward, on the other hand, was represented in a very different light, as antagonistic and reckless, which was equally troubling to expectations of masculinity. He had arrived at the Swan with Two Necks hotel in London at six o'clock in the evening of 13 August 1840, and was observed to have a dispute with his cabman about the charge from the station, although he paid it and went into the hotel in apparently good spirits. He went out on the following Saturday night, and did not return until half past twelve. The next morning, having requested to be called for at half past seven, and having not appeared by eleven, he was found hanging from the rail of his bedstead. At the inquest Lewis Novelli had revealed that Edward was not on friendly terms with their father as a result of his conduct: 'He was of a wild, reckless disposition, and he [the father] much feared that he had formed an acquaintance with persons of disreputable character, and he had become addicted to gaming.' Lewis had previously assisted him in business but for the past nine months he had been 'travelling about the country and on the continent'. He had received a letter from Edward, expressing a desire for a commission in the army or navy, which was about to be purchased for him when he disappeared. The Saturday before the incident Lewis had received another letter, 'couched in desponding terms', requesting money so he could go to sea, a reply had been sent but did not reach his brother in time. Lewis also attested to Edward having 'once threatened to do something desperate'. The verdict returned, once again, had been temporary insanity.[90]

Medical professionals of the nineteenth century understood the dangers of hereditary insanity, but debates around the issue focused on its form and development. Some believed that there was no hereditary disease, per se, but rather a hereditary *predisposition* to disease. This was of little consequence to George Mann Burrows, who stressed that whichever it may be, 'no fact is more incontrovertibly established than that insanity is susceptible of being propagated', with suicide being especially prone to hereditary transmission.[91] There was also medical uncertainty as to whether the transmission of insanity would present itself in every generation, or whether it might skip every other.[92] Regardless of these uncertainties, the key was to minimize the chances of awakening a latent insanity and it was expected that 'wherever a predisposition to insanity is known or suspected to exist, human efforts, judiciously applied, may frequently, perhaps generally, prevent explosion'. It was therefore expected that 'the individual so circumstanced would always be on his guard, and pursue such a course through life as might best ensure exemption; or that the relations who were aware of an hereditary propensity in him would exhibit a watchful anxiety upon the appearance of any symptom indicative of its approach'. However, Burrows lamented that this was often not the case, 'and those who have most to fear appear to be generally the most indifferent to the matter. No preventive measure is adopted: there is no thought of the morrow. Those who are best acquainted with the reasons for apprehension are as careless of every premonition as the patient himself.'[93] Alexander Novelli was just such a person as this. Given the comments made by Mr Harrison regarding Novelli's situation being likely to cause excitement for someone such as he had been described, he had not taken the necessary precautions expected of someone who was aware that insanity ran in the family. Based on the evidence provided, the final verdict returned on Alexander Novelli was 'temporary insanity'. Whilst the insanity verdict was common, not everyone felt it was justified, and for some the Novelli family's history of insanity was insufficient evidence to bring such a verdict. In the week following the Novelli case, one anonymous reader wrote to the editor of *The Manchester Examiner* and *Times* to express their belief that a suggestion of hereditary insanity was not sufficient to justify a verdict of temporary insanity, and that, 'in giving their verdict thus, it was a most flagrant abuse of their high office'.[94]

Historians of crime have noted how juries in criminal trials often looked beyond the immediate events of the crime to inform their verdict, and it is clear that the same can be said of coroners' juries in cases of suicide. Looking at paternal infanticide, Jade Shepherd noted how the criminals' prior conduct was paramount in determining whether they would be convicted, or acquitted on grounds of insanity:

> An examination of press reports and Old Bailey Proceedings Online (OBPO) shows that the nature of the crimes committed by childless men and convicted fathers, their motivations for the crime, their previous character, and demeanour in the courtroom were all subject to scrutiny. In condemning the behaviour of these men the press, judges, and juries helped to define appropriate male behaviour, including what made a good father.[95]

In light of the rarity of the *felo de se* verdict, it is easy to read such verdicts as stark judgements on unacceptable behaviour. Neither James Sproston nor Alexander Novelli had displayed any immoral behaviour previous to committing murder and suicide. Sproston and his wife were upstanding members of society, leading figures in their church and the community in which they lived described them as happily married. Novelli was part of a well-known middle-class family, his brother had entrusted him with the care of his widow, towards whom he had always shown 'the greatest possible kindness'[96] and the two had attended church twice on the day of the incident. Sheppard, in contrast, had been described as 'loose' and unrespectable, and had persistently pursued Ann Smitham to the point of harassment.[97] A suicide's prior character and behaviour played a significant role in influencing a jury's verdict.

The frequency with which suicides were acquitted on account of insanity was a widely debated issue during this period. Whilst many saw insanity verdicts as preferable to *felo de se* on account of the latter inflicting unnecessary pain on the families left behind, others felt that insanity verdicts caused more harm than good. The debate had multiple strands and involved medical professionals concerned with the increasingly simplistic association between suicide and insanity, religious officials concerned that the frequency with which insanity verdicts were returned did nothing to deter further suicide, those who were concerned about the implications for criminal trials, and the wider public who often wrote to the press to express their opinion on the matter. In 1815, the English physician George Mann Burrows, in a pamphlet titled *Observations on the Comparative Mortality of Paris and London*, criticized the jury's habit of returning insanity verdicts:

> It is probably that nine-tenths of those on whose deaths a jury has found a verdict of 'lunacy,' ought to be added to the list of 'suicides.' The motives for returning a

verdict contrary to fact and evidence, may be humane; but it is a dereliction of principle, repugnant to religion, subversive of moral rectitude, and dangerous to society; and if less complaisance were shewn by jurors, fewer suicides would happen.[98]

The debate continued throughout the century with some arguing that insanity in suicides should be judged with the same scrutiny as in criminal trials. In 1833, defending his decision to refuse to bury a suicide, Arthur Phillip Perceval used Charles Wheatley's words to point out how juries acquit a self-murder on the grounds of apparent insanity based on evidence that would not 'acquit the same person of murdering another man' and thus 'there is no reason why they should be urged as a plea for acquitting him of murdering himself'.[99]

In another case of *felo de se*, the suicide of Hiram Simpton in 1839, the importance of prior behaviour in informing a jury's verdict is clear. Simpton was the superintendent of the Bolton police, and had previously been inspector of the police at Liverpool.[100] He was twenty-nine, had been married for four years and had a daughter, Polly. However, it was known by some that he had formed a strong attachment to a young girl, Christina Leader, in Liverpool. On Saturday 21 September 1839, Simpton entered a Liverpool eating house, kept by Eliza Evans and Miss Leader. As the house was busy at the time, Simpton had passed upstairs to the dining room, unnoticed, but soon afterwards rang the bell for Evans. On going upstairs, she noticed that 'he looked very pale and frowned a good deal', he asked her how she was but did not answer her question of the same nature. As she made her way back downstairs, he passed her and rushed up the second flight of stairs to the bedroom and within moments shot himself.

At the inquest, witness depositions describing his character were varied. Eliza commented that she had never known the love affair between Simpton and Leader to cause 'any unpleasantness between him and his wife'. Jane Carr, a servant at the eating house stated, 'I thought the deceased was not a very decent man by the way he went on with me', although no further light seems to have been shed on what was meant by this comment. Frederick Morton Baker, an inspector of the Bolton police, revealed that Simpton had mentioned intentions to shoot himself earlier that day, but he took this to be in jest, after which Simpton showed him a packet of letters addressed to his friends and family. He described him as 'a very passionate man' but had never seen anything amounting to insanity, and like Eliza Evans, he had 'always considered that he lived very happily with his wife, setting aside what I knew privately, that he was very much attached to a girl in Liverpool'. Simpton also told Baker that he was 'heart-broken' that Miss Leader had refused to see him. His father, John, deposed that since an episode of smallpox at the age of twelve he had 'always observed he was very different from the rest' and his brothers used to call him 'mad Harry' when he played with them.

On the day before the incident, Christina Leader had received a letter from Simpton's wife asking to meet at the train station. On her way she encountered Simpton, who had sent his wife home and then proceeded to take Miss Leader by the arm and walk rapidly to the pier-head where they boarded one of the Woodside boats. She stated that 'From his manner altogether I was afraid that he intended something wrong, so I got up from where I was sitting, and told a gentleman that I was afraid he was going to do me some injury, and that he was taking me over the water against my will.'

One of the letters Simpton had written, addressed to his wife, revealed that his marriage had not been entirely a happy one. He had criticized her cleanliness and begged her to learn to write, suggesting that if she had tried she might have 'altered' him, and stated how her conduct in relation to 'Chrissy' had 'added fuel to an already blazing fire'. Excepting this, he owns his part in causing the unhappiness, and states how he 'can blame no one but myself' and revealing how he felt he has been a drawback on both his wife and Chrissy's lives. It is this that he cited as the true reason for his act, and not wholly because of the girl in Liverpool. The Jury returned a verdict of *felo de se*. Yet, the evidence given at the inquest in reference to his behaviour uses much the same language used in other cases which resulted in a verdict of temporary insanity. Words like 'excited', 'passionate', the references to a childhood illnesses or accidents sparking a change in behaviour had all been seen in other cases as enough evidence to support a verdict of insanity.[101]

Conclusion

According to physicians of the nineteenth century, love was prone to operating particularly strongly on the mind, even to the point of insanity and suicide. Nowhere could more evidence of this be found than on the pages of the nineteenth-century press. But the questions of insanity raised by these suicides were often questions of masculine character. Evidence to support verdicts of insanity could be tenuous, but a man's prior behaviour was crucial in determining the jury's verdict. Whilst no questions of insanity were even raised at the inquest on John Sheppard's body, the jury at Alexander Novelli's inquest went out of their way to allow more witnesses to comment on his state of mind, and this in spite of the coroner's initial belief that it was a clear case of willful murder and *felo de se*. A distinct difference between the two was the way their character and previous behaviour had been described. Little could be said to Novelli's detriment outside of his inability to sit down to work like other men, but Sheppard had been described by witnesses as idle and had clearly been harassing and even threatening Ann Smitham.

Moreover, these judgements were made on what was considered appropriate *masculine* character. Over the last several decades, there has been a significant development in putting forward a more nuanced history of gender and masculinity in the nineteenth century, one which has acknowledged the limits of focusing on a middle-class hegemonic masculinity. Early gendered histories of suicide have suggested that the Victorians fixated on an image of suicide embodied by Ophelia, meaning that men who committed suicide were rendered feminine by their actions. In discussing this, Barbara Gates suggests, 'How unmanly such male suicides for love must have seemed to some Victorians becomes clear when one recalls Gilbert and Sullivan's *Mikado* (1885).'[102] Whilst the satire of the *Mikado* certainly transposes the male love-suicide onto a distant culture which was represented as effeminate, it is erroneous to equate effeminacy or 'unmanliness' with femininity in such binary ways. The same has also been said of Werther, whose effeminacy and sensibility is equated with a 'feminine temperament'.[103]

As this chapter has shown, not only were men vulnerable to romantic suicidality in large numbers, but such sweeping conflations of effeminacy with femininity and modern gender categories are misguided. Masculine character was measured not within a binary of masculine and feminine but on its own terms, against other men. Discussions of Wertherism in the British press throughout the century did not label his sensibilities as feminine, but rather against a no-frills English masculinity. These measures of masculinity were made against the hegemonic masculine character of the time and place. None of the men discussed in this chapter were labelled as feminine for their motive to suicide, instead any lack of masculine character is suggested through a more nuanced otherness, whether this be in categorizing them as insane, unrespectable or likening them to an eighteenth-century, European man of sensibility.

Notes

1 Forbes Winslow, *The Anatomy of Suicide* (London: Henry Renshaw, 1840), 55.

2 'Suicide for Love', *Bell's Life in London and Sporting Chronicle*, 17 July 1825: 1.

3 'She Died for Love and He for Glory' was an eighteenth-century ballad written
   by Thomas Dibdin, which tells the tale of a soldier who goes off to war, and in
   order to be by his side, his wife poses as a man and fights alongside him, but,
   ultimately, both of them die in battle. It is a common trope that has been reused
   for illustrations and other poems, such as one by George Cruikshank. Although
   usually revolving around war, the phrase has also been adopted for the discussion
   of suicide to reinforce the gendered trend in suicidal motive, that men chose to
   kill themselves for worldly reasons, such as pecuniary troubles, debt or pride,
   whilst women tend to take their own lives for reasons relating to domestic issues
   and personal relationships. However, this view is increasingly being challenged.
   See Victor Bailey, *This Rash Act: Suicide Across the Life Cycle in the Victorian City*
   (Stanford, CA: Stanford University Press, 1998), 75–6; Silvia Sara Canetto, 'She
   Died for Love and He For Glory: Gender Myths of Suicidal Behaviour', *Omega:
   Journal of Death and Dying* 26, no. 1 (1993): 1–17.

4 For a discussion on depictions of suicidal women, particularly the fallen or the
   lovesick, see Barbara T. Gates, *Victorian Suicide: Mad Crimes and Sad Histories*
   (Princeton, NJ: Princeton University Press, 1988), chaps 7, particularly 131–2.

5 Helen Small, *Love's Madness: Medicine, the Novel, and Female Insanity, 1800–1865*,
   repr. (Oxford: Clarendon Press, 2007), 55.

6 Margaret Higonnet, 'Suicide: Representations of the Feminine in the Nineteenth
   Century', *Poetics Today* 6, no. 1/2 (1985): 107.

7 For example John Tosh, *Manliness and Masculinities in Nineteenth-Century Britain:
   Essays on Gender, Family, and Empire*, 1st edn, Women and Men in History
   (Harlow, England; New York, NY: Pearson Longman, 2005), 63; James Eli Adams,
   Dandies and Desert Saints: Styles of Victorian Masculinity (Ithaca, NY: Cornell
   University Press, 1995), 98; Tim Hitchcock and Michèle Cohen, eds, 'Introduction',
   in *English Masculinities, 1660–1800*, Women and Men in History (New York, NY:
   Addison Wesley, 1999), 5–6; Linda Dowling, *Hellenism and Homosexuality in
   Victorian Oxford* (Ithaca, NY: Cornell University Press, 1994), 5–6; Michael Roper
   and John Tosh, eds, *Manful Assertions: Masculinities in Britain since 1800* (London;
   New York, NY: Routledge, 1991).

8 Inger Sigrun Brodey, 'Masculinity, Sensibility, and the "Man of Feeling": The
   Gendered Ethics of Goethe's Werther', *Papers on Language and Literature* 35, no. 2
   (March 1999): 120.

9 See Robyn L. Schiffman, 'A Concert of Werthers', *Eighteenth-Century Studies* 43,
   no. 2 (2010): quotes from 211.

10   Orie W. Long, 'English Translations of Goethe's Werther', *The Journal of English and Germanic Philology* 14, no. 2 (1915): 171.

11   Kelly McGuire, *Dying to Be English: Suicide Narratives and National Identity, 1721–1814*, Gender and Genre 8 (London; Brookfield, VT: Pickering & Chatto, 2012), 115–17; Kelly McGuire, 'True Crime: Contagion, Print Culture, and Herbert Croft's *Love and Madness; or, A Story Too True*', *Eighteenth-Century Fiction* 24, no. 1 (2011): 62; Al Alvarez, *The Savage God: A Study of Suicide* (London: Bloomsbury, 2002), 230.

12   'Obituary of Considerable Persons; with Biographical Anecdotes', *The Gentleman's Magazine*, November 1784: 876.

13   McGuire, *Dying to Be English*, 116; the reality of the 'Werther-effect', a term popularized by sociologist David Phillips, appears to be a subject of continued debate in sociology, and has a significant influence on media guidance for reporting suicide today. Whilst some studies, such as those conducted by Phillips, found that reports of suicide led to a significant rise in the number of suicides, others have questioned the methodology of these studies and find no significant relationship between suicide numbers and publicity of suicide cases. David P. Phillips, 'The Influence of Suggestion on Suicide: Substantive and Theoretical Implications of the Werther Effect', *American Sociological Review* 39, no. 3 (1974): 340–54; Ira M. Wasserman, 'Imitation and Suicide: A Reexamination of the Werther Effect', *American Sociological Review* 49, no. 3 (1984): 427–36; Klaus Jonas, 'Modelling and Suicide: A Test of the Werther Effect', *British Journal of Social Psychology* 31, no. 4 (1 December 1992): 295–306; James B. Hittner, 'How Robust Is the Werther Effect? A Re-Examination of the Suggestion-Imitation Model of Suicide', *Mortality* 10, no. 3 (1 August 2005): 193–200; Sebastian Scherr and Carsten Reinemann, 'Belief in a Werther Effect: Third-Person Effects in the Perceptions of Suicide Risk for Others and the Moderating Role of Depression', *Suicide and Life-Threatening Behavior* 41, no. 6 (1 December 2011): 624–34.

14   Charles Moore, *A Full Inquiry into the Subject of Suicide*, vol. 2 (London: J. F. and C. Rivington, 1790), 147.

15   Forbes Winslow, *The Anatomy of Suicide* (London: Henry Renshaw, 1840), 85.

16   'Wertherism in England', *The Birmingham Daily Post*, 19 June 1893: 5.

17   Brodey, 'Masculinity, Sensibility, and the "Man of Feeling": The Gendered Ethics of Goethe's Werther', 116–17.

18   Moore, *A Full Inquiry into the Subject of Suicide*, vol. 2, 123.

19   Ibid., vol. 2, 127.

20   William Rowley, *A Treatise on Female, Nervous, Hypochondriacal, Bilious, Convulsive Diseases; Apoplexy and Palsy; with Thoughts on Madness, Suicide, &c.* (London: C. Nourse, 1788), 291.

21   'Mr. Disraeli's Cardinal Virtue', *The Examiner*, 26 August 1876: 6.

22   [No title], *The Times*, 30 December 1878: 7.

23 Francis Espinasse, 'Professor Dowden's New Volume', *Illustrated London News*, 21 September 1895: 370.

24 Kevin Kopelson, 'Saint-Saëns's Samson', in *Masculinity in Opera*, ed. Philip Purvis (New York, NY: Routledge, 2013), 113.

25 McGuire, *Dying to Be English*, 116–17.

26 See ibid., chap. 4.

27 'Nunquam Dormio', *Bell's Life in London*, 22 October 1885: 2; 'Literary Olympic', *Young Folks Paper: Literary Olympic and Tournament*, 30 June 1888: 413.

28 'Love and Suicide—Extraordinary Case', *The Morning Chronicle*, 15 February 1859: 7.

29 'Love and Suicide—Extraordinary Case', *Morpeth Herald*, 19 February 1859: 7.

30 'Love and Suicide—Extraordinary Case', *The Morning Chronicle*.

31 For example, 'Love and Suicide', *The Morning Post*, 9 June 1853: 2; 'Railway Intelligence', *The Leeds Times*, 19 January 1859: 1.

32 Linda Kelly, *The Marvellous Boy: The Life and Myth of Thomas Chatterton* (London: Faber and Faber, 2008), xvii.

33 Michael MacDonald, 'The Medicalization of Suicide in England: Laymen, Physicians, and Cultural Change, 1500–1870', *The Milbank Quarterly* 67 (1989): 81.

34 Kelly, *The Marvellous Boy*, 60.

35 'Love and Duty.—Suicide', *Hampshire Telegraph*, 22 December 1800: 4.

36 'Women and Suicide', *The Ladies' Journal*, 1 January 1896: 29.

37 Winslow, *The Anatomy of Suicide*, 50.

38 Ibid., 134.

39 Ibid., 61.

40 'Shocking Murder and Suicide', *Reynolds's Newspaper*, 4 December 1859: 3–4.

41 'Love, Murder, and Suicide', *Sherborne Post*, 6 December 1859: 8.

42 'Shocking Murder and Suicide', *Reynolds's Newspaper*.

43 'Love, Murder and Suicide', *The Western Daily Press*, 29 November 1859: 3.

44 Noting the lack of *felo de se* verdicts after 1850, Bailey suggests that the 'medium' verdict simply of suicide replaced *felo de se* as a form of moral judgement. Bailey, *This Rash Act*, 69–75.

45 Olive Anderson, *Suicide in Victorian and Edwardian England* (Oxford: Clarendon Press, 1987), 239; Bailey, *This Rash Act*, 69.

46 See Samuel Smiles, *Self-Help: With Illustrations of Character, Conduct, and Perseverance* (London: John Murray, 1868); the complex issue of the breadwinner ideal has been discussed by many historians, particularly highlighting the difficulties in achieving such a status amongst the working classes. See, for example, Megan Doolittle, 'Fatherhood and Family Shame: Masculinity, Welfare and the Workhouse in Late Nineteenth-Century England', in *The Politics of Domestic Authority in Britain Since 1800*, ed. Lucy Delap, Ben Griffin and Abigail Wills (Basingstoke, Hampshire; New York, NY: Palgrave Macmillan, 2009); Marjorie

Levine-Clark, *Unemployment, Welfare, and Masculine Citizenship: 'So Much Honest Poverty' in Britain, 1870–1930* (Basingstoke: Palgrave Macmillan, 2015), chap. 1; Sonya O. Rose, *Limited Livelihoods: Gender and Class in Nineteenth-Century England* (London: Routledge, 1992), chap. 6; Wally Seccombe, 'Patriarchy Stabilized: The Construction of the Male Breadwinner Wage Norm in Nineteenth-Century Britain', *Social History* 11, no. 1 (1986): 53–76.

47　'Murder and Suicide', *London Evening Standard*, 30 April 1855: 1.

48　'Murder and Suicide', *London Evening Standard*.

49　'Shocking Tragedy at Wheelock, in Cheshire', *London Daily News*, 30 April 1855: 2.

50　'Shocking Murder and Suicide in Cheshire', *Liverpool Mercury*, 1 May 1855: 5.

51　James Cowles Prichard, *On the Different Forms of Insanity, in Relation to Jurisprudence, Designed for the Use of Persons Concerned in Legal Questions Regarding Unsoundness of Mind* (London: Hippolyte Baillière, 1842), 164–5.

52　'Murder and Suicide', *London Evening Standard*.

53　'Shocking Tragedy at Wheelock, in Cheshire', *London Daily News*.

54　'District and Local News', *Cheshire Observer*, 5 May 1855: 5.

55　Bridget Walsh, *Domestic Murder in Nineteenth-Century England: Literary and Cultural Representations* (Farnham; Burlington, VT: Ashgate, 2014), 57–9.

56　'Shocking Murder and Suicide in Cheshire', *Liverpool Mercury*.

57　'The Provinces', *Lloyd's Weekly Paper*, 6 May 1855: 2.

58　'Manchester', *London Evening Standard*, 22 January 1850: 3.

59　'Murder and Suicide at Higher Broughton', *The Manchester Guardian*, 23 January 1850: 5.

60　'Awful Tragedy at Broughton', *Manchester Times*, 23 January 1850: 6.

61　'Murder and Suicide at Higher Broughton', *The Manchester Guardian*.

62　'Inquest on Mr. And Mrs. Novelli', *The Times*, 23 January 1850: 4.

63　'Manchester', *London Evening Standard*, 3; 'Supposed Murder and Suicide by a Manchester Merchant', *The Morning Advertiser*, 23 January 1850: 4; Shani D'Cruze, 'The Eloquent Corpse: Gender, Probity, and Bodily Integrity in Victorian Domestic Murder', in *Criminal Converstions: Victorian Crimes, Social Panic, and Moral Outrage*, ed. Judith Rowbotham and Kim Stevenson (Columbus, OH: Ohio State University Press, 2005), 188–90.

64　'Murder and Suicide at Higher Broughton', *The Manchester Guardian*.

65　'Murder and Suicide in Manchester', *The Morning Chronicle*, 23 January 1850: 6.

66　'Murder and Suicide at Higher Broughton', *The Manchester Guardian*.

67　Ibid., 183–5.

68　'Shocking Tragedy at Broughton', *The Manchester Courier and Lancashire General Advertiser*, 26 January 1850: 10.

69　Ibid., 185.

70　'The Adjourned Inquest and Verdict', *The Manchester Courier and Lancashire General Advertiser*, 26 January 1850: 10.

71 'Murder and Suicide in Manchester', *The Morning Chronicle*.

72 'Murder and Suicide Near Manchester', *The Hull Packet and East Riding Times*, 25 January 1850: 8.

73 'Murder and Suicide in Manchester', *The Morning Chronicle*.

74 'Murder and Suicide Near Manchester', *The Hull Packet and East Riding Times*.

75 'Murder and Suicide at Manchester', *The Times*, 25 January 1850: 5.

76 'Supposed Murder and Suicide by a Merchant', *Lloyd's Weekly Paper*, 27 January 1850: 7.

77 'The Murder and Suicide in Higher Broughton. Adjourned Inquest and Verdict', *The Manchester Guardian*, 26 January 1850: 8.

78 'The Adjourned Inquest and Verdict', *The Manchester Courier and Lancashire General Advertiser*.

79 'Awful Tragedy at Broughton', *Manchester Times*; 'The Murder and Suicide at Manchester', *The Times*.

80 Amy Milne-Smith, 'Shattered Minds: Madmen on the Railways, 1860–80', *Journal of Victorian Culture* 21, no. 1 (2 January 2016): 21.

81 Ibid., 23.

82 Ibid., 35.

83 John C Waller, 'Ideas of Heredity, Reproduction and Eugenics in Britain, 1800–1875', *Studies in History and Philosophy of Science Part C: Studies in History and Philosophy of Biological and Biomedical Sciences* 32, no. 3 (1 September 2001): 456.

84 Ibid., 460.

85 'Distressing Case of Suicide with Prussic Acid', *The Bolton Chronicle*, 6 February 1836: 3; 'Suicide of The Son of a Manchester Merchant', *The Morning Post*, 19 August 1840: 4; 'Lunacy Patients Admission Registers', 1850, MH94/8, The National Archives, Kew, Surrey, England.

86 'Merchant's Suicide on a Balcony', *The Manchester Courier and Lancashire General Advertiser*, 5 December 1905: 8.

87 'Distressing Case of Suicide with Prussic Acid', *The Bolton Chronicle*.

88 'Distressing Case of Suicide', *Manchester Times*, 6 February 1836: 3.

89 Esquirol, for example, believed that 'Persons who devote themselves very perseveringly to study, who abandon themselves to the vagaries of their imagination, who fatigue their intellect, either by a restless curiosity, or by turning aside in obedience to theories and hypotheses, or the allurements of speculative ideas, present a condition favourable to the development of mental alienation.' Jean-Étienne Esquirol, *Mental Maladies. A Treatise on Insanity*, trans. E. K. Hunt, MD (Philadelphia, PA: Lea and Blanchard, 1845), 39; Similarly, Forbes Winslow suggested that 'Everything that tends to throw the mind off its healthy balance will, of course, predispose to suicide. Excessive devotion of the attention to any particular branch of study, or to business, often originates cerebral disease and suicidal mania.' Winslow, *The Anatomy of Suicide*, 98; see also, Forbes Winslow, 'The Overworked Mind', *The Journal of Psychological Medicine and Mental Pathology* V (1852).

90 'Coroner's Inquest', *The Morning Chronicle*, 1 August 1840: 4; 'Suicide', *The Examiner*, 23 August 1840: 541.

91 George Mann Burrows, *Commentaries on the Causes, Forms, Symptoms, and Treatment, Moral and Medical, of Insanity* (London: Thomas and George Underwood, 1828), 91; Winslow, *The Anatomy of Suicide*, 152.

92 Hugh Grainger Stewart, *On Hereditary Insanity* (London: Printed by J. E. Adlard, 1864), 3.

93 Burrows, *Commentaries on the Causes, Forms, Symptoms, and Treatment, Moral and Medical, of Insanity*, 108.

94 'Awful Tragedy At Broughton', *Manchester Times*.

95 Jade Shepherd, '"One of the Best Fathers until He Went Out of His Mind": Paternal Child-Murder, 1864–1900', *Journal of Victorian Culture* 18, no. 1 (March 2013): 14.

96 'Inquest on Mr. And Mrs. Novelli', *The Times*.

97 'Murder Through Love and Suicide', *Manchester Courier and Lancashire General Advertiser*, 3 December 1859: 4; 'Shocking Murder and Suicide', *Reynolds's Newspaper*, 4 December 1859.

98 George Mann Burrows, 'Observations on the Comparative Mortality of Paris and London', in *The History of Suicide in England, 1650–1850*, ed. Daryl Lee, vol. 8 (London: Pickering & Chatto, 2013), 75.

99 Arthur Phillip Perceval, *A Clergyman's Defence of Himself, for Refusing to Use the Office for the Burial of the Dead Over One Who Destroyed Himself, Notwithstanding the Coroner's Verdict of Mental Derangement* (London: J. G. Irvington, 1833), 21.

100 'Determined and Extraordinary Suicide at Liverpool', *London Evening Standard*, 25 September 1839: 4.

101 Determined and Extraordinary Suicide at Liverpool', *London Evening Standard*.

102 Gates, *Victorian Suicide*, 146.

103 McGuire, *Dying to Be English*, 123; Higonnet, 'Suicide: Representations of the Feminine in the Nineteenth Century', 107; Margaret Higonnet, 'Speaking Silences: Women's Suicide', in *The Female Body in Western Culture: Contemporary Perspectives*, ed. Susan Rubin Suleiman (Cambridge, MA: Harvard University Press, 1986), 71.

2

Poverty and unemployment

A labouring man was found dead in St. Mary's Cemetery, Dover, this morning with his throat cut. He had been out of work.
> – 'Supposed Suicide of a Labourer', *The North-Eastern Daily Gazette*, 23 May 1890

The suicide of the labourer was a common story in the newspapers of the nineteenth century. In just two short sentences – only twenty-three words – the article above tells a thousand stories of unemployment, masculinity and suicide that are acted out again and again on the pages of the press.[1] A man out of work is unable to feed his family, or he might even be unable to feed himself. Perhaps his wife and children have to work, undermining his masculine credibility as the primary breadwinner. He might be forced to resort to charity or poor relief, or in extreme cases he might have to go into the workhouse, forfeiting his independence. These stories all share one narrative: a failure to meet the expectations of normative masculinity and the internalized shame that comes with it. This had become a well-established narrative by the end of the century. Many of these suicides appear to have been given little space in reports of crime and suicide during the period, with many as short as thirty to a hundred words. In some cases, though, newspapers provided a detailed account of the turmoil that led to the final rash act.

The landscape of work was changing rapidly throughout the nineteenth century. For many working-class men employment was cyclical – reliant on fair weather or the cycle of the seasons to bring demand for labour. For others, the introduction of machinery rendered their labour superfluous and displaced swathes of men from the factory and the field, throwing many of them out of employment and into poverty.[2] This state of things rendered the 'separate spheres' model of the Victorian family, and the breadwinner ideal of hegemonic masculinity largely unattainable for many working-class men.[3] Whilst the notion of 'separate spheres' has long been critiqued as unrepresentative of the Victorian family, it nevertheless remained a powerful ideology in working-class cultures of respectability.[4] This is evident across cultural spheres as diverse as working-class melodrama and the calls for a 'family wage', and features heavily in the suicide narratives of working-class men.[5] This chapter is about the power of this breadwinning ideal, and the feeling of shame and failure that could accompany poverty and unemployment. The power of this ideal was compounded by the rampant individualism of the nineteenth century and the language of burden used in discourses of unemployment.[6]

The stories of suicide examined in this chapter provide insight into the overbearing pressures of hegemonic masculinity and the anxieties it engendered. For the most part, they constitute a failure to live up to an idealized model of masculinity that is able-bodied, able-minded and able to provide. They reveal the violence inflicted on the poorest of society by the rampant individualism of the nineteenth century, the damage of a masculinity that puts its onus on productivity and the resultant feelings of shame, guilt and failure that this cultural climate engendered. This individualism, championed by theorists such as Thomas Malthus and Samuel Smiles, was enshrined in the New Poor Law system of 1834, which sought to emphasize that financial security 'was an individual obligation in the natural order of the economic market'.[7] As such, productive labour became a symbol of personal morality. This new system aimed to lessen the 'burden' of poor relief for the parish and ratepayers, by reducing the scope of outdoor relief and requiring the able-bodied poor to enter the workhouse in order to receive it. Workhouse conditions were purposely harsh in order to deter parishioners from resorting to state welfare; families were separated and lodged in crowded dormitories, inmates were put to useless work like picking oakum and made to wear the workhouse uniform. Entering the workhouse, as David Englander highlights, was seen as 'a public admission of personal and moral failure'.[8] This cultural climate measured masculinity and men's moral worth by their participation in productive labour, and utilized a language of burden in discourses of unemployment and poverty that served to shame those out of work.

Shame has been described as 'the premier social emotion', one that has the potential to occur in any social interaction and is triggered by even the slightest threat to the social bond.[9] In this way, as David Nash and Anne-Marie Kilday have pointed out, it has also been an integral part of punishment and social control throughout history, and one that persists despite claims that modernity replaced 'shame cultures' with 'guilt cultures'.[10] Shame, then, plays a key part in understanding the experiences of unemployment in a society that conflated productive labour with individual moral worth. So far, the discussion on the role of shame in punishment has been focused, primarily, on institutions of criminal punishment, but the same principles can be seen in the function of the workhouse. Whilst Englander has noted that shame was not uniformly attached to the workhouse across all working-class communities, it was a powerful deterrent in those communities where this sense of shame was deeply entrenched.[11] In these communities, shame was key in enforcing the utilitarian principles of the nineteenth century, even among those who found themselves unemployed through no fault of their own. It is also, as Jennifer Biddle discusses, a learned emotion, and these suicide narratives provide a stark demonstration of this fact.[12] Not only is this shame taught and learned through the language of burden used in utilitarian discourses of poverty, but the shame of unemployment was acted out again and again on the pages of the press, in showing suicide as a rational response to such hardship. Kali Israel has suggested that 'people enact as well as write the stories they inherit', and in turning to look at these narratives of poverty and suicide, we see how the shame of unemployment and poverty was learned, re-enacted and reinforced.[13]

In some reports of these unemployed suicides, however, we can see attempts to counter these feelings of shame and moral failure, through the way in which these stories were narrated. Looking at workplace accidents, Jamie Bronstein has highlighted how they were interpreted and reported by 'deploying one of a small number of literary genres' and were described by middle-class observers in ways that evoked middle-class sympathies.[14] One example of this is through the use of a melodramatic narrative in newspaper reports.[15] In both Bronstein's workplace accidents, and these suicides, journalists often highlighted the plight of widows and children left behind – 'The deceased has left a widow and a large family unprovided for'[16] – to create a narrative of domestic melodrama that was popular throughout the nineteenth century. Melodrama was political. It saw the home become a sight of tragedy, under threat from an outsider, usually embodied by an upper- or middle-class villain who represented the wider social forces at work behind domestic tragedy. By reading these reports of working-class suicides through a melodramatic lens, we can see how suicide represented the threat posed to the working-class family by invisible forces at work in modern capitalist and industrial society. In doing so, the melodramatic framing in some reports of suicide attempted to alleviate the guilt and shame felt by working-class men out of work.

Whilst Bronstein suggests that references to widows and children in these melodramatic narratives are evidence of the imposition of middle-class family ideals and gender roles, these 'middle-class' values were embraced by the working classes, and indeed domestic melodrama was a popular form of working-class entertainment.[17] The rhetoric of family was not just a middle-class narrative tool imposed on the working classes. As others have demonstrated, workers drew on the ideals of breadwinner masculinity and separate spheres for their own ends, to protest women's entry into the workplace and make demands for a 'family wage'.[18] Building on this work, this chapter looks at how masculinity was an integral part of the way work-related suicides were conceptualized in the press and by the public. Whilst women also committed suicide because of poverty – most famously Margaret Moyes who jumped from the London Monument in September 1839[19] – these narratives of working-class suicides were inflected with the gendered ideal of the breadwinner that reinforced hegemonic masculinity, whilst their unemployment served to undermine it.

A Malthusian framework for suicide

For the majority of these suicides, there is a distinctly Malthusian element to their stories. By looking at the political thought and social commentary of the period we are better able to understand the pressures facing the men who chose to take their own lives. In 1798, Thomas Malthus published his *Essay on the Principle of Population* (which was expanded in a second edition published in 1803), raising concerns over a growing population that appeared to be growing at an unsustainable rate, and criticizing the poor laws for encouraging the working classes to reproduce beyond their means and have larger families than they are able to maintain. Malthus' conflation of the concepts of population and labour and the idea of surplus population is key to reading these suicides.[20] Following in the fashion of Adam Smith, Malthus implies that only those who were useful to society were deserving of financial aid, and this was to be given as benevolent *charity*, rather than being a *right*.[21] In the controversial 'Nature's mighty feast' passage (which was removed in later editions),[22] Malthus wrote:

> Man who is born into a world already possessed, if he cannot get subsistence from his parents on whom he has a just demand, and if the society do not want his labour, has no claim of *right* to the smallest portion of food, and, in fact, has no business to be where he is. At nature's mighty feast there is no vacant cover for him. She tells him to be gone, and will quickly execute her own orders, if he do not (*sic*) work upon the compassion of some of her guests.[23]

In Malthus' theory, nature executes her orders through 'positive checks' on population: disease, famine, war and other causes of premature death. He also identified 'preventive checks' which he considered to be a form of moral restraint, such as delaying marriage and having children.[24] Malthus believed, for example, that those on wages as low as 'eighteen pence or two shillings a day', would think twice before marrying and starting a family on a wage that 'seems to be not more than sufficient for one'. And whilst he acknowledged that he might be willing to work harder to live with a woman he loves, he would be conscious that should ill-fortune befall him 'no degree of frugality, no possible exertion of his manual strength, would preserve him from the heartrending sensation of seeing his children starve, or of being obliged to the parish for their support'.[25]

Malthus never wrote on the issue of suicide, but his principles pervade the welfare provision of the New Poor Law providing an important context in which to interpret suicides as a response to unemployment. In a utilitarian context, those committing suicide because they are unable to find unemployment can be considered as part of the surplus population: those whose labour society does not appear to need nor want. Whilst the 'Nature's mighty feast' passage above talks about nature executing her own orders, the suicide obeys these orders and carries them out himself.

The best-known example of such suicide is found in Thomas Hardy's *Jude the Obscure* (1895), in which Little Father Time kills his two siblings and then himself. The episode is described by Gillian Beer as a 'late-Malthusian tragedy'[26] and the note left by Father Time, 'Done because we are too menny',[27] explicitly frames the suicide in Malthusian terms. Father Time's actions are the result of a seemingly rational utilitarian consideration. He sees himself and his half-siblings as a burden on his parents, Jude and Sue, who are unemployed and have another child on the way and feels they would be better off without them to care for. The murders and suicide come following Sue's failed attempts to find lodgings, as 'Every householder looked askance at such a woman and child inquiring for accommodation' and recognizing his role in this failure, Father Time exclaims 'I ought not to be born, ought I?' The conversation between Sue and Father Time that follows continues in the same vein, the child asking, 'It would be better to be out o' the world than in it, wouldn't it?'.

One of the novel's most Malthusian sentiments comes only moments later when Father Time suggests that 'whenever children be born that are not wanted they should be killed directly, before their souls come to 'em, and not allowed to grow big and walk about!'. It is at this point that Sue reveals, to Father Time's horror, that she is expecting another child.[28] Father Time's actions operate as a 'positive check' on the family's population where the preventative check – celibacy – has failed, and as Emily Steinlight has noted, the Malthusian sentiment is recognizable even to readers who are only 'passingly familiar' with Malthus' work.[29]

Many real suicides had felt themselves to be an unnecessary burden upon families by the time *Jude the Obscure* was published. When Walter Swallow, an elderly man who had been out of work for four months, attempted suicide by cutting his throat in 1886, his letter revealed that he felt he 'were only a burden to my mother', whom he lived with.[30] A note left by John Joseph Perkins after committing suicide on 8 September 1891 explained how he could not 'be a burden' on his family any longer and believed that they would 'get along better' without him. He had been suffering with crippling pains in his limbs, which left him unable to work and as a result, he and his children were entirely dependent on the earnings of the woman he had been living with for eleven years.[31] Others felt the burden they would incur on the wider community by depending on the parish in times of unemployment. William Lenny, who was seventy-two and had been a farmer in Romford, committed suicide after coming into serious pecuniary difficulties. The *Chelmsford Chronicle* reported that, as his circumstances became more embarrassed he had had to borrow 'various sums of money' from his neighbours, and 'after being reduced to great distress' he 'determined to commit suicide, rather than become a burden to the parish, which must have been the result had he survived'.[32] In this rhetoric of burden, people's worth is measured in terms of their productivity.

Malthus' views on the right of people to subsistence reinforce the notion that an individual's value is intrinsically linked to their labour power. In his view, the laws of nature do not allow for a universal right to subsist because nature is unable to provide unlimited resources. Disagreeing with Thomas Paine's *Rights of Man* (1791), Malthus declares, 'there is one right which man has generally been thought to possess, which I am confident he neither does not can possess, *a right to subsistence when his labour will not fairly purchase it*' (emphasis added).[33] When those without labour power claim from the Poor Laws they are directly or indirectly interfering with their neighbours' rights to live. This point is made by implication in a passage analogizing the right to subsist to the right to live indefinitely: 'Undoubtedly he had then, and has still, a good right to live a hundred years, nay a thousand, *if he can*, without interfering with the right of others to live; but the affair in both cases is principally an affair of power, not of right'.[34] What this also makes clear is that power is also linked to labour; those without labour have no power, and no right to claim from the state. As Gregory Claeys neatly summarizes the argument: 'No "right to charity" consequently existed, separate from the ability and willingness of the poor to make a contribution to common produce.'[35] Many of the suicides in this chapter, according to Malthus, would have had no right to subsistence due to their state of unemployment. Unable to find employment, they saw suicide as their last option.

The utilitarianism that underpins Malthus' work was common in discussions of suicide. But whilst Malthus' view could theoretically provide an argument in support of suicide in certain cases, this utilitarianism also underpinned the vehement religious arguments against it. In a sermon preached at the anniversary of the Royal Humane Society on 26 March 1797, the Anglican clergyman George Gregory spoke of the guilt of the suicide, for 'a breach of his duty to his neighbour'. The sermon expressed this viewpoint explicitly in terms of labour, preaching that the suicide 'disobeys the first of social laws, that order by which God appropriated his labours to the welfare of society'.[36] Similarly, the Anglian cleric Sydney Smith concluded his sermon *On Suicide* by reinforcing that it is man's 'duty to remain':

> That he owes it to the will of the supreme being, to the Christian law, to worldly endearments, *to general utility*, to individual magnanimity, to brave every vicissitude of fortune, while he extracts from those vicissitudes, of every nature, and in every degree, fresh sources of solid improvement, and new occasions for pious, and resigned obedience to the will of God. (emphasis added)[37]

According to Christian doctrine, each individual had a duty to carry out the post assigned to him by God, to contribute his skill and labour to society for the sake of the universal good. Caught between the religious and utilitarian values of the time, men in poverty found themselves in the paralyzing situation of being seemingly useless but unable to access relief.

Many of these sermons stressed the importance of hard work, self-discipline, perseverance and a life in service to God and society, either as a way of protecting against suicidal tendencies, or as a deterrent for those contemplating taking their own lives. The idea of 'duty', and its fulfilment, became a moral code to live by. This is something that Max Weber identified as being particular to Protestant faith, linking the concept of the 'calling' – defined as 'the fulfilment of the obligations imposed upon the individual by his position in the world' – to the rise of capitalism.[38] Weber highlights a change in conceptualization of asceticism, which rejected the accumulation of wealth as an end in itself, but saw its attainment through labour and hard work as a blessing. What is important in this, according to Weber, is the high value placed on 'restless, continuous, systematic work in a worldly calling, as the highest means to asceticism' but also as 'the surest and most evident proof of rebirth and genuine faith'.[39] In this sense, asceticism is less a self-denial of wealth in favour of religious devotion, and becomes more a self-punishing work ethic that denies pleasure and inactivity. Again, moral value is being placed on labour and productivity; to be unproductive is to be immoral.

Suicide, then, was seen as an immoral act because it was unproductive, denying society of an individual's *potential* utility. But, there are some who, through old age, infirmity, injury or ill-health, were unable (or at least felt themselves unable) to perform their duty and contribute to society in any useful way. It was along these lines that David Hume challenged the religious condemnation of suicide in his essay *On Suicide* in 1755 (posthumously published in 1777):

> … suppose that it is no longer in my power to promote the interest of society; suppose that I am a burden to it; suppose that my life hinders some person from being much more useful to society. In such cases, my resignation of life must not only be innocent, but laudable.[40]

In this case, those who could not find work would be justified in committing suicide if they required subsistence without being able to contribute. In such circumstances, suicide might even become a moral duty. This was the belief of Thomas Owen Bonser. Bonser was a supporter of Malthus' work, a member of the Malthusian League and the author of a paper defending the act of suicide.[41] In his paper *The Right to Die*, he maintained that 'in many cases it is justifiable, or even a moral duty, to retire from life' and challenged the religious notion that life, in itself, is sacred.[42] Echoing Malthus, he wrote that nothing in nature was cheaper or incurred more waste than life, and that the rate of population growth far exceeded any increase in the provision of sustenance. Bonser concluded that 'the places at the board of life are quite insufficient for the number brought in. The superfluous lives come simply to be eliminated.'[43] In accordance with this logic, those who are found to be superfluous were morally justified, if not morally *obliged*, to commit suicide. In utilitarian terms, unemployment might consequently a justifiable reason for suicide.

The question then arises how men negotiated these two perspectives, between the work ethic that Samuel Smiles described as 'that honest and upright performance of individual duty, which is the glory of manly character',[44] and the inability to find work, which suggested that his labour is not needed, that there is 'no room' for him. As can be seen through the cases in this chapter, many negotiated this uneasy position by removing themselves from the world, removing their own suffering and helping to alleviate the 'burden' they would place on others who might support them. Perhaps these acts of suicide themselves suggest that many were unable to reconcile this contradiction between the expectations and reality. Above all, this is a question of productivity, and what it means to be an unproductive male in the nineteenth century. These suicides are a testament to the importance of labour and productivity as components of respectable masculine identity.

Distress and suicide

The rhetoric around independence and individualism espoused by Smiles and Malthus was central to the breadwinner ideal of hegemonic masculinity. Men who conformed to this hegemonic masculinity were able to provide for and protect those dependent on them. Whilst there has been a concerted effort amongst historians to question how representative this hegemonic model of masculinity was and highlight other, alternative models of masculinity available to men in the nineteenth century, it is pervasive in these narratives of suicide. Based on this ideal, which was underpinned by Evangelical rhetoric at the time, work has been seen as central to masculine identity, both as a signifier of masculine status and as a site of masculine identity formation. Having work meant a man should be able to support himself and even provide for a family. It is clear that this was not always the case, and for the many who lived their lives on the borderlands of poverty and subsistence, it was an impossibility.

For the working-class man, (un)employment could be a constant source of anguish. Reports of working-class suicides often detailed the length of time workers had been without employment, sometimes for as long as eight years.[45] For many, however, even just a few weeks was enough to plunge the family into distress. George Saville, sixty-two, had been a foreman for the Midland Railway but in the month previous to his suicide he had had no work and entertained no hope of getting any. After just one month of unemployment Saville and his wife were destitute, their furniture had been seized and sold and the neighbours commented that this had caused Saville to 'become gloomy and desponding'. The article concluded by declaring that, 'It is generally stated in Kilton street and the neighbourhood that the deceased committed suicide because of being in want; but as he had only been out of work a month his condition could hardly have been that of absolute want.'[46] This report came from the local *Sheffield Independent*, and contrasts starkly with the report of the suicide found in the London papers, which acknowledged the Sheffield suburb of Brightside, where Saville lived, was an area 'where distress among the working classes largely prevails'.[47] The former shows an apparent disregard for the struggles of the local population. But it also reflects Samuel Smiles' belief that the respectable and honest working man should possess savings that protected himself and his family from want in times of unemployment or sickness. A lack of such forward thinking leads to failure.[48] Despite the rising popularity of savings banks and other informal means of savings, the reality, of course, was that saving was not always a possibility for those at the bottom of the social ladder.[49] For those living hand-to-mouth, one month without work absolutely could render them destitute. Regardless of such realities, savings, as Beverly Lemire outlines, were praised as the best tool for a man to reach the domestic comfort that was his right, and were key to reaching the 'acme of respectable manhood'.[50] The assumption made by the paper, that four weeks would not be long enough to plunge Saville into such desperate circumstances, casts an aspersion on his masculinity by highlighting his failure to save. The passing of this judgement also demonstrates an element of public shaming by highlighting the result of such a failing to others.

The nineteenth-century press played an important role in the policing of behaviour and the maintenance of shame culture. As David Barrie's work on reports of police court trials in Scotland has shown, this was particularly true of reports of criminal proceedings, but these principles are also visible in reports of suicides.[51] Following the inquest, another report of Saville's suicide from the *Sheffield Independent* added further colour to his story, by noting a history of drinking. At the inquest, it appears that his wife stated that he 'had not been drinking heavily of late but at one time he used to drink a great deal'.[52] In contrast with some of the lengthier reports on suicide inquests, this report appears to be a brief summary of the proceedings, paraphrasing the depositions of only Ann Saville, his wife, James Turner, the keeper of the beer-house where Saville took his life, and Inspector Smith, who had presumably been called to the scene. It may be that details have been left out, but the inclusion of the comment on past drinking habits, which does not appear to be relevant to his suicide, is telling of the way in which newspapers policed behaviour. In light of the Smilesian ethic of the time, the mention of his history of drinking reads as a comment on the irresponsible use of money – wasted on drink rather than put aside in case of hard times – and thus reflecting the importance of principles of respectability. Respectability was an important part of working-class culture and respectable working-class masculinity encompassed saving and protecting oneself and family against hard times, rather than spending wages on excessive drinking.[53]

The report also revealed that Saville had told Turner how he had 'expected to get fresh employment' earlier that week 'but had been disappointed', although he had not mentioned that he was out of work. His wife 'supposed' his unemployment had preyed on his mind, although she noted that he 'discussed his affairs at home very little'. In making note of the items found on Saville's person after his death, the report noted that 'There was nothing to throw light upon the reason the deceased had for laying violent hands upon himself.' Despite not explicitly attributing his unemployment to his decision to take his own life, the narrative given of Saville's life and death in the press implies his poverty and lack of employment had been a key factor. The jury reached an open verdict of suicide, feeling that there was insufficient evidence to account for his state of mind at the time.[54] This was an unusual verdict for suicides, and one that was more commonly reserved for community outsiders where little was known about the deceased.[55] The details of the inquest as reported in the press are limited, and it may be that the evidence on his mental state was lacking, but as others have suggested, juries could usually find evidence to support insanity verdicts in descriptions of 'gloominess' and 'despondency', and it appears that several witnesses mentioned that his unemployment or the fact that his home 'had been nearly stripped of the furniture'.[56] Even the fact of the suicide itself could be seen as sufficient evidence of insanity.[57] Olive Anderson, however, has suggested that such verdicts could 'represent a kind of suspended moral judgement'.[58] Ultimately, there is insufficient detail in the reports to conclude with any certainty whether this true of Saville's suicide, but given some of the comments passed on Saville's life, it does leave room for readers to exercise their own moral judgement.[59]

This interpretation of the verdict seems all the more plausible when we consider how the *Sheffield Independent* reported George William Short's 'distressing suicide through want of work' only a year and a half later. Short, a labourer of only twenty-three, had lived on Rutland Road, less than a mile from Kilton Street, and had faced similar problems with unemployment. He had been married for nine months, but for almost the entirety of this time – with the exception of six weeks doing odd jobs – he had been unable to find steady employment, and not for want of effort. The report highlighted how, at the inquest, his wife Clara detailed his efforts to look for work every day, but to no avail. She noted how he would return 'from these fruitless journeys tired and apparently ill' and was 'ashamed of walking about the streets'. His inability to find work had apparently preyed on his mind, but he had never threatened suicide. When asked by the coroner how they had lived, given her husband's lack of employment, Clara revealed that they had been forced to sell the furniture in their home in order to get money to maintain themselves, and had used 'some little money [Short] had'. They had then lost £12 of this after Short had paid for passage to America, but was then unable to bring himself to go once they had boarded the boat. After this, they had been taken in by his sister, who described him as 'a steady man' who, although not being a teetotaller, had 'never bought a gill of ale in his life'. When his wife discovered that he had cut his throat, she heard him say he was 'sorry that he had done it, and wanted to get well'. The doctor who was called to attend to Short's injuries professed his belief that the suicide had been 'owing to his want of employment preying on his mind'. The report also highlighted the coroner's reflections on what he described as a 'pitiable' case. He noted how Short had clearly been 'willing and anxious to work' having clearly made efforts to find employment. He believed that 'selling his furniture naturally would oppress him, as no doubt he had intended to spend his days in his home. To see, bit by bit, that home being broken up, for little or nothing, as was generally the case, would make a great impression upon him', with the loss of the £12 serving as 'the finishing touch to his trouble of mind'. The verdict was 'suicide during a state of temporary insanity'.[60]

Despite the similarities between these two cases – both are narratives of unemployment and suicide, both occurred within close geographical and temporal proximity, both reported in the same paper – there are, of course, some key differences. Although both had resorted to the selling of furniture to provide some income, Short appears to have had some money saved that they were able to fall back on. Adding to the contrast is the fact that Short was significantly younger, with Saville having had more work from which to, ideally, accumulate savings. Having been at least nine months without work, compared to Saville's one month, Short had also clearly persevered and had painstakingly tried to find work. Both included comments on the impact of unemployment on the men's states of mind, yet evidence in Short's case appears to have been more compelling, perhaps bolstered by the words of the doctor who had attended him. And in contrast to Saville's history of drinking, Short appears to have drunk very little, having not 'bought a gill of ale' his entire life. In other words, the report of Short's suicided describes a man who conformed to standards of respectability, and appears to have had an unblemished moral character. Although there was nothing in the report of Saville's suicide that overtly disparaged his character (with the exception of the comment on past drinking habits), there was also nothing that actively praised him either. Here, as in the cases of the previous chapter, it appears that character and prior conduct were key in informing the verdicts of coroner's juries, policing and shaming behaviour even after death. In a similar manner to reports of police court trials, the reports of these suicide inquests served as an 'extrajudicial shaming resource' in providing examples of what kind of behaviour warranted sympathy and what did not.

A further blow following unemployment was that a wife's employment could become the primary income for a family, whether through casual work or as part of organized labour. One such case was that of William Abraham Elliot, a horse-keeper who hanged himself after illness had left him 'incapacitated from work'. The report followed this revelation with the, rather blunt, statement that 'His wife had to be the bread winner'.[61] A working wife was far from uncommon amongst the working classes, but the rise of working-class respectability had grown to encompass the ideal of a male breadwinner able to support the whole family independently. Historians have analysed the impact women's entry into the industrial workplace had on working-class gender relations.[62] Employers looking to maximize profit often found cheaper female labour the preferred option, especially with the introduction of machinery which reduced the need for the physical strength of a man's labour power in trades that became increasingly machine-assisted. As Sonya Rose has pointed out, employers even used gendered rhetoric to defend their employment of women, branding the work being done by them as 'women's work' or having brought women's machines, and representing certain occupations, such as weaving, as light work that able-bodied men should be ashamed to do.[63] The entry of women into the workforce served to drive wages down and render men unemployed. In reaction, male worker began using a gendered rhetoric in their efforts to call for a 'family wage', which would allow a man to sustain his entire family without the need for wives and children to contribute to the household economy. These calls for higher wages were grounded on principles that, as Wally Seccombe has argued, 'the propertied classes found morally unassailable'.[64] In this short, blunt sentence, then, is contained a multitude of tensions and underlying issues of the changing nature of Britain's industry, family dynamics and gender relations.

Similarly, George William Lock, who had previously been an iron safe maker, had been out of work 'for some time' before he committed suicide in 1886, and 'as a last resource' his wife, 'who is a mere girl' had gone out to work at umbrella making. As the article made clear, this was a last resort. She earned just 7s a week and, out of this, 2s was spent on child nursing whilst Mrs Lock worked, and 3s 6d for rent, leaving only 1s 6d for food and other provisions.[65] The following year, Charles Booth famously distinguished 'the poor' as those, with a moderate family, living on a 'bare income' of between 18s and 21s a week and the 'very poor' as those living with less than this.[66] Similarly, in 1888, an article in *The Nineteenth Century* titled 'Life on a Guinea A Week', claimed that a wage of 21s per week was an 'impossible' scheme,[67] and the report of Lock's inquest described his wife's 7s as a 'small pittance', acknowledging that it was 'impossible to carry on any longer on such a small sum'.[68] In order to alleviate their want, they ceased paying rent for a week or two, but this only added to their anxieties. George's unemployment 'had troubled him greatly, and produced sleepless nights and despondency during the day time' and the thought of getting into debt began to prey on his mind. Their material condition will have had a significant impact of their physical health alone. Although we do not know how long Lock had been out of employment – the article only generalized that it had been 'for some time' – we know that Lock's wife was used to regularly going without breakfast. Such a constant state of hunger would have undoubtedly have caused severe mental distress. The coroner, Mr Hawkes, concluded the inquest by turning attention to considering Lock's state of mind at the time of his suicide, revealing that, '[h]e could not imagine anything more likely to overbalance a man's mind than being in such a dreadful state of destitution with a young wife and child'.[69] In referencing Lock's wife and child this way, Hawkes frames Lock's anxieties and suicide in terms of his role as provider and protector of his family.

The melodramatic narrative

Wives and children left behind were often an important part in the emotional narratives of these suicides, reinforcing the providing role of men inscribed in hegemonic masculinity by revealing that the suicide had 'left a wife and family totally unprovided for'.[70] By invoking the image of a family broken up, these suicide narratives present a severe rupture in domestic life which adds a melodramatic reading to the texts. David Mayer describes melodrama as

> a theatrical or literary response to a world where things are seen to go wrong, where ideas of secular and divine justice and recompense are not always met, where suffering is not always acknowledged, and where the explanations for wrong, injustice, and suffering are not altogether understandable. Melodrama tries to respond with emotional, rather than intellectual, answers to a world where explanations of why there is pain and chaos and discord are flawed or

deeply and logically inconsistent, where there are all-too-visible discrepancies between readily observed calamities and palliative answers.[71]

The melodramatic mode was not just confined to literature and the stage, but permeated culture, acting as a tool for expression, understanding and meaning-making. As Rohan McWilliam argues, it also shaped journalism, through the sensationalization of the news, using the 'language and categories of the stage' to make sense of events and scandals.[72] Narratives of suicide follow along similar lines. Both the unemployment and the suicides fit into what Mayer above refers to as the suffering and injustice that is not always understandable. Unemployment was a structural problem. Trades were seasonal and rapid technological advancement was rendering a large portion of physical manpower obsolete. But the New Poor Law and the emergence of an individualistic, capitalist society created an environment where unemployment was seen to be the result of personal moral failure, exemplified by the writings of Thomas Malthus and Samuel Smiles.

The melodramatic mode in suicide narratives helped to challenge the idea that unemployment was the result of personal moral failure. As Martha Vicinus states, the 'emotional effectiveness' of melodrama is in the way it makes the moral visible: 'The good is made visible in the passive suffering of virtuous characters.'[73] The reports of many of these suicides present stories of respectable working people desperately searching for employment and, through no fault of their own, being unable to find any. Many of these reports emphasized the good or respectable character of those at the heart of these domestic tragedies, that they had searched tirelessly for work, and were hardworking when they were in employment, made personal sacrifices so their children might not go without, and recall the neighbours' kind words about them. J. Challiner, who suffered constitutional fits that prevented him from working and committed suicide in 1845, was described as bearing 'a very good character'.[74] George William Short, who committed suicide in 1879, had been out of employment for nearly nine months but 'had tried to get work every day' without success.[75] James Ilott, who committed suicide in 1885, after months of unemployment, was described by those who knew him as a 'respectable man'.[76] Papers explained that George William Lock, mentioned above, had 'striven hard to earn a livelihood'.[77]

Whilst these narratives did not necessarily offer clear answers as to why poverty happened, they did go some way in showing those trapped in it that their situation was not due to their own laziness or wastefulness, as the individualistic dogma of the times suggested. Melodrama appeals to those who feel powerless, 'who feel that their lives are without order and that events they cannot control can destroy or save them'.[78] As Rohan McWilliam suggested, it could offer 'a form of psychic healing by dramatizing anxieties such as the fear of not being able to pay the rent'.[79] Suicide reports of the unemployed provided evidence of blameless suffering which often went unacknowledged and was not easily understood. By acknowledging this suffering, which the New Poor Law system blamed on the individual, such reports offered an alternative form of knowledge to Malthusianism, utilitarianism and individualism.[80]

One case which offers the perfect example of the melodramatic narrative at work was the 'Tooting Horror' or 'Tooting Tragedy', as papers variously described it.[81] Frank Taylor awoke at an early hour on Thursday 7 March and proceeded to cut the throats of his wife and six of their children, before committing suicide in the same manner. The eldest boy, Frank, only fourteen, who survived his father's attempt to cut his throat but sustained injuries on his neck and arms where he had raised his hands to protect himself, rushed to his neighbours to raise an alarm. The neighbour, Mr Hawkins (or Hockins according to some papers), was woken by the young boy knocking at his door at six in the morning, bleeding from his throat and hands, who told him 'Father's cut all our throats, and mother is dead'.[82] After bandaging the boy's throat, he sent his wife for the police, who arrived almost immediately. On entering the house, the scene was described as 'having the appearance more of a slaughter-house than a human habitation, the furniture and walls being splashed with blood, while pools of it lay upon the floor'. The father was found to be still alive on arrival at the house and was immediately removed to the Clapham Infirmary, but he died on the way.[83]

The family was well thought of amongst the local community. Taylor and his wife had been married for fifteen years and appeared to live together happily, and neighbours commented that they were 'highly regarded by the local clergy'.[84] The reports of the incident and the inquest made sure to highlight the positive words said about Frank Taylor himself. He was described as a teetotaller (or at least a very infrequent drinker), a 'kind father', an 'affectionate husband', 'a most loving man', 'hard working but very unfortunate' and a 'steady, industrious man'.[85] But despite being 'active and willing to work if work could be found',[86] he had been out of employment since Christmas. With a severe frost in the winter, the family had been 'plunged into distress', subsisting on what they could grow in their allotment but having to rely on the penny dinners provided at the local church and the charity of clergymen, who offered them milk, bread and meat.[87] It appears he had recently found some work at Tooting Junction, and it was noted how, as soon as he had been paid, he 'stocked the larder and purchased boots for some of the children'. Unfortunately, only a week after starting work again he was taken ill with influenza, once again throwing him out of work. He resumed work the day before he killed his family and, although he was not fully recovered and appearing 'out of sorts', it was noted that there was nothing to suggest that he had been seriously affected by the illness.[88] That is to say, there was no reason to suspect that his illness had affected his mind in any way.

The reports of the Tooting case, as with many other working-class suicides, was laced through with the trappings of domestic melodrama. This is highlighted in details of their households, the family circumstances and threat to domesticity which unemployment posed. Evidence of this has already been seen in the previously mentioned suicide of George William Short, in which the coroner described the anguish Short must have felt at seeing his home broken up 'bit by bit' as they sold furniture in order to maintain themselves. Here, the threat to domesticity is shown not only through the suicide itself, but in the imagery of the home physically being broken up. The 'Tooting Tragedy', in particular, provides a vivid illustration of this through the descriptions of the Taylor family's home and the scene of the crime: 'The bedding in the front room was saturated with blood, and the apartment was bespattered with it in all directions';[89] Mrs Taylor's 'thumbs were nearly cut off, and she had evidently been injured about the body before the death wound in her throat had been given'.[90] Another report revealed how,

> More revolting still was the sight of six children lying lifeless, four of them upon the floor, and two of them, both girls, hanging over the side of the bed with their heads nearly severed from their bodies. It was only too apparent that the little victims had put forth all their feeble strength to resist the furious onslaught of their murderer, and had died struggling hard against dreadful odds.[91]

This graphic illustration of a home turned into a deeply disturbing crime scene was not only part of nineteenth-century sensationalism. As Shani D'Cruze has exemplified through her work on domestic murder, such violence taking place inside the home threatened the ideological space of the home as a safe haven.[92] Whilst D'Cruze's discussion is focused more explicitly on violence within the middle-class home, such domestic tragedy was felt just as keenly amongst the working classes. Domesticity was not monopolized by the middle classes, and it had a central place in working-class rhetoric. As Anna Clark has convincingly shown, Chartists used images of domesticity in their political rhetoric, drawing on melodramatic plots that shifted the blame of poverty and domestic misery from the immorality of the working-class individual to 'the aristocratic libertine, symbolizing capitalism and corruption'.[93] What makes the tragedy more horrific is that, not only did Taylor implicitly threaten the security of the domestic environment by committing suicide and thereby removing the main source of income, but he directly destroyed it by murdering his family in their own home.

Where these narratives differ from melodrama is in the absence of a clear, identifiable villain. The villain was a key figure in melodrama and was usually a representation of wider social issues affecting working-class lives, embodied in a greedy middle-class character.[94] In these suicide narratives, however, the 'villain' of the narrative is often unembodied. In Taylor's case, despite being the murderer, he was not presented as the melodramatic villain in this narrative, as he himself was the victim of the real villain – the forces of capitalism and liberalism that perpetuated the poverty of the working classes. Here, low wages, increasing mechanization and the precarious nature of many working-class jobs threatened not just a man's masculinity, but the welfare of the entire household. Unemployment, and by implication capitalist society, murdered the family.

Moreover, the way in which Taylor's story was marked by distinct periods of employment, unemployment, sickness and health reflects the pacing of melodramatic performances. Juliet John describes 'the emotional economy of melodrama' as 'best figured in a series of waves',[95] alternating, literally, between music and pictures, music and speech, but also between movement and stasis.[96] To this we can also add calm and crisis especially when we are dealing with melodrama's written form. The Taylor case, for example, alternates between relative calm and security and moments of crisis. We learn that Taylor had been a hard worker when in work, but thrown out of work the family is plunged into crisis, Taylor again finds work but is again thrown into a crisis when he contracts influenza, he returns to work despite not having fully recovered and the ultimate crisis comes with the murder of his family. The narrative itself follows the form of melodramatic performance.

Suicide coupled with family murder was by no means an unfamiliar combination in murder-suicides.[97] Many unemployed men appear to have believed their families to be better off without them, but for others, rather than leaving their families in more distress without a breadwinner, murder might be seen as a further way to protect them from poverty. It might also be a way of keeping the family together rather than breaking them up. The *Bristol Mercury*, which gave one of the most sensational accounts of the case, framed the tragedy in this way. The report framed the narrative in terms of Taylor's mind becoming unhinged on account of concern for his family's situation, and described his actions as an attempt to relieve them 'from the hard battle of life' and allow them to 'all retire together'.[98]

As more details of what *Reynolds's Newspaper* described as the 'Tooting Horror' were uncovered, the press began to report that letters had been found on Taylor's body, which indicated that he had initially only contemplated his own suicide. The first, addressed to his wife and children, revealed that 'People have accused me of many wrong things, but the Lord has washed them away in His precious blood. I can't bear the shame that I am accused of. May God protect you and my dear children when I am gone … May God bless you all, and keep you all from shame!' On the back of this was another, written apparently several days later, when his 'mind had become even more unhinged than before, and his suicidal intent had developed into the infinitely more terrible determination to take the lives of the whole of his dear ones at once', which began, 'To-night we depart from this life of trouble' and ended 'It is finished'. The envelope in which the letter was found was written, 'I love my wife and children too dearly to allow people to jeer them. They are all pure.'[99]

None of the reports picked up on these 'shameful accusations', so it is unclear what they may have been, whether they were real or imagined. But despite the journalistic attempts to relieve the blame of poverty from the working classes, the sense of shame that surrounded the experience of poverty was keenly felt by many. Vivienne Richmond's study of working-class clothing has shown how important appearances – cleanliness and clothing – was in creating and maintaining respectability. Having, or not having, appropriate clothing was an important marker of respectability; for example, the Sunday best was the 'sartorial barometer' of respectability, and those without would even keep themselves and their children cooped up inside all day long for fear of the shame.[100] With his first new wages, the papers reported how in addition to stocking the larder, Frank Taylor had immediately bought new boots for some of the children, shinning boots being a 'blazon of family respectability'.[101] *The Standard* also reported that the house itself was barely furnished and dirty: there was hardly any bed-clothing, and none at all in the room where the children slept, the bed was only a single and the 'mattress was very dirty'. All rooms were scantily furnished, with the exception of the front, ground-floor room which, the report noted, had a piano; and in the cupboards there was only two loaves of bread, some butter, one egg and 'a small piece of roast mutton'.[102] The description of Taylor's efforts as a father to provide boots and the description of the house suggest that the family had been doing all they could to keep up appearances and mask the shame of poverty.

'Death before the workhouse': suicide and masculine shame

One of the biggest markers of shame in working-class communities was entry into the workhouse. The Tooting relieving officer, George William Phillips, revealed that Taylor had applied to him for relief the previous month and had confessed that he owed six weeks rent and his son was working for 2*s* 6*d* per week. Phillips had said he could get a job at the stone-yard for 15*s*–16*s* a week, but Taylor never took up the offer.[103] This form of outdoor relief, which despite emphasis on the use of indoor relief was still being used widely by the end of the century, did not quite carry the same level of shame as entering the workhouse, but would still have been degrading and 'a cause for self-reproach and private humiliation'.[104]

The workhouse, and particularly its uniform, were part of the ritual of public shaming to regulate moral behaviour that persisted into the nineteenth century.[105] In discussing the punitive role of institutional uniform during the nineteenth century, Vivienne Richmond has argued that the workhouse uniform became more punitive with the Poor Law Amendment Act of 1834, acting as part of the aim to instill a desire never to return. For some Poor Law reformers, such as George Nicholls, the workhouse was intended to act as a shame punishment, and would entail reproach so strong that it would be 'extended downwards from Father to Son'.[106] The shame and punitive nature of the workhouse and its uniform, then, was clearly recognized by contemporaries as a key part of such institutions even near the end of the century. In 1892, when the Islington workhouse introduced plain clothes for elderly workhouse residents on their walks outside the workhouse, the *Bristol Mercury* praised the move as 'revolutionary' and one that helped to relieve the stigma of the workhouse for those who, they felt, had entered the 'House' through no fault of their own. Nonetheless, they clearly supported the use of uniforms as a punitive measure, feeling that those who found themselves in the workhouse because they were 'loafers' and had a 'distaste for work', should be made to 'bear some badge that they are maintained at the public expense'.[107]

The notion of the workhouse uniform as a badge of shame was clearly felt by the working classes. One of Henry Mayhew's interviewees, a blind street-seller, described the workhouse coat as a 'slothful, degrading badge', that forever changed a man who wears one.[108] It also shattered any notion of respectability, stripped men of their civil rights, cast shame over generations to come and broke up their families, undermining their position as head of the household.[109] In the context of Smilesian self-help and Malthusian utility, the workhouse also represented individual moral failure. Samuel Smiles believed that a sense of individualism should be cultivated from youth; it was important that man felt 'that his happiness and well-doing in life must necessarily rely mainly on himself and the exercise of his own energies, rather than upon the help and patronage of others'. The necessity of hard work was preferable to having 'everything done ready to our hand', and even set down that a 'start in life with relatively small means' was so important a stimulus to work that it should be considered 'essential to success in life'.[110] Entering the workhouse meant relying upon the help and patronage of others and insinuated failure.

So shameful was the workhouse that headlines such as 'Death Before the Workhouse' were not uncommon in narratives of men's suicides.[111] The suicide of Benjamin Klimcke, a watchcase polisher from Coventry, forty-seven years of age, which was widely reported in the north of England, in Wales and Scotland, was used to comment variously on the 'false pride' of the working classes, the workhouse system, the distress and suffering that pervaded in Coventry at the time and to criticize William Gladstone's free-trade principles for throwing hundreds of watchmakers out of employment.[112] Klimcke had been out of work for six months before taking his own life; recently he had been surviving on only bread, and, at the inquest, his daughter commented that lately 'his manner had become strange'. According to the letter he left on the table in his sitting room, Klimcke had become 'almost wild through no work' and seeing no prospects of finding employment in the near future, he wrote, 'I prefer death to the workhouse'.[113] Twelve out of the fifteen papers reporting Benjamin Klimcke's suicide included the following commentary:

> It adds a touch to the pathos of the story to learn on the authority of Alderman Worwood that Klimcke, who was a member of a local 'Early Morning Class', would have been relieved had he made his case known. Some feeling of false pride had restrained him from telling his sorrows to the outside world.[114]

But, at a time when independence was a marker of success, dependence on parish relief was antithetical to respectable working-class masculinity. A letter to the editor of the politically radical *Reynolds's Newspaper*, decrying the Poor Laws and the Charity Organization Society, used Klimcke's suicide to highlight the degradation that accompanied entry into the workhouse and call for reform. The author, a regular columnist operating under the pseudonym 'Northumbrian',[115] lambasted 'the gentlemen of the Charity Organization Society' for failing to understand why the working classes refused to apply for relief, by answering to these suicides by 'saying that the poor wretch should have applied to them'. 'Northumbrian' outlined how 'before he could do that he would have to conquer that curious pride which makes decent and honest men shirk the workhouse'; this aversion to the workhouse was a result of the simple fact that 'the workhouse is a badge of disgrace' and branded them as paupers.[116] As Claudia C. Klaver has noted, there was an important distinction between pauper and labourer (including the labouring poor). 'Pauperism', Klaver points out, 'entailed laziness, drunkenness, and thriftlessness'.[117] This distinction engaged with the individualistic and utilitarian conflation of labour and morality where independence epitomized a high moral character and dependence was a sign of immorality. Being unable to 'honestly' maintain oneself and one's family necessitated 'living dishonestly upon the means of somebody else'.[118] Entering the workhouse, then, was symbol of personal moral failure, as it placed the burden of personal and family maintenance on others. For the working man, the workhouse was a profound symbol of masculine shame as it represented the loss of independence that was an important marker of manhood and masculinity.[119]

Entering the workhouse also entailed a loss of a man's status as head of his household. Families would be broken up on admission, and aside from the emotional distress this might cause, this separation undermined a man's position as provider and protector by placing his wife and children (as well as himself) under parish authority. This breaking-up of families was a very real concern. In the suicide note of Alfred Allen, who was charged with attempting suicide in 1887 after being unemployed for two months, he revealed his concern at seeing his family separated in the workhouse. Allen had worked at Bacton Gasworks for twelve years, where he had lost sight in one eye after an explosion and was discharged when work became 'a little slack'. After returning home one night to see his 'wife fainting at her needlework and the children crying for bread', he could see only death in front of him. The note, addressed to his wife, recounted this and continued, 'We must part ... But where? At the workhouse gate? No, little darling, "till death us do part" was the promise we made, and death is the kindest and the best.'[120] For Allen, breaking up his family in the workhouse was inconceivable. The family was important in the formation of masculine identity. Having a family was a marker of maturity and economic independence, which were important in masculine identity formation, and the ability to maintain his family represented his honourable labour.[121] The workhouse represented a man's failure by making him dependent upon the state for the maintenance of himself and his family, by taking away his autonomy and independence and by the implication of immorality represented in the individualistic economy.

For many of these men, suicide offered a rational path out of hardship, avoiding the shame cast over them by poverty or the workhouse. Suicide notes sometimes pleaded the jury not to return verdicts of insanity, insisting they were in full possession of their reason and presenting the suicide as logical response to their situation. J. Challiner, for example, wrote a postscript to his suicide note pleading the 'Gentlemen of the Jury' not to 'return a verdict that I destroyed myself being at the time insane, for I am sensible to the time of dropping the pen to present the pistol to my mouth'.[122] The jury returned a verdict in accord with his request. A similar plea was made in a case in 1890. Arthur Charles Selby Hilton, only twenty-three years of age, committed suicide after being made redundant from his job as a solicitor's clerk. He had been given a week's holiday to find other employment, but to no avail. On visiting an old friend and sharing his situation, the friend revealed he would have been able to find him work for 35s a week if he had come to him only two days earlier. The 'ill-luck completely upset' him and he determined he 'would stand no more of it', hoping his family would see that he 'did this for the best' of them. In a postscript to the letter he had left explaining his circumstances to his mother, he stated how he was 'a long way from being mad, although everyone will say so'. The jury, however, returned the verdict of temporary insanity.[123] These cases conform to typical narratives of male suicide, which frame the act as a rational choice and downplay the emotional and psychological trauma that can accompany unemployment, poverty and financial anxiety.[124]

Many of these narratives were also replete with emotional signifiers. Witnesses attest to the distress caused by unemployment, and the despondency that so often accompanied it. James Ilott 'became very depressed, refused to eat anything, and was very strange in his behaviour' as a result of his months of unemployment, and committed suicide by throwing himself under a train.[125] The mother of Charles Brown, a 28-year-old miner, 'believed that the only reason for the rash act was he had been heartbroken because he had been out of work'.[126] In some cases, the men themselves were open about their emotional distress in their final letters. Blackburn's *Weekly Standard* and *Express* reported the 'pathetic letter' of John Crane, a dock labourer who drowned himself at the age of forty-eight, having been discharged by the London and South-West India Dock Company, after eighteen years in their employ, because he was suffering a 'skin complaint'. After being dragged from the water, a letter describing his emotional distress was found in his pocket. It detailed how he was unable to find food for his children, was unable to work and wished love to his mother and wife. The letter concluded emotionally, stating: 'This misery is too much for me. There is not one bright star in the clouds—all is dark.' The jury's verdict was 'suicide whilst temporarily insane, brought on through loss of work and mental worry'.[127]

The experience of unemployment and poverty were, and remain, a continuous cause of insanity, mental illness and suicide in Britain and the wider world.[128] Yet some believed that the experience of being reduced from poor to a state of poverty was not as devastating as being reduced from great to moderate wealth. Charles Mercier believed that a reduction in circumstances among the wealthy members of society was likely be accompanied by enough stress to bring on insanity, but the same did not apply to the working-class man reduced to poverty:

> A person who lives always on the verge of penury; whose means of subsistence suffice, at the best of times, to procure for him only the bare necessaries of life; who seldom enjoys the satisfaction of having quite enough to eat; whose clothing in winter is seldom substantial enough to be a full protection against the weather; whose dwelling is at the best of time destitute of all comforts, and of many things which are regarded by the majority of people as necessaries;—such a person will suffer less stress from a complete withdrawal of his scanty means of subsistence, than will another person who is accustomed to live in the lap of luxury, and who, from loss of the greater part of his fortune, is compelled to remove from a lordly mansion to a cottage of six rooms. Although the condition of the first man, who is reduced to sleeping under a haystack, and who knows not, when he awakes in the morning, whether or no he will taste food that day, is absolutely worse than that of the second, who has a neatly furnished cottage, and enough saved out of the wreck of his fortune to provide him with a living for the rest of his life; yet the amount of vicissitude experienced by the first is not so great as that experienced by the second.[129]

By the standards of Charles Mercier, the men in this chapter, whose suicides were explained as the result of insanity brought on through poverty, would not have been liable to such aberrations of mind. This is despite the fact that, as Akihito Suzuki has shown, prospects of unemployment, poverty and the workhouse were regularly given as explanations for insanity amongst labouring men.[130] Mercier's views indicate a clear class distinction in how insanity was perceived and understood and presents a failure to recognize the psychological and emotional effects of extended and extreme poverty. However, this is not necessarily reflective of the medical view of insanity as a whole. Earlier in the century an article in the *Provincial Medical and Surgical Journal* (later to become the *British Medical Journal*) reported that, in England and Wales, pauper asylum patients numbered 7,482, whilst the number of private asylum patients stood at 3,790.[131]

Denying that poverty can result in insanity again reinforced the notion of suicide being a rational response to the practical problem of living without enough money, and denies the emotional and psychological suffering that accompanies poverty. Such experiences, however, become clear through the narratives used to write about suicide, and the notes printed by the press. The men writing of their distress in suicide notes painfully describe the effects of unemployment. William Gowar Dean, who committed suicide in Liverpool in August 1895, whose 'most assiduous' efforts to find employment were unsuccessful, wrote to his wife that he felt 'completely heartbroken. Employment seems to be denied me everywhere I go. I am almost starving; therefore you cannot wonder at my committing such an act.' He also appears to have blamed himself for his family's distress, signing off the letter begging his wife 'to forget the unhappy wretch who has embittered your days so long, but who still dearly and devotedly loves you'.[132] A similar letter was written by John Joseph Perkins, who wrote his last letter to his wife 'with a broken heart' and told her that she was 'worth her weight in gold to any man that is able to work and do well by you'.[133] Both letters display evidence of the men's shame at failing in their duties to support their wives and children. Rather than understanding their failure as the result of structural unemployment, or an illness out of personal control, Dean and Perkins appear to see their inability to work as a personal moral failure, something to be personally ashamed of.[134]

Conclusion

Whilst the workhouses of the nineteenth century have long disappeared, stories of suicide from poverty and unemployment have not. However, with strict media guidelines on the reporting of suicides, the direct links between worldly suffering and suicide has been blurred.[135] In recent years, work has been done to highlight the impact of government policies on increasing suicide rates, and to challenge the pathologizing and internalizing of suicide which distances it from 'other cultural meanings' and wider social causes.[136] Looking at economic crises throughout the twentieth century to the present day, David Stuckler and Sanjay Basu have demonstrated how austerity measures have a direct impact on suicide rates across the world, whilst China Mills has drawn on reports of suicides directly linked to the UK government's austerity measures and benefits cuts to demonstrate how benefit claimants are made to feel they are a burden by 'neoliberal market logic'.[137] This was a familiar feeling to the working-class men of the nineteenth century who, after losing employment, being unable to support their families and refusing to degrade themselves and their families by submitting to the workhouse, chose to take their own lives. These stories of hardship were picked up and amplified by radical papers such as *Reynolds's* who utilized melodramatic tropes to provide recognition to the blameless suffering that many experienced.

The liberalism of the nineteenth century embraced utilitarian measures of value, and measured moral worth in terms of labour power, whilst Tory paternalism reconceptualized the helping of the poor as a benevolent act of charity, rather than a moral obligation. This was also the ethos of the individualism captured in Samuel Smiles' *Self-Help*, which placed responsibility for one's situation on the individual.[138] As Peter Mandler notes, the elites came to see free-markets 'as Providentially-designed mechanisms for the cultivation of true morality', which, he notes, Boyd Hilton has attributed to Evangelical influences, which placed faith in a 'natural order' to 'discipline the weak and punish the vicious'.[139] As a result, the unemployed, who were unable to make a contribution to general utility, were deemed to be less worthy of help, idling rather than working, a burden on the state and parish.

Although these suicide narratives were mediated by editors and journalists, the reporting of inquest proceedings offered a way for the working classes to regain some control over their identities and have their voices heard. By recounting the tireless searches and miles walked many went through in desperate attempts to find work and the recognizable appeals made to symbols of respectability, the narratives help to challenge the idea espoused by Thomas Malthus and Samuel Smiles that the unproductive were immoral. The melodramatic language and motifs found in the reports also offered a way to acknowledge and understand the suffering experienced by these working-class men that might otherwise go unacknowledged; it allowed them to see that the suffering was through no fault of their own, but that they were victims of the changing social and economic landscape.

The suicides throughout this chapter represent only a small proportion of those who struggled in the face of severe stress, to the point that they could no longer bear it. Whether their suicidal actions were a reaction to the poverty endured by the unemployed working-class man, or as a result of the nervous breakdown of the over-working middle-class man, the issues of labour and productivity are key to understanding them.

Notes

1   For example, 'Suicide Through Want of Work', *Yorkshire Herald*, 19 September 1894: 14; 'Distressing Suicide Through Want of Work at Neepsend', *Sheffield Independent*, 2 June 1879: 3; 'Suicide Through Starvation', *Star*, 19 August 1879;

'Attempted Suicide Through Want of Work', *Blackburn Standard* and *Weekly Express*, 18 February 1893: 7; 'An Out-Of-Work's Suicide', *Weekly Standard and Express*, 4 August 1894: 7; 'Attempted Suicide from Want', *Morning Post*, 16 March 1846: 3; 'Attempt at Suicide Through Distress', *Morning Post*, 5 November 1818: 2.

2 For a more extensive discussion of the causes of unemployment, see John Burnett, *Idle Hands: The Experience of Unemployment, 1790–1990* (London; New York, NY: Routledge, 1994), 5–8.

3 See, for example, Megan Doolittle, 'Fatherhood and Family Shame: Masculinity, Welfare and the Workhouse in Late Nineteenth-Century England', in *The Politics of Domestic Authority in Britain Since 1800*, ed. Lucy Delap, Ben Griffin and Abigail Wills (Basingstoke, Hampshire; New York, NY: Palgrave Macmillan, 2009); Claudia C. Klaver, *A/Moral Economics: Classical Political Economy and Cultural Authority in Nineteenth-Century England* (Columbus, OH: Ohio State University Press, 2003), chap. 5; Marjorie Levine-Clark, *Unemployment, Welfare, and Masculine Citizenship: "So Much Honest Poverty" in Britain, 1870–1930* (Basingstoke: Palgrave Macmillan, 2015).

4 Leonore Davidoff and Catherine Hall themselves stressed, in their extended introduction to the revised edition of *Family Fortunes*, that their 'intention was always to move beyond the public/private divide'. Leonore Davidoff and Catherine Hall, *Family Fortunes*, rev. edn (London; New York, NY: Routledge, 2002), xvi; John Tosh, *A Man's Place: Masculinity and the Middle-Class Home in Victorian England* (New Haven, CT; London: Yale University Press, 1999), 92.

5 See, for example, Wally Seccombe, 'Patriarchy Stabilized: The Construction of the Male Breadwinner Wage Norm in Nineteenth-Century Britain', *Social History* 11, no. 1 (1986): 53–76; Sonya O. Rose, *Limited Livelihoods: Gender and Class in Nineteenth-Century England* (London: Routledge, 1992), 142; Anna Clark, 'The Rhetoric of Chartist Domesticity: Gender, Language, and Class in the 1830s and 1840s', *Journal of British Studies* 31, no. 1 (1992): 62–88.

6 This language still permeates contemporary debates around poverty, austerity and suicides today; see China Mills, '"Dead People Don't Claim": A Psychopolitical Autopsy of UK Austerity Suicides', *Critical Social Policy* 38, no. 2 (2017).

7 David Englander, *Poverty and Poor Law Reform in Britain: From Chadwick to Booth, 1834–1914* (London: Routledge, 1998), 44.

8 Ibid., 38, 44 (quote on 44).

9 Thomas J. Scheff, 'Shame and the Social Bond: A Sociological Theory', *Sociological Theory* 18, no. 1 (1 March 2000): 96–8 (quote on 98).

10 See David Nash and Anne-Marie Kilday, *Cultures of Shame: Exploring Crime and Morality in Britain 1600–1900* (Houndmills, Basingstoke; New York, NY: Palgrave Macmillan, 2010); Anne-Marie Kilday and David Nash, *Shame and Modernity in Britain: 1890 to the Present* (London: Palgrave Macmillan, 2017); David G. Barrie, 'Naming and Shaming: Trial by Media in Nineteenth-Century Scotland', *Journal Of British Studies* 54, no. 2 (2015): 350.

11 Englander, *Poverty and Poor Law Reform in Britain*, 44.

12 Jennifer Biddle, 'Shame', in *Emotions: A Cultural Studies Reader*, ed. Jennifer Harding and E. Deidre Pribram, 1st edn (Oxford; New York, NY: Routledge, 2009), 115.

13 Kali Israel, *Names and Stories: Emilia Dilke and Victorian Culture* (New York, NY: Oxford University Press, 1999), 14.

14 Jamie L. Bronstein, *Caught in the Machinery: Workplace Accidents and Injured Workers in Nineteenth-Century Britain* (Stanford, CA: Stanford University Press, 2008), 3.

15 Rohan McWilliam, 'Melodrama', in Pamela K. Gilbert, ed., *A Companion to Sensation Fiction* (Malden, MA: Wiley-Blackwell, 2011): 59.

16 'Melancholy Suicide at Bury St. Edmund's', *Ipswich Journal*, 20 June 1857: 4. See also 'Suicide at Slaithwaite', *Huddersfield Chronicle and West Yorshire Advertiser*, 27 May 1882: 5; 'Suicide Through Want of Work', *Bury and Norwich Post*, 1 September 1885: 3; 'Attempted Murder and Suicide', *Nottinghamshire Guardian*, 13 May 1893: 4; 'Suicide Through Poverty', *North-Eastern Daily Gazette*, 3 November 1886: 4.

17 Bronstein, *Caught in the Machinery*, 62.

18 Rose, *Limited Livelihoods*, 130–2.

19 'Suicide of A Young Lady, by Leaping Off The Monument', *The Examiner*, 15 September 1839: 588; for a discussion of poverty and female insanity, see Marjorie Levine-Clark, '"Embarrassed Circumstances": Gender, Poverty, and Insanity in the West Riding of England in the Early-Victorian Years', in *Sex and Seclusion, Class and Custody: Perspectives on Gender and Class in the History of British and Irish Psychiatry*, ed. Johnathan Andrews and Anne Digby, (Amsterdam: Rodopi, 2004), 123–48.

20 Bob Shenton, 'Suicide and Surplus People/Value', *Identities* 18, no. 1 (1 January 2011): 64.

21 Gregory Claeys, 'Malthus and Godwin: Rights, Utility and Productivity', in *New Perspectives on Malthus*, ed. Robert J. Mayhew (Cambridge: Cambridge University Press, 2016), 66–8.

22 Ibid., 66.

23 Thomas Malthus, *An Essay on the Principle of Population: Or. A View of Its Past and Present Effects on Human Happiness*, 2nd edn (London: J. Johnson, 1803), 531.

24 Thomas Malthus, *An Essay on the Principle of Population: Or. A View of Its Past and Present Effects on Human Happiness*, 4th edn, vol. 1 (London: J. Johnson, 1807), 15–21.

25 Ibid., 451–2.

26 Gillian Beer, *Darwin's Plots: Evolutionary Narrative in Darwin, George Eliot, and Nineteenth-Century Fiction*, 2nd edn (Cambridge; New York, NY: Cambridge University Press, 2000), 240.

27 Thomas Hardy, *Jude the Obscure* (London: Penguin, 1998), 336.

28 Ibid., 332–3; child-murder as a form of population control had, controversially, been raised earlier in the century, in a work published pseudonymously which proposed a theory of 'painless extinction' and gained notoriety. Marcus, *On the Possibility of Limiting Populousness* (London: John Hill, 1838); the work is discussed in Josephine McDonagh, *Child Murder and British Culture, 1720–1900* (Cambridge: Cambridge University Press, 2003), 101–2.

29 E. Steinlight, 'Hardy's Unnecessary Lives: The Novel as Surplus', *Novel: A Forum on Fiction* 47, no. 2 (1 June 2014): 224.

30 'Attempted Suicide in Sheffield', *Sheffield Independent*, 2 August 1886: 3.

31 'A Suicide's Letter', *Huddersfield Daily Chronicle*, 10 September 1891: 4.

32 'Melancholy Suicide', *Chelmsford Chronicle*, 23 April 1858: 3.

33 Malthus, *Principle of Population*, 1807, 306.

34 Ibid., 307.

35 Claeys, 'Malthus and Godwin: Rights, Utility and Productivity', 68.

36 George Gregory, *A Sermon on Suicide* (London: J. Nichols; and sold by C. Dilly, Messrs. F. and C. Rivington, J. Johnson, and J. Hookham, 1797), 12–13.

37 Sydney Smith, 'On Suicide', in *Two Volumes of Sermons*, vol. II (London: T. Cadell and W. Davies, 1809), 142.

38 Max Weber, *The Protestant Ethic and the Spirit of Capitalism*, Routledge Classics (London; New York, NY: Routledge, 2001), 40.

39 Ibid., 116.

40 David Hume, 'Essay I' [On Suicide], in David Hume, *Two Essays* (London, 1777): 20.

41 Bonser went on to commit suicide in 1898 after his mind had become 'unhinged', although the cause of this was not given in the reports of his death. 'Practiced What He Preached', *South Wales Daily News*, 19 July 1898: 3; 'The Theory And Practice Of Suicide', *Northern Daily Telegraph*, 19 July 1898: 3; 'Suicide at Malvern', *St. James's Gazette*, 19 July 1898: 12; 'Shocking Suicide of an Author', *Grantham Journal*, 23 July 1898: 7; 'A Student of Suicide!', *Hull Daily Mail*, 19 July 1898: 2; 'A Follower of Malthus Commits Suicide', *Dundee Courier*, 19 July 1898: 5.

42 Thomas Owen Bonser, *The Right to Die* (London: Freethought Publishing Company, 1885), 3.

43 Ibid., 7.

44 Samuel Smiles, *Self-Help: With Illustrations of Character, Conduct, and Perseverance* (London: John Murray, 1868), xi.

45 'Double Murder and Suicide', *Belfast News-Letter*, 22 January 1895: 5.

46 'The Distress in Brightside', *Sheffield Independent*, 19 January 1878: 3.

47 'Suicide', *The Times*, 19 January 1878: 11; 'Suicide', *Evening Mail*, 21 January 1878: 3.

48 Smiles, *Self-Help*, 291–7.

49 See Beverly Lemire's discussion of the rise of savings culture in chap. 6 of Beverly
    Lemire, *The Business of Everyday Life: Gender, Practice and Social Politics in
    England, c.1600–1900*, Gender in History (Manchester: Manchester University
    Press, 2005), 141–86.
50 Ibid., 161, 175.
51 On the nineteenth-century press as an extrajudicial instrument and its role in
    upholding shame culture, see Barrie, 'Naming and Shaming: Trial by Media in
    Nineteenth-Century Scotland'.
52 'The Suicide at Brightside', *Sheffield Independent*, 26 January 1878: 12.
53 Samuel Smiles devoted a whole chapter to the 'use and misuse' of money: Smiles,
    Self-Help, chap. 10.
54 'The Suicide at Brightside', *Sheffield Independent*.
55 Anderson, *Suicide in Victorian and Edwardian England*, 223.
56 'The Supposed Suicide Through Want in Sheffield', *Sheffield Daily Telegraph*,
    22 January 1878: 2.
57 The question of whether the act of suicide alone was evidence of insanity was
    debated throughout the century, and there was concern around this assumption
    that all suicides were necessarily insane. Gates, *Victorian Suicide*, 12–16; Georgina
    Laragy, '"A Peculiar Species of Felony": Suicide, Medicine, and the Law in Victorian
    Britain and Ireland', *Journal of Social History* 46, no. 3 (1 March 2013): 733–4.
58 Anderson, *Suicide in Victorian and Edwardian England*, 223.
59 Matthew MacDonald has also suggested that the increase in insanity verdicts
    provides evidence that moral judgement shifted from juries to newspaper readers.
    MacDonald, 'Suicide and the Rise of the Popular Press in England', 42.
60 'Distressing Suicide Through Want of Work At Neepsend', *Sheffield Independent*,
    2 June 1879: 3.
61 'Suffering and Suicide', *The Morning Post*, 20 June 1899: 3.
62 Rose, *Limited Livelihoods*, 127–9; Anna Clark, *The Struggle for the Breeches: Gender
    and the Making of the British Working Class*, Studies on the History of Society and
    Culture 23 (Berkeley, CA: University of California Press, 1995), chap. 7; Seccombe,
    'Patriarchy Stabilized', 55.
63 Rose, *Limited Livelihoods*, 133–4.
64 Seccombe, 'Patriarchy Stabilized', 55; Karl Ittmann, *Work, Gender and Family in
    Victorian England* (Basingstoke: Macmillan, 1995), 146.
65 'Suicide through Poverty', *North-Eastern Daily Gazette*, 3 November 1886: 4.
66 Charles Booth, 'The Inhabitants of Tower Hamlets (School Board Division),
    Their Condition and Occupations', *Journal of the Royal Statistical Society* 50, no. 2
    (1887): 328.
67 Although, in referencing the type of clothing needed and the frequent restaurant
    meals, it is clear that this was aimed at those of a much higher social position than

the Lock family. W Roberts, 'Life on a Guinea a Week', *The Nineteenth Century: A Monthly Review* 23, no. 133 (March 1888): 464–7 (quote on 464).

68 'Suicide Through Poverty', *North-Eastern Daily Gazette*.

69 Ibid.

70 For example, 'Melancholy Case of Suicide', *Cheshire Observer*, 14 April 1855: 5; 'Melancholy Suicide at bury St. Edmund's', *The Ipswich Journal*, 20 June 1857; 'Attempted Murder and Suicide', *Nottinghamshire Guardian*, 13 May 1893.

71 David Mayer, 'Encountering Melodrama', in *The Cambridge Companion to Victorian and Edwardian Theatre*, ed. Kerry Powell, Cambridge Companions to Literature (Cambridge; New York, NY: Cambridge University Press, 2004), 148.

72 McWilliam, 'Melodrama', 59.

73 Martha Vicinus, '"Helpless and Unfriended": Nineteenth-Century Domestic Melodrama', *New Literary History* 13, no. 1 (1981): 137.

74 'Shocking Case of Suicide', *Berrow's Worcester Journal*, 14 August 1845.

75 'Distressing Suicide Through Want of Work at Neepsend', *Sheffield Independent*, 2 June 1879: 3.

76 'Suicide Through Want of Work', *Bury and Norwich Post*, 1 September 1885: 3.

77 'Suicide Through Poverty', *North-Eastern Daily Gazette*.

78 Vicinus, '"Helpless and Unfriended"', 131–2.

79 McWilliam, 'Melodrama and the Historians', 72.

80 Ibid., 74.

81 'The Tooting Horror', *The Evening News*, 8 March 1895: 3; 'The Tooting Horror', *South Wales Daily News*, 9 March 1895: 5; 'A Tooting Horror', *Reynolds's Newspaper*, 10 March 1895: 1; 'The Tooting Tragedy', *Birmingham Daily Post*, 11 March 1895: 5; 'The Tooting Tragedy', *Sheffield Independent*, 11 March 1895: 5.

82 'A Tooting Horror', *Reynolds's Newspaper*.

83 'Terrible Tragedy in London', *Liverpool Mercury* etc., 8 March 1895.

84 'A Tooting Horror', *Reynolds's Newspaper*, 10 March 1895; 'Murder of A Wife and Six Children', *The Standard*, 8 March 1895.

85 'Terrible Tragedy in London', *The Liverpool Mercury*; 'Terrible Tragedy in London', *Northern Whig*, 8 March 1895: 5; 'Terrible Tragedy in London', *The Yorkshire Herald* and *The York Herald*, 8 March 1895: 5; 'The Tooting Tragedy', *The Liverpool Mercury*, 11 March 1895: 5.

86 'Murder of A Wife and Six Children', *The Standard*.

87 'Terrible Tragedy in London', *The Liverpool Mercury*.

88 'Murder of A Wife and Six Children', *The Standard*; 'Terrible Tragedy in London', *Liverpool Mercury* etc.

89 'Terrible Tragedy in London', *The Yorkshire Herald* and *The York Herald*, 5.

90 'The Murders at Tooting', *London Evening Standard*, 11 March 1895: 2.

91 'Terrible Tragedy in London', *The Yorkshire Herald* and *The York Herald*: 5.

92   Shani D'Cruze, 'The Eloquent Corpse: Gender, Probity, and Bodily Integrity in Victorian Domestic Murder', in *Criminal Converstions: Victorian Crimes, Social Panic, and Moral Outrage*, ed. Judith Rowbotham and Kim Stevenson (Columbus, OH: Ohio State University Press, 2005), 181.

93   Clark, 'The Rhetoric of Chartist Domesticity: Gender, Language, and Class in the 1830s and 1840s', 62–4; it is worth noting that Kristen Leaver also identifies a shift from the upper-class villain to a middle-class one. See Kristen Leaver, 'Victorian Melodrama and the Performance of Poverty', *Victorian Literature and Culture* 27, no. 2 (1999): 444.

94   Mayer, 'Encountering Melodrama', 151; Leaver, 'Victorian Melodrama and the Performance of Poverty', 444.

95   Juliet John, quoted in Carolyn Williams, 'Melodrama', in *The Cambridge History of Victorian Literature*, ed. Kate Flint, The New Cambridge History of English Literature (Cambridge; New York, NY: Cambridge University Press, 2012), 193.

96   Ibid.

97   C. M. Milroy, 'Homicide Followed by Suicide: Remorse or Revenge?', *Journal of Clinical Forensic Medicine* 5, no. 2 (1 June 1998): 61–4; John L. Oliffe et al., 'Men, Masculinities, and Murder-Suicide', *American Journal of Men's Health* 9, no. 6 (7 October 2014): 473–85.

98   'A Terrible Tragedy', *Bristol Mercury*, 8 March 1895.

99   'A Tooting Horror', *Reynolds's Newspaper*.

100 Vivienne Richmond, *Clothing the Poor in Nineteenth-Century England* (Cambridge; New York, NY: Cambridge University Press, 2013), 132–3.

101 Robert Roberts, *The Classic Slum: Salford Life in the First Quarter of the Century* (Manchester: Manchester University Press, 1971), 23.

102 'Murder of A Wife and Six Children', *The Standard*, 3.

103 Ibid., 3.

104 Englander, *Poverty and Poor Law Reform in Britain*, 44.

105 Nash and Kilday, *Cultures of Shame*, 4–11; Doolittle, 'Fatherhood and Family Shame', 87; Pamela Fox, *Class Fictions: Shame and Resistance in the British Working-Class Novel, 1890–1945* (Durham: Duke University Press, 1994), 15.

106 Quoted in Richmond, *Clothing the Poor in Nineteenth-Century England*, 273.

107 'Workhouse Dress', *Bristol Mercury*, 18 April 1892: 5.

108 Henry Mayhew, *London Labour and the London Poor: The Condition and Earnings of Those That Will Work, Cannot Work, and Will Not Work*, vol. 1 (London: George Woodfall and Son, 1851), 344.

109 Doolittle, 'Fatherhood and Family Shame', 96.

110 Smiles, *Self-Help*, 267–8.

111 For example, 'Distressing Suicide in A Workhouse', *Morning Post*, 7 May 1841: 2; 'Suicide in The Work-House', *Yorkshire Gazette*, 23 June 1821: 3; 'Suicide in

A Workhouse', *Evening Mail*, 19 April 1844: 3; 'Suicide in Clerkenwell Workhouse',
London Daily News, 24 February 1847: 3; 'Death Before The Workhouse', *North-
Eastern Daily Gazette*, 2 August 1894; 'Death Before The Workhouse', *South
Wales Daily News*, 30 March 1899: 8; 20 November 1869: 3; 'Death Before The
Workhouse', *Gloucester Citizen*, 26 January 1895: 4; 'Death Before The Workhouse',
Lancashire Evening Post, 20 June 1891: 2; 'Death Before The Workhouse', *Western
Gazette*, 10 August 1894: 2. This narrative was not exclusive to men, women
also chose to commit suicide rather than enter the workhouse, but I will not
be commenting on them here. For example, 'Death Before The Workhouse',
The Globe, 9 August 1881: 2; 'Death Before The Workhouse', *Cheshire Observer*,
16 January 1869: 7; 'Death Before The Workhouse', *South London Chronicle*,
20 November 1869: 6; 'Death Before The Workhouse', *Manchester Courier and
Lancashire General Advertiser*, 29 July 1895: 7.

112   The *Lincolnshire Chronicle*, reported that 'Owing to Mr. Gladstone's French treaty
admitting foreign made watches duty free, times are bad for the watch trade'.
'A Victim of Free Trade', *Lincolnshire Chronicle*, 24 November 1893: 6. And a letter
to the editor of *Reynolds's Newspaper* noted that, as a result of the international
competition in the watch-making trade 'hundreds of workmen have been thrown
out of employment'. 'Death Rather Than The Workhouse', *Reynolds's Newspaper*,
26 November 1893: 2.

113   'Starvation And Suicide', *Yorkshire Evening Post*, 22 November 1893: 3; 'Starved
Into Suicide', *South Wales Echo*, 22 November 1893: 2; 'Death Better Than The
Workhouse', *Dundee Evening Telegraph*, 23 November 1893: 2; 'News of the Day',
Shields Daily News, 23 November 1893: 2; 'A Father's Sad Suicide', *Glasgow Evening
Post*, 23 November 1893: 7; 'Sorrows, False Pride, and Suicide', *Daily Gazette
for Middlesbrough*, 23 November 1893: 4; 'A Victim Of Free Trade', *Lincolnshire
Chronicle*, 6; 'A Pathetic Story Of Depression', *Nuneaton Advertiser*, 25 November
1893: 2; 'Preferring Death To The Workhouse', *Wellington Journal*, 24 November
1893: 2; 'Death Rather Than The Workhouse', *Worcestershire Chronicle*, 25
November 1893: 6.

114   'Starvation and Suicide', *Huddersfield Chronicle*, 4.

115   'Northumbrian' was eventually identified as 'Mr Macintosh'. Laurel Brake et al.,
eds, *Dictionary of Nineteenth-Century Journalism in Great Britain and Ireland*
(Gent: Academia Press, 2009), 541.

116   'Death Rather Than The Workhouse', *Reynolds's Newspaper*, 2.

117   Klaver, *A/Moral Economics*, 114.

118   Smiles, *Self-Help*, 297.

119   Doolittle, 'Fatherhood and Family Shame', 88–90; Joanne Bailey, "'A Very Sensible
Man": Imagining Fatherhood in England c.1750–1830', *History* 95, no. 3 (319)
(2010): 291.

120   'Poverty and Crime', *York Herald*, 11 June 1887: 5.

121   Joanne Bailey, 'Masculinity and Fatherhood in England c. 1760–1830', in *What Is Masculinity?: Historical Dynamics from Antiquity to the Contemporary World*, ed. John Arnold and Sean Brady, Genders and Sexualities in History (Houndmills, Basingstoke, Hampshire; New York, NY: Palgrave Macmillan, 2011), 168; Klaver, *A/Moral Economics*, 117–18.

122   'Shocking Case Of Suicide', *Berrow's Worcester Journal*.

123   'Suicide Through Want of Work', *Royal Cornwall Gazette*, 20 November 1890: 3.

124   For discussions of how male suicides are narrated in ways that downplay mental illness, see Christabel Owens and Helen Lambert, 'Mad, Bad, or Heroic? Gender, Identitty and Accountability in Lay Portrayals of Suicide in Late Twentieth-Century England', *Culture, Medicine, and Psychiatry* 36 (2012): 348–71; David Stuckler and Sanjay Basu, *The Body Economic: Eight Experiments in Economic Recovery, from Iceland to Greece* (London: Penguin Books, 2014), chap. 7.

125   'Suicide Through Want Of Work', *Bury and Norwich Post*, 3.

126   'Poverty and Suicide At Rotherham', *Sheffield Independent,* 27 May 1887: 8.

127   'An Out-Of-Work's Suicide', *Weekly Standard and Express*, 4 August 1894: 7.

128   Akihito Suzuki, 'Lunacy and Labouring Men: Narratives of Male Vulnerability in Mid-Victorian London', in *Medicine, Madness and Social History: Essays in Honour of Roy Porter* (Basingstoke: Palgrave Macmillan, 2008); Levine-Clark, '"Embarrassed Circumstances": Gender, Poverty, and Insanity in the West Riding of England in the Early-Victorian Years'; Catherine Cox, *Negotiating Insanity in the Southeast of Ireland, 1820–1900* (Oxford: Oxford University Press, 2018), 62, 121, 223; A. Kuruvilla and K. S. Jacob, 'Poverty, Social Stress & Mental Health', *Indian Journal of Medical Research* 126, no. 34 (2007): 273–8; Mills, '"Dead People Don't Claim": A Psychopolitical Autopsy of UK Austerity Suicides'; Stuckler and Basu, *The Body Economic*, chap. 7; William C. Kerr et al., 'Economic Recession, Alcohol, and Suicide Rates: Comparative Effects of Poverty, Foreclosure, and Job Loss', *American Journal of Preventive Medicine* 52, no. 4 (1 April 2017): 469–75; Valentina Iemmi et al., 'Suicide and Poverty in Low-Income and Middle-Income Countries: A Systematic Review', *The Lancet Psychiatry* 3, no. 8 (1 August 2016): 774–83; sociologists have noted that the relationship between poverty and suicide is complex, with the association varying across different levels of study, i.e. the individual, regional, national and international. See Christian Baudelot and Roger Establet, *Suicide: The Hidden Side of Modernity* (Cambridge, UK; Malden, MA: Polity Press, 2008) particularly chap. 1.

129   Charles Mercier, *Sanity and Insanity* (London: Walter Scott, 1890), 267–8.

130   See Suzuki, 'Lunacy and Labouring Men: Narratives of Male Vulnerability in Mid-Victorian London'.

131   'Statistics of Insanity', *British Medical Journal* s1-9, no. 51 (1845): 739.

132 'Suicide In Liverpool', *Daily News,* 11 August 1854.

133 'A Suicide's Letter', *Huddersfield Daily Chronicle*, 10 September 1891: 4.

134 Fox, *Class Fictions*, 15.

135 The World Health Organisation discourages framing suicide as a 'constructive solution to problems'. WHO, *Preventing Suicide: A Resource for Media Professionals* (Geneva: WHO, 2017), 6; earlier editions of these guidelines more explicitly discourage depicting suicide as a method of coping with personal problems, such as financial trouble or relationship breakdown. WHO, *Preventing Suicide: A Resource for Media Professionals* (Geneva: WHO, 2008), 7; WHO, *Preventing Suicide: A Resource for Media Professionals* (Geneva: WHO, 2000), 7–8.

136 See particularly chap. 3 of Marsh, *Suicide*, quote on 47.

137 Mills, '"Dead People Don't Claim": A Psychopolitical Autopsy of UK Austerity Suicides', 317.

138 Smiles, *Self-Help*, ix, 6–7.

139 Peter Mandler, ed., *Liberty and Authority in Victorian Britain* (Oxford: Oxford University Press, 2006), 5, 9.

3

Fraud and speculation

If the poor wretch has, up to his last days, been apparently living a decent life; if he be not hated, or has not in his last moments made himself specially obnoxious to the world at large, then he is declared to have been mad ... But let a Melmotte be found dead, with a bottle of prussic acid by his side—a man who has become horrid to the world because of his late iniquities, a man who has so well pretended to be rich that he has been able to buy and to sell properties without paying for them, a wretch who has made himself odious by his ruin to friends who had taken him up as a pillar of strength in regard to wealth, a brute who had got into the House of Commons by false pretences, and had disgraced the House by being drunk there,—and, of course, he will not be saved by a verdict of insanity from the cross roads, or whatever scornful grave may be allowed to those who have killed themselves, with their wits about them.

–Anthony Trollope, *The Way We Live Now*, 1875[1]

For by that time it was known that the late Mr Merdle's complaint had been simply Forgery and Robbery. He, the uncouth object of such wide-spread adulation, the sitter at great men's feasts, the roc's egg of great ladies' assemblies, the subduer of exclusiveness, the leveller of pride, the patron of patrons, the bargain-driver with a Minister for Lordships of the Circumlocution Office, the recipient of more acknowledgment within some ten or fifteen years, at most, than had been bestowed in England upon all peaceful public benefactors, and upon all the leaders of all the Arts and Sciences, with all their works to testify for them, during two centuries at least—he, the shining wonder, the new constellation to be followed by the wise men bringing gifts, until it stopped over a certain carrion at the bottom of a bath and disappeared—was simply the greatest Forger and the greatest Thief that ever cheated the gallows.

–Charles Dickens, *Little Dorrit*, 1857[2]

It was not just on the pages of Victorian literature that nineteenth-century readers could find swindlers like Augustus Melmotte and Mr Merdle. These characters were equally as prevalent in the newspapers of the period, and readers often encountered them through the reports of their suicides. In his study on suicide throughout the lifecycle in Victorian Hull, Victor Bailey suggests that *felo de se* verdicts were often returned on those who had 'escaped punishment for an earlier or concurrent crime', a statement that would appear to bear out the above claim made by Anthony Trollope, reflecting on the self-inflicted death of his central character.[3] Both Trollope's contemporary fiction and Bailey's critical history read suicide verdicts as moral character judgements and, where the suicide's prior character was questionable, juries could use the *felo de se* to pass harsh judgement. In cases of suicide following financial crimes, juries appear to have been less willing to accept hearsay evidence such as a change in character following illness or injury, irritability, memory loss or pains in the head, as proof of insanity despite this being sufficient in many other cases. For example, Alexander Maas, a clerk charged with embezzling £20,000 was found to be *felo de se*, despite evidence from his wife and doctor that he had not been the same man since having two bicycle accidents that had resulted in serious injuries which kept him from work and 'might have affected his brain'. Yet, when Alfred Dimsey, a medical student, committed suicide a few years later, the revelation that 'he had never been the same man' since suffering from scarlet fever the year before appears to be enough to have supported the verdict of insanity.[4]

For those like Melmotte and Merdle, whose suicides followed financial crimes and who sought to escape through death, the *felo de se* verdict appears to have been utilized more frequently than in the other narrative types discussed in this work, particularly if they had already been apprehended. In 1832 a man named Thomas Pelham Hollis committed suicide in his cell, whilst awaiting a trial for the extensive forgery and circulation of Bank of England notes. The report of the inquest clearly framed this as an act committed in desperation by a man who was 'dreading ... to face his accusers'. After noting the jury's verdict of *felo de se*, the article referred to the coroner's words of approval. He had never, it was reported, known 'a more deliberate act of self-murder ... the deceased having committed it in the full possession of his faculties, and to anticipate the law'.[5] Towards the end of the century, Charles Middleton Cox was a well-known bookmaker shot himself whilst awaiting trial for fraud after bringing a false action against a Mr Wood for a bill of £600. His suicide was read as an escape of justice and accordingly received a verdict of *felo de se*.[6] The report on Cox's case suggested that 'He has now escaped trial by self-destruction.'[7] Again, the suicide of a chemist, Bruno Behrandt, who was wanted for fraud in Southampton, was reported as a 'suicide to avoid arrest'.[8] These *felo de se* verdicts reflect the point made by Barbara Gates that suicides could not, and did not, satisfy the 'Victorian sense of justice'.[9] As Dickens' commentary on Mr Merdle suggests, suicide could be regarded as a way of cheating justice and exhibited a failure of masculine character in the inability to face up to the consequences of one's actions. This is not to say that all cases of suicide following financial crime resulted in a *felo de se* verdict, purely on the basis of their criminal actions. This verdict still appears to have been returned in a minority of these cases and most of the time some convincing evidence could be found to support insanity.[10] What has been noticeable is that reports of suicides following this narrative appear to end in this verdict more frequently when compared to those of the other narrative types found in my research.

This chapter is focused, specifically, on the discourse of masculinity amongst the growing middle classes. This was tied up with the growth of commercial and entrepreneurial society that Harold Perkin suggests placed value on the idea of meritocracy, moral character and hard work.[11] In the first half of the nineteenth century, this discourse saw a move away from the importance of reputation, as conferred through the esteem of others, to an emphasis on an Evangelical notion of character, as guided by one's inner conscience.[12] The power of the evaluative idea of character, Stefan Collini argues, was greater in the Victorian period than at any other time, to the extent that it became 'the favoured explanatory element' for the cause of differences in human fate.[13] The 'core' qualities invoked in the idea of (good) character were 'self-restraint, perseverance, strenuous effort, courage in the face of adversity' and 'sense of duty'.[14] These characteristics constituted the backbone of the middle-class masculinity that took ascendancy in the nineteenth century, but this Evangelical notion of character as an internalized quality was unable to resist commodification. Character became a central currency in the world of commerce and society, which could be used as a tool to gain influence, respect and business.[15] On this basis, a man's success in business attested to his moral character and, as Barbara Weiss explains, the association between success and virtue necessitated that failure was the result of 'moral inadequacies'.[16] In this chapter, I look at how the narratives of suicide following financial crimes like fraud and embezzlement, as well as those around failed speculations, reveal the centrality of money, business and character to middle-class masculinity. I suggest that the decision to return a verdict of *felo de se* served as an indictment against a man's masculinity for his failure to abide by the middle-class standards, in which commercial success was built on merit and hard work.

Character was important in business and economic thought – a term which I use here to encompass both common and specialist understanding of economic issues. According to Alfred Marshall, the study of political economy was as much the study of man as it was of wealth, because 'man's character has been moulded' by his work and material resources 'more than by any other influence' apart from religion. For Marshall, the character of man was 'formed by the way in which he uses his faculties in his work, by the thoughts and the feelings which it suggests', and by relationships with those he works with.[17] Taking Marshall's belief that a man's character was influenced by his work, I suggest that these suicides reflect a sense of uneasiness about the rapid advancement of a credit economy and the dangers that participation in an increasingly competitive market posed to men's health and moral character. These anxieties were only exacerbated by the economic crises, booms and busts of speculative ventures, recurrent failures of banks and exposés of fraud that punctuated the century. This theme has been picked up by Kirsten Guest in her analysis of late-nineteenth-century melodrama. Guest explains the emergence of the privileged male victim in genteel melodramas as a result of the contradictory expectations that men participated in the 'aggressive and competitive capitalist economy' whilst at the same time maintaining the 'private, moral rectitude' expected of middle-class men.[18] Commentary surrounding these suicide narratives in the press often alluded to the moral degradation of the nation resulting from what they saw as the love of Mammon. In this context, suicides following fraud or bad business speculations became morality tales warning of the perils of what was described as Mammon-worship.[19] This concern was underpinned by shifts in distinctly middle-class notions of masculinity and the rhetoric of work as a 'calling'.

Character, economy and the Protestant ethic

An important part of the shift in expectations of middle-class masculinity was the reconception of work as a 'calling' – a feature of capitalist development that Max Weber outlined in his *Protestant Ethic and the Spirit of Capitalism* (1905) and which has been taken up by historians examining the relationship between masculinity and work.[20] Under the guise of the calling, work became a moral duty and the wealth it accumulated, so long as it was acquired through legal business, was a by-product of toil in worldly duty rather than the aim of it. In this sense, wealth was a symbol of man's virtue;[21] whether this was through having enough money to simply support oneself, enough to support one's family, or having enough money, as Dickens' Mr Dombey professed, to cause men 'to be honoured, feared, respected, courted, and admired', and to make one 'powerful and glorious in the eyes of all men'.[22] But nineteenth-century attitudes towards money were contradictory. Whilst wealth earned as a by-product of man's a calling to work was evidence of good, middle-class masculine character, excessive wealth could undermine masculinity through the association with greed, Mammon-worship, luxury and idleness. This kind of wealth offered never-ending temptation to greed, and provided a financial security that inculcated relaxation and idleness, 'a distraction from the pursuit of a righteous life'.[23] This, Max Weber believed, was the real objection to wealth, in that it induced idleness when man should be carrying out the work set for him by God. The only relaxation was the everlasting rest in the next world.[24] The relationship between wealth and idleness that are exemplified through this ethic also come with connotations of effeminacy, associated as it was with the luxury and idleness of the eighteenth century.[25] The accumulation of wealth as a by-product of steady and honest hard work was an admirable quality that conformed to the middle-class standards of masculinity – hard work, activity, moral integrity – but the pursuit of wealth for its own sake was morally dubious.

Gambling and speculation in particular were seen as morally hazardous in the way they eschewed these principles of hard work and patient accumulation of wealth in favour of amassing a quick fortune. This rhetoric was pushed in newspaper coverage of suicides who had suffered bad speculations. In 1864, the suicide of a bank manager named Robert Williams, who had used bank funds to meet £25,000 in liabilities for his speculations on the Stock Exchange, prompted a lengthy commentary on 'Mammon and Suicide'. It was not the 'circumstances of the commercial world' itself that was to blame for suicides like Williams', but 'the spiritual and ethical atmosphere' in which 'wealth is worshipped' and 'gold is deified'. These suicides were evidence of the 'sincerity of our worship of Mammon' and a willingness to give up life in its service.[26] In 1890, the suicide of Jack Scrivener, who drowned himself after losing his fortune to gambling and left a letter warning other young men against the habit, inspired a sermon by Reverend J. K. Nuttall. In it, he lamented that the 'vice of betting and gambling' exercised the same influence on man as drink: 'It demoralised him, it *unmanned him*' and 'fostered selfishness'. The pleasures of gambling, Nuttall believed, were 'at the cost of some other person's pain'.[27] Nuttall's words echoed those of Samuel Smiles who, earlier in the century, urged the importance of every man living within his means, proclaiming that 'if a man do not manage to live within his own means, he must necessarily be living dishonestly upon the means of somebody else'.[28] Quick wealth, gained by gambling or speculation, was morally dubious on several grounds. In the first instance it could encourage idleness and a rejection of pious hard work central to middle-class masculine identity, in the second it was a dishonest way of living seen as putting others at a disadvantage for one's own gain.

The rise of 'stock market villains', to use Tamara S. Wagner's phrase, like Melmotte and Merdle, attests to the troubled relationship that Victorians had with money throughout the nineteenth century. In addition to these two, perhaps the most (in)famous, we see Mr Carker in Dickens' *Dombey and Son* (1848) run the business beyond its means; George Vavasour of Trollope's *Can You Forgive Her?* (1864–5); Dobbs Broughton in *The Last Chronicle of Barset* (1867) whose social position is, like Melmotte's, founded on the *appearance* of wealth and who speculates (unsuccessfully) with other people's money; Ferdinand Lopez in *The Prime Minister* (1876), and Bennet Frothingham in George Gissing's *The Whirlpool* (1897), whose name 'stood for criminal recklessness, for huge rascality'.[29] All represent financial 'villains' of sorts. The rise of a credit economy, the emergence of paper money, the decline of personal responsibility for company behaviour, the railway mania of the 1840s and the recurring financial crises all served to raise concerns about the morality of the market place and the value of money. The Limited Liability Act of 1855 further brought up questions about morality in the competitive market place. It meant that company shareholders were only responsible up to the amount they had invested, rather than being liable for unlimited company debts, therefore decreasing the risks of speculation. Further concern was brought on by the increasing scale of business organization, putting distance between business owners, the running of the company and the effects on the rest of the population. The result was increased opportunities for dishonest conduct within a business, and the lessening of personal accountability.[30]

This depersonalization of business was part of a broader shift in economic thought in the nineteenth century, that sought to push the idea that the economy was an autonomous, self-regulating system that should not be interfered with. In doing so, political economists like David Ricardo separated 'economic' concerns from the social, political, psychological, cultural and, importantly, from moral concerns.[31] As political economy developed, attempts were made to establish it as a scientific discipline by drawing on the methods and authority of sciences such as geology, chemistry, physics, mechanics and biology. Drawing on geological metaphors, for example, financial crashes were described as 'earthquakes' and the economy was increasingly viewed in terms of natural rhythms.[32] By categorizing the economy as an independent and autonomous entity and discouraging external interference, it became easier to distance economic behaviour from personal morality. So, too, did the growing size of companies increase the distance between personal morality and company behaviour.

The management of companies became increasingly stratified and the nominal owners became less and less involved in the everyday running of business; a series of shareholders, directors, managers and clerks all stood to remove personal responsibility and opened up the system to abuse.[33] Business had traditionally operated on the basis of personal character and reputation, but as business practice became increasingly separated from the personality of the business owner, the relationship between the private and the public became confused. Importantly, for the middle-class man, the separation of work and home also proved to separate the public and private personality.[34] Although this simplified characterization of 'separate spheres' is not without its problems, the detachment of work and home, as John Tosh suggests, increased the association of work with 'a heartless commercial ethic'.[35] Whilst men might conform to moral expectations of middle-class masculinity in their private lives, the competition of the commercial world allowed for the evasion of these moral principles, directly damaging his own character. I suggest that the narratives of these suicides suggest that separation of the moral and the economic was not only morally hazardous, but hazardous to a man's health, causing a fatal rupture in his character.

In the context of financial suicides – where the suicide had suffered bankruptcy, committed fraud or been involved in a failed speculation – an analogy can also be made between the economy and medicine. The specialization of economic knowledge and the formation of political economy as a scientific discipline created the idea that the economy was a 'distinct entity' and had clear distinctions between inside and outside. In this formulation what was inside was seen as 'natural' and acted 'in the natural self-regulation of the economy', whilst any external interference was seen to be 'unnatural' and potentially disastrous.[36] Such external interference included, for example, government interference with prices or the money supply, which was a topic of intense debate among political economists and often blamed for the periodic economic crises. It also included government efforts to prevent company fraud through legislation, which some believed would extinguish the habit of self-regulation and 'private vigilance' – as George Robb points out there was a belief that the market would regulate itself and naturally drive out bad business practices and corruption.[37] The regularity with which these economic crises occurred – roughly every ten years (1825–6, 1836–7, 1847–8, 1857 and 1890) – was seen as evidence of a natural cycle of the economy, suggesting that it was an entity not to be interfered with. This belief in self-regulation, rooted in classical political economy of Adam Smith and John Stuart Mill, was not without its critics but generally informed the *laissez-faire* attitude towards the economy and the market that persisted until the latter half of the century.[38]

Just as the economy was seen to be a self-regulatory system, so too were men expected to exert self-regulation over themselves; it was a habit integral to masculine identity.[39] Without it men were susceptible to personal crisis, just as the economy was susceptible to recession. The most critical and public form this personal crisis could take was suicide, which medical opinion believed resulted from the failure of self-regulation. Although some thought suicide must always be an act of madness, as it perverted the most natural instinct of survival, the physician James Cowles Prichard believed that it was 'frequently … the result of rational motives' such as the desire 'to escape from anticipated evils, from the sufferings of life protracted under circumstances which promise only shame or misery and disappointment'. In such cases, suicide was the act 'of a person possessed of reason, though under the influence of despair, of passions habitually ill-regulated, and uncontrolled by a sense of duty and religion'.[40] Opening his chapter on the mental causes of suicide, Forbes Winslow wrote that in the voyage through life, unregulated passions 'drive the vessel on the rocks and quicksands of life, and ruin us'.[41] Failure to exercise self-regulation would thus result in self-destruction. Transposing this idea of regulation of passions and desires into economic contexts, the consequences of unchecked greed were felt to be particularly disastrous.

Speculation was a prime example of such greed; it was the antithesis of a masculine compulsion to work. The steady accumulation of wealth that accompanied this work ethic was to be seen as a side effect rather than the goal itself.[42] Speculation rejected these principles. Clearly prioritizing wealth over duty to work, it was seen as 'a ready way to get rich' which launched men into a 'destructive sea'.[43] Whereas legitimate business was conducted within the limits of one's capital and involved 'solid commerce', speculation was selfish and illegitimate, which would ultimately 'incur God's wrath and punishment as he visited the preventive check of bankruptcy on these earthly sinners'.[44] As Boyd Hilton has convincingly argued, bankruptcies were not inexplicable accidents of misfortune, they 'evinced economic guilt' and were 'the logical outcome of sin'.[45] In these situations, Hilton suggests, the payment of debts was the highest order of Christian duty, but following spectacular financial failures this was often impossible and, for many, death was preferable to debt.[46] Suicide, then, became the physical manifestation of financial self-destruction, both seen to be caused by a failure to adhere to the principles of self-regulation that underlined hegemonic conceptions of middle-class masculinity.

Melmottes and Merdles

Suicide as a response to financial crimes or financial failures is, by now, a well-worn trope and there has been a lot of interesting work on how the financial 'suicide myth' was, as Nancy Henry has suggested, 'part of a broader critique of capitalism', exposing the 'meaninglessness' of capitalist life.[47] Barbara Weiss, in her discussion of how suicide fits into the narrative of bankruptcy, draws on Durkheim to suggest that financial suicides were an external expression of the social and economic conditions of the time.[48] For Tamara Wagner, the suicidal speculators of Victorian literature embodied 'the self-destructiveness of "mighty Shares"'.[49] Opening her chapter on suicide and finance in Victorian literature, Henry draws on John Kenneth Galbraith's analysis of the 'suicide myth' circulating in the London press following the New York stock market crash of 1929, which made exaggerated claims about pedestrians having to carefully pick their way through the bodies of suicidal financiers who had thrown themselves out of windows. Galbraith comes to the conclusion that the newspapers had 'merely seized on such suicides as occurred to show that people were reacting appropriately to their misfortune'.[50] However, tracing the financial suicide from the mid-1850s through Dickens, Trollope, Gissing and, across the Atlantic, Edith Wharton, Henry argues that this trope was 'prepared by Victorian novelists', rather than the 'occasional' reports of the London penny press.[51]

Whilst it is undeniable that Victorian literature did much to perpetuate the financial suicide, it was more than just a literary metaphor invented by Victorian authors to be used as a tool for social commentary; the financial suicide had been a feature of the press long before the mid-nineteenth century.[52] One high-profile case was the suicide of Abraham Goldsmid, a well-known banker, who shot himself after suffering a devastating bankruptcy. Goldsmid had been a joint contractor for a government loan of £14 million, but fluctuations in the stock market and the depreciation of Omnium funds, which he held to the value of £3–4 million, plunged him into ruinous bankruptcy.[53] Goldsmid's spirits had apparently been 'progressively drooping' as a result of the depreciation of Omnium, but once it had reached a discount of 5 and 6 per cent, without probability of recovering, he 'appeared evidently restless in his disposition and disordered in his mind'.[54] He was also reported to have been irritable and subject to sudden 'paroxisms' since the death of his partner in the loan, Sir Francis Baring, who had died only a few days previously, putting him under even more pressure.[55] According to reports on the inquest, witnesses also deposed that since the death of his brother in 1808 he had been subject to 'occasional depression of spirits' and that a recent accident, in which he had been 'beaten down by an over-drove ox', appeared to have 'contributed to the derangement of his nervous system.'[56] The jury immediately returned a verdict of *temporary insanity*.

Most accounts of Goldsmid's suicide made efforts to point out that he 'had determined, if possible, to perform all his contracts at the Stock exchange … He had already commenced his retrenchments by discharging all the work-men and out-door labourers employed on his extensive premises.'[57] The reported efforts to pay his debts were an integral part of this narrative because, as Boyd Hilton and Leeann Hunter have shown, the repayment of debt was a sign of moral integrity. Although debt itself was seen as sinful, Hilton's work has shown how a bankruptcy could be made honourable when the bankrupt paid his debts.[58] Looking at Victorian novels of bankruptcy, Hunter explains how, even when bankruptcy laws absolved debtors of a portion of their debt, many still endeavoured to pay their debts in full 'to avert the shame of bankruptcy'. Dickens' Mr Dombey is a prime example of this, as 'a gentleman of high honour and integrity', he was 'resolved on payment to the last farthing of his means.'[59] In suicides of bankrupts or financial failures, then, reporting attempts made at repayment of debt signalled virtue and honour on the part of the suicide, characteristics that were central to middle-class masculinity. This was in complete opposition to the Melmottes and Merdles of Victorian literature and real life, whose failure to recompense for their frauds and failures attested to their failure to live up to standards of a masculinity based on moral integrity.

Of course, Nancy Henry is right to highlight the importance of this trope in the literature of the period. The fictional suicides of financial men have been established as 'either inevitable moral justice' or a broader reflection on capitalist society, especially the economy of credit, speculation and shares.[60] Even the deaths of financial villains that were not self-inflicted followed in the tradition of financial suicides, for example *Dombey and Son*'s Carker. After running Dombey's business into the ground and running away with Dombey's wife, Edith, Carker finds himself face-to-face with Dombey on the station platform: 'turning in his walk, where it was bounded by one end of the wooden stage on which he paced up and down, he saw the man from whom he had fled, emerging from the door by which he himself had entered. And their eyes met.' Physically taken aback by the surprise of seeing Dombey, Carker stumbles backwards onto the tracks. However, he immediately recovers his footing and takes a few steps back in order to 'interpose some wider space between them, and looked at his pursuer, breathing short and quick'. At the same moment a train is rushing towards him:

> He heard a shout—another—saw the face change from its vindictive passion to a faint sickness and terror—felt the earth tremble—knew in a moment that the rush was come—uttered a shriek—looked round—saw the red eyes, bleared and dim, in the daylight, close upon him—was beaten down, caught up, and whirled away upon a jagged mill, that spun him round and round, and struck him limb from limb, and licked his stream of life up with its fiery heat, and cast his mutilated fragments in the air.[61]

Although Carker's death was not a suicide, it follows the common narrative of other literary suicides of financial men. The passage describing Carker's death is similar to the description of Ferdinand Lopez's suicide in Trollope's later novel *The Prime Minister*, who 'walked down before the flying engine—and in a moment had been knocked into bloody atoms'.[62] Most importantly, though, is the way in which Carker's death fits the narrative of this type of suicide. Olive Anderson, in her study of Victorian and Edwardian suicides, points to the trope of male suicide as an 'escape of the proud, the weak, or the wicked from financial ruin, disgrace, or retribution' and further argues that male suicides were 'most often shown simply as the fitting end of a villain or a weakling'.[63]

The literary convention of financial suicides is part of this narrative reflecting the character of financial men whose suicides act, as Dickens notes about Mr Merdle, as an escape of justice and an unwillingness to face the consequences of their actions. Carker's actual death may not have been deliberate, but his steps back were a purposeful attempt to escape Dombey. Carker's avoidance of confronting, and facing up to, what he has done follows the tradition of the financial suicide and reflects the perceived moral character of business and money in an age of credit, bankruptcy and almost constant financial crises. The rise of the 'stock-market villain' and financial failure as a plot device has been the subject of rich and valuable research into Victorian literature. The use of the stock market in literature, Wagner suggests, was more than a mere reflection of contemporary crises, but 'formed a new cultural imaginary' that expressed the changing concepts 'of moral probity and indeterminate identity, creditworthiness and the management of financial risks, the experience of instability'.[64] But the genealogy of financial villains was not just literary, and neither was literature the only place in which these themes of creditworthiness, identity, instability and risk were mediated upon. Newspaper reports of real suicides following frauds and failures provided ample space for these discussions and constituted a wealth of material for moralizing on the subject of money.

The suicide of John Sadleir

At twenty to nine in the morning, on Sunday 17 February 1856, a labourer named Joseph Bates came across a body lying on the ground near Jack Straw Castle, Hampstead Heath. Another man, named Rudge, appeared and ordered Bates to stand by the body whilst the former went to fetch a police officer. An officer arrived at the scene, and Bates discovered a bottle labelled 'Essential oil of bitter almonds' lying next to the body, along with a silver tankard. The police officer, Richard Hewson, searched the body, finding various coins and notes, razors, a latch-key and a piece of paper, which was addressed to 'John Sadleir, 11, Gloucester-square, Hyde-park'. The body was removed to Hampstead workhouse. After a medical examination, which also revealed traces of opium, it was clear that death had 'undoubtedly' been caused by taking poison, and the body was identified as that of Irish financier and former MP for Sligo, Ireland, John Sadleir.[65]

John Sadleir's suicide caused a sensation, and is the most infamous case of suicide following financial crime throughout the nineteenth century, being cited as inspiration for Dickens' Mr Merdle and Trollope's Augustus Melmotte.[66] Sadleir's story has been the subject of interest in the history of white-collar – specifically financial – crime, and, in 1999, James O'Shea published his biography, *Prince of Swindlers: John Sadleir M.P. 1813–1856*. However, his suicide, how it was represented and how it feeds into the wider narratives of male suicide during the period, has not received sustained analysis, his name often being little more than a footnote.[67]

At the inquest, the butler, Joseph Elwin, deposed that Sadleir had left the house on Saturday morning with many papers, as was quite usual, but had to return to his room several times, as if having forgotten something. In the evening he returned home for dinner unexpectedly – it was his usual habit to dine at his club – and asked him to purchase £1 worth of essential oil of bitter almonds from Mr Maitland, a chemist, supposedly at the request of his groom. Mr Maitland informed the butler that the quantity would be about half a pint and he would send for it, as he did not currently have it. By half past nine the poison had not arrived and Sadleir asked Elwin to collect it, but, as he was busy he sent the kitchen maid. On her way, she posted a letter that the butler had given to her, addressed to Sadleir's sister-in-law. On returning, the kitchen maid passed the bottle, wrapped in paper, to Elwin who delivered it to Mr Sadleir, who was 'looking over some writings'. Elwin also testified to Sadleir's 'sober' and 'temperate' character; he drank only a little sherry with dinner, but not more than two glasses at most. There had apparently been no change in his manner during the previous few months, he had not complained of his head or being unable to sleep and had not been under any medical treatment.[68] He had, however, been very pressed with business, and lately had 'a great deal of writing to do'.[69]

In response to a question regarding the razors found on the body, the butler suggested that it was unusual for Sadleir to carry razors unless he 'went out to sleep' and had never known him to take opium. The kitchen maid also deposed that she had never been sent to buy opium for Sadleir. On being recalled, the butler added that three letters addressed to Robert Keating MP, and one to Anthony Norris, a solicitor, had been found in the hall on Sunday morning, which were sent out as instructed by the note left. The coroner enquired as to the whereabouts of the letters mentioned, but as the letter to Mrs Sadleir was only posted on Saturday evening, would have only reached its destination the morning of the inquest. The coroner asked whether the jury wished to see it, adding that 'I have no desire for it. Nothing can be plainer than that Mr. Sadleir's death was caused by poison, and that it was administered by his own hand.' The only question left for the jury to decide was regarding Sadleir's state of mind at the time of suicide.[70]

Evidence from a solicitor, Anthony Norris, who knew the deceased intimately and had last seen him on Saturday night, suggested that he 'was pressed by his undertakings' being the 'chairman of the London and Country Bank, chairman of the Royal Swedish Railway, a director of an Irish bank', amongst other 'public concerns'. He had visited him on Saturday afternoon and noticed 'a remarkable peculiarity about the eyes as though he had been weeping' and asked him to return at eleven o'clock the next day. He had noticed an 'extraordinary change in his appearance' throughout the last week, describing him as looking 'haggard', with blood-shot eyes and appearing 'to be quite borne down during the last few days' on account of the extent of his business and some sudden and severe pecuniary losses. He described Sadleir as 'a man of extraordinary coolness and strength of mind' but had remarked to a Mr Stevens, in relation to Sadleir's losses, that 'I should not be surprised if Sadleir were to shoot himself'. *The Tyrone Constitution*, however, reported that Sadleir had been at his club until half past ten on Saturday night, and that his friends there had 'observed nothing strange in his manner' and when he returned home 'he seemed in his usual calm self'.[71] One of the letters had been addressed to Mr Norris, but when the coroner asked after it, Norris replied that he had not got it with him. Suspecting that it had been left behind 'designedly', the jury concluded that the inquest should be adjourned in order to obtain the letters. Having been written the night before his death, they felt they might provide some evidence as to his state of mind prior to his rash act.[72]

News of Sadleir's death quickly circulated in the British press, and, as James O'Shea points out, initial reaction was sympathetic.[73] They spoke of his kind disposition, his 'amiable and benevolent character',[74] his 'tact, ability and signal success' in his chairmanship of the London and County Bank and lamented that the various railway companies he was involved with had lost 'the benefit of his counsel and services'.[75] Most accounts attributed the act to his heavy financial losses, although one paper, the *Leicester Journal*, put it down to 'insanity brought on by excessive intellectual exertion'.[76] *The Standard*'s report of his suicide included details of his pecuniary affairs, stating that his losses were to such an extent that not only had they 'completely dissipated' his large fortune, but also reduced him to 'hopeless and inextricable ruin'. He was, they noted, one of the 'few men outside the house of Rothschild who speculated to such an extent in foreign and continental railways and mining undertakings'.[77]

The following day, the same paper printed some 'further particulars' to the case, directly ascribing the 'rash act' to 'his having become heavily involved by losses and liabilities which he was utterly unable to meet'. The report indicated that his losses included the entirety 'of his own private property, amounting sometime back to above 200,000*l*.' as well as having added 'a very heavy amount o[f] liability'.[78] Even before details of the inquest had been reported, *The Times* stated that, although the motive for Sadleir's suicide cannot be positively stated, 'there seems to be an impression that the deceased had disordered his mind by over-speculation'.[79] And as the Irish *Freeman's Journal* noted, the timing of the announcement of Sadleir's 'sudden' death, coupled with the news that the Tipperary Joint-Stock Bank, of which Sadleir was Chairman, had had its drafts refused by their London agents and the Bank of Ireland had refused to honour them, 'left little doubt on the public mind as to the immediate cause of death'. The paper believed that this news had 'produced the despondency under the influence of which the fatal course was adopted'.[80] That idea that sudden pecuniary changes could cause insanity and suicide was not uncommon. Medical opinion believed that the loss of a sizeable fortune, even when it did not reduce a man to absolute poverty, could be particularly dangerous for the wealthy.[81] But speculation in particular had regularly been linked to suicide in the newspapers in the first half of the nineteenth century. Newspapers of the late 1830s and 1840s reported the suicides of those whose speculations, often on the railways, had proved disastrous.[82] This connection between suicide and speculation was so entrenched by 1839 that *The Somerset County Gazette* described speculation as the chief cause of suicide in England.[83]

The language used in the initial reports of Sadleir's suicide, and indeed the message of all the reports of suicide from speculation I have read, is suggestive of the link between economic and personal health. Writing in 1840, Forbes Winslow outlines the effects that speculation and reverses of fortune can have on the mind of a man:

> In great commercial communities, where men may be reduced, in a few minutes, from affluence to beggary; where the hopes and aspirations of years are levelled in a moment to the dust, and the individual finds himself exposed to the insulting pity of friends, and the searching curiosity of the public, we need not feel surprise, when all the circumstances rush upon a man's mind in the sudden convulsion and turbulence of its elements, that he should welcome the only escape from the abyss into which he has been hurled.[84]

Similarly, a sudden accession of wealth was believed to provoke insanity. Burrows believed that 'no impression is more calculated to subvert ordinary minds than the sudden and unexpected influx of great wealth. When thus acquired, many become deranged from being elevated to a sphere for which they were never intended.'[85] The artificial tampering with wealth that speculation involved and the sudden losses it could incur both resulted in disordered pecuniary conditions. With disordered finances came a disordered mind. Making a more direct connection between speculation and insanity, Henry Maudsley explained that 'in the higher departments of trade and commerce speculations of all sorts are eagerly entered on, and that many people are kept in a continued state of excitement and anxiety by the fluctuations of the money market'.[86] In order to survive in the competitive marketplace, men required the strength of character and calm nerves typical of the idealized middle-class masculinity in order to survive the anxieties of market fluctuations. As Melmotte explicates, 'It is only the strong ships that can stand the fury of the winds and waves. And then the buffeting which a man gets leaves him only half the man he was.'[87] Financial speculation and the fluctuations in the market were capable of testing a man's masculinity. The speculations made by the press that Sadleir's mind had been disordered through financial losses, as well as witness testimony to his having lost his strength of mind, imply that Sadleir's masculinity had come up short.

At the same time as news of Sadleir's suicide was circulating, reports began to emerge in the press of troubles with various firms in which John Sadleir had been involved. On Wednesday 13 February the *Morning Chronicle* reported that drafts of the Tipperary Joint-Stock Bank had been returned by their London agents, Messrs. Glyn and Co., with the words 'not provided for'.[88] The report was followed by a number of notices reassuring the public that this was simply down to an accident.[89] But the news had 'thrown a doubt on the bank' and produced the 'natural consequence' that 'a severe and sudden demand for repayment from their numerous depositors' ensued; the Bank of Ireland had continued to meet demands until the end of the week, but on Monday 18 February – the same day that news of Sadler's suicide broke – the *Evening Freeman* announced that the bank was now refusing to pay the drafts.[90] Then came the news that shares for the Royal Swedish Railway Company, of which Sadleir was also Chairman, had been improperly issued.[91] The first paper to hint that something was amiss was the *Morning Chronicle* on Wednesday 20 February, whose announcement is worth quoting in full. In the Money Market and City News column, the paper reported that:

> The peculiar circumstances attending to the decease of Mr. John Sadleir appear destined, from his position with several joint-stock projects, to create much public attention in the elucidation of his pecuniary difficulties. As a public man his death would necessarily be talked of with some interest, but when it is known that he was either chairman or director to several undertakings, and took an active part in their proceedings, the circumstances surrounding his sudden decease are invested with more than ordinary interest. It appears desirable, if not imperative, for the respective shareholders and directors in some of the companies with which he was connected, to consider their position. Not only does rumour ascribe to the latter a deficiency of care, prudence, and attention to the interests of the concerns over which they are supposed to have exercised the vigilance the proprietary had invested them with the power of exercising, and to whom they are accountable for any irregularity in their own duties, or in the general administration of the affairs of each undertaking—but circumstances are hourly coming to light which will place them in a very unenviable position if they do not promptly come forward and investigate matters with which they are supposed to be negligently ignorant. A bill, bearing the signature of the late Mr. Sadleir, accepted by him as Chairman of the Swedish Railway, and made payable at the offices of the company, fell due on Saturday, and was dishonoured.

A similar became due yesterday, and shared the same fate. The interests of shareholders must not now be neglected from false delicacy to the feelings and position of the deceased. Another bill for upwards of £6,000, bearing Mr. Sadleir's and other names, fell due to-day at Messrs. Masterman's, and was not paid. It was on account of a foreign railway.[92]

Then, on 23 February, as the news of his death was still spreading across the regional papers, the *Morning Advertiser* announced 'the most startling facts which ever perhaps appeared relative to the extent of frauds and forgeries committed by one individual' and that they could not recollect 'ever having heard or read of anything, in the form of frauds and forgeries, which could be at all compared with those which we are about to specify as having been committed by the late Mr. John Sadleir'.[93] It was still early days, and the paper admitted that the full extent of the forgeries was, as yet, unknown, but speculated that it 'will not be much under 1,000,000*l*'. The over-issue of Royal Swedish Railway shares turned out to be Sadleir's work, having forged at least 50,000, for 5*l*. each, amounting to no less than 250,000*l*., although they had not yet determined how much he had raised on these shares. He had also forged deeds and mortgages for estates in Ireland, the extent of which was unknown. He had further defrauded private individuals of about 100,000*l*. and was 'guilty of the assignment of deeds held in trust by him'. But, as the *Advertiser* described it, 'the boldest and most daring' of his forgeries were those relating to deeds for the purchase of properties in the Encumbered Estates Court of Ireland. These bore the signatures of Commissioners, the Registrar, the Chief Clerk, solicitors and the Commissioner's Seal, all forgeries, which were 'said to be so perfect, that the most experienced eye could not detect the forged deeds from the genuine'.[94] The news spread quickly and Sadleir's suicide was no longer a rash response to heavy financial losses. Instead, the *Advertiser* had reported that it had been precipitated by a holder of one of the deeds for the purchase of one of the encumbered estates, who had already given 10,000*l*. to Sadleir, going to Ireland to attempt to register the deed. 'Hence, it is presumed, the commission of suicide at the particular time it took place, — longer concealment of his crimes being seen to be impossible'. Sadleir's suicide was now being narrated as an inability or unwillingness to face responsibility for his crimes. One, the paper hinted at, which he had been contemplating, as evidenced by his purchase of the book *Taylor on Poisoning*, which had been turned down at the page relating to the essential oil of bitter almonds 'as if he had made up his mind that that was the means to which he would resort'.[95]

By the time that the inquest readjourned on Monday 25 February, there was no doubt that Sadleir had been involved in extensive frauds and forgeries, and that he had been turned from an unfortunate speculator to a villain. The inquest opened with Mr Manning, the solicitor representing the family, stating that he 'proposed to put in two letters' which had been referred to at the first inquiry, one to Mr Keating, and another to Mr Norris, adding that, 'Under ordinary circumstances they were letters that ought not to be made public', but, after the revelation of the forgeries, it was the wish of the family 'that nothing should be concealed'. It was wished that the names of some individuals mentioned in the letters be omitted, to which the coroner agreed, as 'he was of opinion that it would be highly injurious to those individuals if their names were made public, as he said they were ruined men by his *villainy*' (emphasis added).[96] In the letters Sadleir confessed that he had 'swindled and deceived, without the knowledge of anyone', and wrote that he was unable to live to see the 'agony' of those he had ruined by his 'villainy', and the 'shame' and 'distress' he had brought on his family. In his letter to Robert Keating he also admitted how he felt 'for those on whom all this ruin must fall! I could bear all punishments; but I could never bear to witness the sufferings of those on whom I have brought ruin. It must be better that I should not live'. This was also reiterated in the letter sent to his sister-in-law when he wrote, 'Oh, what would I not suffer with gladness to save those whom I have ruined' and he believed that his suicide would 'prove at least that I was not callous to their agony'.[97]

Josiah Wilkinson, an occasional solicitor to Mr Sadleir, also deposed that Sadleir had visited him on Saturday, the day before he was found dead, asking him to raise some money to aid the failing Tipperary Bank, and when he was unable to do so, Sadleir became excited and exclaimed 'Good God, I shall be the ruin of thousands!'[98] Wilkinson was the aforementioned deed-holder who had attempted to get the deed registered after his suspicions were raised that it might be a forgery. He deposed that 'since his death I attribute the excitement he displayed in my office partly to the failure of the Tipperary Bank, and partly to my having insisted upon sending over my deed for registration'.[99] However, he did not believe that matters were as bad as the letters implied. Although the papers had suggested that 'there were a great many forged deeds in existence', he had not heard of any of them and, having seen many of Sadleir's deeds, believed them all to be genuine with the exception of the one in his possession.[100] As only one case of forgery had thus far been proved, the coroner asked the jury 'whether it would not be expedient to adjourn the inquiry' as, if Sadleir was not guilty of forgery to the extent implied in his letters, this would be evidence enough that he was not of sound mind at the time of his suicide. The jury agreed with this opinion and the inquest was adjourned for a second time.

In the meantime, further news of the extent of Sadleir's frauds unfolded. 'Every day', *Reynolds's Newspaper* reported, 'develops some fresh frauds and forgeries on the part of the late suicide, Sadleir, M.P.',[101] and it had become the subject of 'absorbing interest'.[102] By the time the inquest readjourned, for the final time, there was no doubt that the forgeries alluded to in Sadleir's letters were far from the figment of his imagination. His frauds were unprecedented. Several papers compared it to the failure of the private bank, Paul, Strahan and Bates, and the discovery of forgeries committed by the partners John Paul, William Strahan and Robert Bates in 1855. Described by financial journalist David Mourier Evans as being 'characterized by circumstances of so unparalleled a nature, as to remove it altogether from the category of ordinary delinquencies',[103] Strahan, Paul and Bates had been borrowing customers' money since 1816, and the bank had also suffered from financing Welsh coalmines. When the bank became insolvent by 1849, Paul, Strahan and Bates attempted to rescue the situation through 'speculative Italian railway loans' which were funded by fraudulently converting customers' security deposits to the tune of over £100,000.[104] The *Morning Advertiser* wrote that their forgeries were 'not only much smaller in amount, but ... are tame compared with his', pointing out that 'no ingenuity or management was required' compared to Sadleir's;[105] the *Leeds Times* were also of the opinion that the Strahan, Paul and Bates swindle 'sinks into insignificance when compared with this, the latest illustration of commercial honesty'.[106]

At the final inquiry, Mr Manning attempted to persuade the jury that only one forged deed had been found amongst those relating to the Encumbered Estates Court, suggesting that the extent of the forgeries outlined in the letters were certainly 'exaggerations and unfounded', but thought it would be 'impossible' to produce evidence to disprove the claims that he had ruined thousands and committed diabolical crimes. It became clear that the family were hoping for a verdict of insanity. On the coroner pointing out that the case had 'assumed a more serious aspect' since the last inquiry, of which they were aware through the newspaper reports, Manning pleaded that the case would be judged 'by the evidence brought before it, and not by reports flying about',[107] and 'urged that the depression of mind consequent upon taking opium, and the distressing circumstances in which he was placed, justified the assertion that ... Mr. Sadleir at the time of his death was not responsible for his acts', based on the evidence produced in court.[108] Manning had appealed to the jury to consider the effect of their verdict.

The coroner, at length, summed up the case before them, labouring particularly on the question of Sadleir's state of mind, making it clear that he believed Sadleir's suicide did not deserve the mercy that was often shown to suicides by way of an insanity verdict. He lamented that they had 'had to make the investigation [into his state of mind], for he believed that such inquiries were generally useless, and in some cases most mischievous, for verdicts of insanity in cases of suicide were almost always returned as a matter of course'. He also believed that, '[t]he familiarity of jurymen with such verdicts had a most injurious effect, for they went to the Old Bailey, and there, on very slight grounds, returned verdicts of insanity, and the result was that the worst criminals escaped from justice, and now and then a madman was executed'.[109] He highlighted that the last person to see John Sadleir alive could give no strength to the argument for insanity, and after reading some portions of a letter Sadleir sent to his brother, requesting £20,000–£30,000 to prevent widespread ruin, he asked the jury to consider what insanity was, '[w]as it grief, was it remorse, was it despair?'. The coroner admitted that it was a difficult matter. Whilst he was aware that juries would often lean on the side of 'mercy', 'justice and humanity' by returning an insanity verdict, he added that if these were due to an individual 'it must not be forgotten that justice and humanity were also due to society'. Again, he reinforced his belief that insanity verdicts proved disastrous to the criminal justice system.[110] The revelation of the crimes committed by John Sadleir, and the extent of the ruin they would throw upon his victims, undoubtedly informed the coroner's words in his attempt to sway the jury against a verdict of insanity. His reference to the trials of the Old Bailey paint Sadleir as one of those 'worst criminals' who, he believed, escaped justice through the verdict of insanity. In this way, the inquest on Sadleir's body was turned into a criminal trial. As Barbara Gates has pointed out, suicide did not satisfy the 'Victorian sense of justice' in the same way that a murder could;[111] whereas a murderer could be convicted and sentenced to death or imprisonment, the best they could do with a suicide is deem them *felo de se*. After only half an hour of deliberation, the jury unanimously returned the verdict that John Sadleir had 'died by his own hand, while in a perfectly sane state of mind'.[112]

The letters Sadleir wrote the night of his death clearly espoused remorse and were full of self-reproach, yet the jury still saw Sadleir deserved a criminal verdict. Gates has suggested that it was these notes that 'ultimately convinced' the jury of Sadleir's sanity, suggesting that they believed that no one 'could so clearly realize the harm that he had done to others and be intellectually impaired'.[113] Gates' reasoning is logical, an admission of guilt and an acute awareness of the consequences suggests Sadleir was in full possession of mind, and provides a reasonable basis to reject a verdict of insanity. But I would argue the judgement was influenced more by his commission of crime than his expressing remorse at having done it. Introducing an analysis of the Sadleir case, Gates suggests that coroners' juries 'tended to deal harshly with the greedy, especially with shady financiers and embezzlers', of which Sadleir is the prime example.[114] To suggest, then, that the jury was influenced more by the letters than the extensive crimes committed seems inconsistent with her earlier evaluation. As is the assertion that with Sadleir's decision to suicide, 'the Victorian sense of justice seemed well-satisfied',[115] which undermines Gates' earlier claim that suicide failed to satisfy the Victorian sense of justice.

Far from Sadleir's suicide satisfying this sense of justice, his inquest turned into a criminal trial in which he was judged guilty of the crimes his letters confessed to. As the coroner pointed out to the jury, it was common for verdicts of insanity to be returned as an expression of sympathy, and they have certainly been returned on the kind of evidence given by Mr Norris. The suicide of a Robert Henry Williams, Bank Manager, for example was deemed an act of temporary insanity on the basis that he 'was not as usual', had 'seemed depressed', which was attributed to being 'harassed' about the affairs of the bank, and that witnesses had noticed a 'difference in him' for the last few weeks. Although witnesses were concerned about his state of mind, there was nothing that had suggested that he was 'labouring under insanity', and it was said that 'he appeared in his usual health'.[116] It was also a common assumption that losses in speculation were enough to disorder the mind and lead to suicide. When William Cowell, a clerk, committed suicide, letters were produced at the inquest, containing what was 'apparently the outpouring of a disordered mind'. The letters told the story of Cowell's life, blaming his troubles on 'overindulgence' since birth. He reprimanded his parents, who he suggested should have tried to curb his 'wayward thoughts at the start', and others who had 'misled me over shares, stocks, etc.', and even blaming a man, whose name was removed in press reports, 'for the magnificent salary' he had given him. The article concluded that it was 'evident the deceased had speculated, and lost, and this had unhinged his mind' and the jury returned a verdict of temporary insanity, with no other evidence given regarding his state of mind.[117] None of these men, however, had committed large-scale fraud.

In Sadleir's case, the coroner had initially expressed that he had 'no desire' to see the letters written by Sadleir, as it was clear that he had committed suicide by taking poison, and that the jury simply needed to determine his state of mind, implying he believed that enough evidence had been presented.[118] It was the jury who wished to see the letters, in the hope that they might produce more evidence as to his state of mind. With the revelation of his crimes, and their being proven to be true, the inquest took on a new dynamic. Furthermore, the coroner's lengthy speech at the conclusion of the evidence, urging the jury to consider the need for justice on behalf of the public, was remarkable in its condemnatory tone; rarely did a coroner attempt to influence the jury to such an extent. The suicide of Henry Salmon, an agent for the Falkirk branch of Commercial Bank of Scotland, is a case in point. Salmon had embezzled £30,000, over a period of fifteen years, having successfully passed the scrutiny of 'the Argus-eyes of directors, depositors, inspectors, secretaries ... and every man that had a right to be suspicious, and every one that might be expected to perform the functions of a detective' – the local newspaper declared it a case of 'Sadleirism in Scotland'.[119] Yet the coroner in this case appeared to lean in favour of insanity. Although his suggestion was by no means the impassioned speech of Sadleir's coroner, he referred back to a letter found in Salmon's pocket which had been read in court and was described as being 'written in a very disjointed and unconnected style'. This, he believed, showed 'that there was an awful pressure upon him' at the time he committed suicide and the jury returned a verdict of 'temporary insanity'.[120] The key point of contrast (apart from the extent of his fraud) was that Salmon had been described as an upstanding member of the community, he had confessed his crimes as soon as they were discovered, and reportedly he had attempted to come to an arrangement with the directors of the bank (which had been refused).[121] Sadleir's whole character, on the other hand, had been fraudulent.

At the inquest and in the newspapers, Sadleir's character was put on trial. As James Taylor has noted in his work on company fraud, 'the perceived character of the offender' played an important part in criminal trials for frauds and forgeries.[122] Lawyers played on the notion of a defendant's good or bad character in trying to sway the jury; for example, in 1862 when it was discovered that Reverend Fletcher, as both secretary and treasurer of the local savings bank at Bilston, had embezzled £9,000, his defence counsel Henry Matthews 'played on Fletcher's good character' during the trial.[123] In another case, the manager of the Oriental Commercial Bank, Demetrio Pappa, had embezzled £10,000 of the bank's money, and owed a further £6,000, but the jury 'recommended him to mercy on account of his previous good character'.[124]

In an age when character was a favoured explanation of deeds and tragedies during the nineteenth century, this is perhaps no surprise. As Stefan Collini notes, 'to be known as a man of character was to possess the moral collateral which would reassure potential business associates or employers'; but when businesses failed, speculations proved imprudent or disastrous, or frauds were exposed, these stories were utilized as moral fables that linked the moral failing of character to the financial failing.[125] A suicide, similarly seen as a morally culpable act and a failure of character, added extra weight to these moral exposés.[126] In *The Anatomy of Suicide* Forbes Winslow described suicide as being among 'the black catalogue of human offences' before arguing that suicide was a crime against God and man. Later, exploring the influence of different mental states in inducing the suicidal disposition, he laments how a defective education, replaced 'sound morals' and cultivation of the heart and mind with 'polished manners' and 'external accomplishments', and explains that the origination of the suicidal disposition is allowed by a weakening of moral principles.[127] In 1832 the Society for Promoting Christian Knowledge had circulated a tract that described how the 'alarming frequency of the crime of suicide' was 'mournful proof of the want of religious and moral principle'.[128] In light of Sadleir's fraudulence and financial recklessness, his suicide no longer seemed surprising.

In the aftermath of the revelations, and with the inquest brought to a conclusion, reports of Sadleir's suicide in the press were no longer espousing words of sympathy. Sadleir's suicide was held up as a rash escape of justice, and a reflection of his immoral character. *The Ulsterman* described the implications of this verdict to its readers in the following manner: 'that John Sadleir, swindler and forger, did, in the full possession of his sense, lay violent hands on himself, and did (without the excuse of insanity) rashly face the awful vengeance of Heaven, to avoid the condemnation of his fellow-mortals'.[129] Similarly, *The Evening Packet* jumped on the evidence that opium had been found in his stomach (although no witness could confirm an opium habit), as evidence of his 'effort to escape from the inquietude of mind, which, when things reached their climax, produced his deliberate *resolve to die*' (emphasis in original).[130] Here, Sadleir is framed as lacking the moral integrity to face up to the consequences of his own actions, which was a cornerstone of middle-class masculinity. His suicide, essentially, is framed as a coward's escape. This was not an unfamiliar narrative. A curious letter regarding Sadleir appears in the Dublin-based newspaper, *The Nation*, on 29 March, suggesting that Sadleir had not actually committed suicide but had fled with the money he had embezzled. Introducing the case, the author of the letter asserts how there was '[n]o inconsistency between the antecedents of the individual and *this*—the abrupt [c]lose of his career—nothing very extraordinary in such a consummation of the destiny of *such* a man' (emphasis in original).[131]

What this suggests is an already well-established narrative in which suicide follows speculation and forgery.

The suicide became 'fiction's conventional ending' for the financial villain, and as Barbara Weiss suggests, it arises out of 'the necessity for the villain to pay for his crimes at the end of the melodrama'.[132] But, as this chapter makes clear, this was more than just a literary and dramatic convention written into the financial plots of Victorian fiction, a metaphor for the contemporary economic climate; it was grounded in real life. Sadleir's suicide and inquest came just a year before Dickens published the self-inflicted conclusion to Mr Merdle's criminal career, and, according to Norman Russell, only two days before he began writing the fifth instalment in which the Merdles first appear. Sadleir's story thus 'provided Dickens with an excellent, immediately contemporary model' for Mr Merdle.[133] In fact, these implications upon Sadleir's character – that his suicide is not unsurprising given the type of man he was now revealed to be – are echoed in the comments made by Merdle's butler on being informed of his master's suicide. After receiving the news of Mr Merdle's self-inflicted death, and being questioned about his lack of shock or surprise, the Chief Butler 'replied in these memorable words. "Sir, Mr Merdle never was the gentleman, and no ungentlemanly act on Mr Merdle's part would surprise me".[134] As long as Sadleir appeared to be solvent his character was thought to be respectable, but with the revelation that his wealth was fraudulent and he was heavily in debt, his character was cast into doubt.

The moral problem with speculation was that it was fast money obtained with high risk in a pursuit of wealth beyond needs, rather than the steady accumulation of wealth as a by-product of honest and steady work. The *Faversham Gazette* published an article on 1 March detailing how Sadleir's entire career and 'high commercial, social, and political position' had been held up by a 'gigantic system of fraud'. He had commenced the world without fortune 'yet determined to be rich', but 'the path of patient industry and regular gains was too slow for him'.[135] An article in the *Glasgow Herald* later that month disparaged the dishonest means by which he earned his fortune by highlighting how '[m]uch vaster fortunes have been made with less beginnings, where the possession of capital has been accompanied by intelligence, energy, and prudence'.[136] The criticisms these articles put forward were underlined by expectations of middle-class masculinity, in which wealth was earned through honest, hard work. Sadleir, on the other hand, had cheated his way to his position. Sadleir had begun his career in relative obscurity as an Irish attorney and within only eight years had attained a position in Lord Aberdeen's government as Junior Lord of the Treasury. Such a rapid ascension within society warranted suspicion. In his study of the influence of Evangelicalism on economic thought in the first half of the nineteenth century, Boyd Hilton demonstrates that, in an age of speculation, wealth could be viewed with suspicion. Fast riches were always morally culpable, but the 'slow and sure' growth of fortune was 'virtuous'. Extravagant speculation, it was believed, brought more ruin than deliberate fraudulence. Hilton suggests that this 'explains how fraudulent rogues like … John Sadleir could be regarded in a romantic and almost an heroic light, while those who tried to jump above their proper economic stations were invariably castigated as sinful.'[137] Based on the reports of his suicide, however, Sadleir does not appear to have been regarded in the 'romantic and almost heroic light' that Hilton suggests. Instead, I suggest that he was branded part of the latter group, who tried to advance their economic position without merit. Sadleir's wealth was artificial and had been acquired through unnatural means, indicative of a greed unchecked by proper self-regulation. Returning to the earlier analogy made between economy and mind, then, Sadleir's suicide is an example of how financial destruction is manifested, physically, in self-destruction. The *Faversham Gazette* article went on to state that it was believed that, had he withdrawn from business at the height of his career, he would have 'retired on a handsome estate', and raises the question: 'If the fact be so, one must needs wonder at the suddenness with which he became so rich; if otherwise, one may wonder more at the spectacle of a man standing, or rather seeming to stand, so high upon nothing.'[138] The suspicion of Sadleir's wealth displayed here was rooted in both the values of middle-class masculinity and in a deeper ambiguity about value in an age of credit and paper money.

This ambiguity of value has now become an important theme in scholarship on the literature and economics of the nineteenth century. Margot C. Finn has looked at the importance of character in the new credit economy, explaining how the idea of an individual's character was used in discourses of debt, with credit acting as a moral evaluation of character. Before the rise of the credit economy, Finn argues, credit and debt were dependent upon 'conceptions of mutual trust', but during the eighteenth and nineteenth centuries credit relations came to be 'shaped most decisively by notions of personal character'. Character became the basis upon which credit was given, and acted as 'a broader social and cultural measure of personal worth'.[139] The problem, as Finn points out, is that the measures creditors used in their evaluations of character were fluid and unstable: clothing, manner, social status, marital relations, which were rarely accurate representations of personal wealth.[140]

The *Faversham Gazette*'s questioning of Sadleir's wealth illustrates this point. As chairman of the London and County joint-stock bank and the Royal Swedish Railway Company, an MP for both Carlow (1847–53) and Sligo (1853–6) and Lord of the Treasury, Sadleir had enjoyed the reputation of a respectable character. According to David Mourier Evans, it was generally believed by shareholders that the name John Sadleir 'at the head of the board' was 'equivalent to a rise of at least one per cent. in the market value of their shares'.[141] Yet he was £288,000 overdrawn with the Tipperary Bank.[142] Sadleir's greatest qualification – much like that of Augustus Melmotte – was that 'he had the power of impressing upon others a high opinion of his own value'.[143] Early reports, before his frauds were known to the public, had praised his character. *The Belfast News-Letter* described his character as 'amiable and benevolent', and stated that he had 'possessed very considerable talent, and was distinguished by superior address'.[144] *The Standard* described him as being 'greatly respected by the class of capitalists among whom he moved',[145] and *The Times*, seemingly using his monetary affairs as a representation of his character, reported that 'he was a purchaser to a large amount of lands sold in the Encumbered Estates Court in Ireland, and that he was extensively connected with various commercial undertakings of magnitude, but that he was under no heavy liabilities' to the London and County Joint-Stock Banking Company'.[146] Sadleir's reputation as a man of moral character had allowed him to raise credit and carry on business despite being insolvent. By the end of February 1857, however, he had been exposed. *The Morning Post* published a lengthy diatribe of Sadleir's life and character:

> He had passed for a man whose energy and acuteness had won him station and wealth. How rapidly these seeming properties passed from him; how speedily his ill deeds clustered avenging before his face; how short a time he enjoyed even the reputation of those things, to gain which he sacrificed so much ...[147]

Whilst Sadleir passed for a man of wealth, who had built his reputation on the back of commercial talent, he was lauded as an exemplar of the values that underpinned middle-class masculinity. The revelations of his frauds and forgeries revealed a fatal flaw in the estimation of moral character by the extent of one's wealth. The wonder expressed by the *Faversham Gazette* that a man could stand 'so high upon nothing', cuts right to the heart of this. That someone could rise to such high position on nothing but the *appearance* of wealth, highlighted a fatal flaw in the moral measure of creditworthiness.

These suicides demonstrate how the physical body was closely tied into the association between character and credit. Finn has looked at how credit is conflated with the person through debt law which seized men's bodies for their debts, 'allowing the human body to serve as collateral for goods obtained … through the operation of consumer credit'.[148] So too is the body offered up as collateral in suicide. Commenting on the motive for his suicide, *The Morning Post* of 27 February 1856 concluded that it had been committed out of fear of exposure and punishment, but revealed other possible interpretations. Whilst clearly stating that Sadleir's suicide was not committed out of the feeling that 'he had nothing left except his wretched and worthless life to offer as a sacrifice to those whom he had injured so grievously', the fact that this was a possible interpretation of his suicide suggests how much the body and identity is tied to the notion of credit.[149] In suicide, as in debt law, the body served as a replacement for money when the money has run out.

Mary Poovey's work on the ambiguity of value focuses mostly on the unstable and uncertain value of paper credit, such as banknotes, paper shares and bills of exchange. As Poovey points out the bursting of the South Sea Bubble demonstrated how shares could fluctuate from 'magical' to 'nonexistent' value, and the Restriction Act of 1797, when the Bank of England ceased to exchange paper money for gold, or the printing of banknotes to satisfy demand, the value of paper money became fictitious. No longer was money rooted in any tangible form of worth, and it bore little relation to what it was supposed to represent.[150] In such an environment, moral character became an important signifier of value. In an analysis of the value of money, Claudia Klaver has argued how economic and moral value were inextricable. Fictions such as *Dombey and Son* and the journalistic responses to the Bank Charter Act of 1844 – which restricted the issuing of bank notes to the Bank of England, and required them to be backed by gold or up to £14 million of government debt – argued that 'individual moral integrity … was the only stable basis for economic value'.[151] This value is also tied to personal identity, not only through the value signifiers mentioned by Finn, such as clothing or manner, but through the physical body. As Klaver has pointed out in relation to Mr Dombey's bankruptcy in *Dombey and Son*, loss of fortune, or fortune-based status, shatters Mr Dombey's identity, one which reaches suicidal proportions.[152] Once the real value of Sadleir's money, or lack thereof, is exposed Sadleir himself disappears. As Roger L. Slakey has commented regarding Anthony Trollope's Melmotte, which is equally befitting for Sadleir, his business has no grounding in 'real' value, his entire identity is a fiction based on paper which purports to represent value, his death becomes 'an assertion of his reality, that is of his nothingness'.[153] Although not fictional, Sadleir's suicide equally represents how integral wealth was to masculine identity.

Conclusion

John Sadleir was, in the words of Evans, 'one of the greatest, if not the greatest, and … most successful, swindlers that this or any other country has produced'. Evans' summary of his life and character encompasses some of the key concerns surrounding wealth during the nineteenth century,

> That he was a man of high talents, few who knew him personally can doubt; and had he been content to apply those talents to honest courses, the brilliant opportunities which opened for their exercise would have enabled him to attain the highest position in the State, But his impetuosity would not brook the labour, and the toil, and the delay of gratifying his ambition in a legitimate manner. He sought the short road to fortune, and, like all who have travelled that delusive path, miserably failed.[154]

Sadleir had once stood as a pillar in middle-class commercial society, whose character had been valued so highly on the intangible basis of his apparent financial success. But he had eschewed the values that were central to middle-class masculinity – moral integrity, virtue and patient industry – and instead had sought to advance his position in society through, not just speculation, but extensive fraud. The man who speculated and lost in the 'rough sea' of the market might have been unmanned, but he could be viewed with pity as a victim who did not possess the steady nerves required in the competitive market. But the man who had cheated his way to such a position as Sadleir's evidenced not only the corruption of the market, but a flagrant disregard for the values of honest hard work upon which middle-class masculinity was built.

But looking beyond Sadleir, financial suicides serve as an illustration of the anxieties around men's participation in a competitive capitalist market, whilst trying to retain the moral character that was supposed to be central to middle-class masculinity. The suicides that followed these exposés and financial failings served as an example of how, in the words of Boyd Hilton, the economy acted 'as an arena of great spiritual trial and suspense' and those guilty of 'economic peccadilloes might stand in greater danger than murderers'.[155] In these narratives of suicide following financial fraud and ruin, the press found moral fables of the consequences of the hasty pursuit of wealth.

Notes

1 Anthony Trollope, *The Way We Live Now* (Hertfordshire: Wordsworth Editions, 1995), 670–1.

2 Charles Dickens, *Little Dorrit* (Hertfordshire: Wordsworth Editions, 2002), 672.

3 Victor Bailey, *This Rash Act: Suicide Across the Life Cycle in the Victorian City* (Stanford, CA: Stanford University Press, 1998), 75–6.

4 'Suicide of A Clerk', *Cardiff Times* and *South Wales Weekly News*, 23 December 1893: 6; 'Suicide of A London Medical Man', *The Falkirk Herald and Midland Counties Journal*, 28 April 1897: 6.

5 'Inquest on Thomas Pelham Hollis', *Morning Advertiser*, 27 November 1832: 3.

6 'Fraud and Suicide', *Carlisle Patriot*, 11 November 1887: 3.

7 Ibid.

8 'Suicide To Avoid Arrest', *Southampton Herald*, 20 August 1892: 3.

9 Barbara T. Gates, *Victorian Suicide: Mad Crimes and Sad Histories* (Princeton, NJ: Princeton University Press, 1988), 38.

10 As Matthew MacDonald as shown, even by the start of the nineteenth century insanity was by far the favoured verdict, being returned in 97 per cent of cases between 1780 and 1800. Michael MacDonald, 'The Medicalization of Suicide in England: Laymen, Physicians, and Cultural Change, 1500–1870', *The Milbank Quarterly* 67 (1989): 75.

11 See Harold James Perkin, *The Origins of Modern English Society* (London: Routledge, 2002), 182–90.

12 John Tosh, *Manliness and Masculinities in Nineteenth-Century Britain: Essays on Gender, Family, and Empire*, 1st edn, Women and Men in History (Harlow, England; New York, NY: Pearson Longman, 2005), 74.

13 Stefan Collini, *Public Moralists: Political Thought and Intellectual Life in Britain* (Oxford: Clarendon, 1991), 94–6.

14 Ibid., 100.

15 Tosh, *Manliness and Masculinities in Nineteenth-Century Britain*, 76; Collini, *Public Moralists*, 106; see also Margot C. Finn, *The Character of Credit: Personal Debt in English Culture, 1740–1914*, Cambridge Social and Cultural Histories 1 (Cambridge; New York, NY: Cambridge University Press, 2003), particularly 18–21.

16 Barbara Weiss, *The Hell of the English: Bankruptcy and the Victorian Novel* (Lewisburg; London; Cranbury, NJ: Bucknell University Press; Associated University Presses, 1986), 30–1.

17 Collini, *Public Moralists*, 92; Alfred Marshall, *Principles of Economics*, vol. 1 (London; New York, NY: Macmillan, 1890), 1–2.

18 Kristen Guest, 'The Subject of Money: Late-Victorian Melodrama's Crisis of Masculinity', *Victorian Studies* 49, no. 4 (2007): 636.

19 For example, 'Worship of Mammon', *Coventry Herald,* 19 May 1865: 4, and 'Mammon and Suicide', *Falkirk Herald,* 10 November 1864: 3.

20 Max Weber, *The Protestant Ethic and the Spirit of Capitalism,* Routledge Classics (London; New York, NY: Routledge, 2001); Leonore Davidoff and Catherine Hall, *Family Fortunes,* rev. edn (London; New York, NY: Routledge, 2002), 111–12; Tosh, *Manliness and Masculinities in Nineteenth-Century Britain,* 76–7; the concept of work as a 'calling' underpins Tosh's understanding of middle-class masculinity throughout. John Tosh, *A Man's Place: Masculinity and the Middle-Class Home in Victorian England* (New Haven, CT; London: Yale University Press, 1999).

21 Weber, *The Protestant Ethic and the Spirit of Capitalism,* 19.

22 Charles Dickens, *Dombey and Son* (Hertfordshire: Wordsworth Editions, 1995), 87.

23 Weber, *The Protestant Ethic and the Spirit of Capitalism,* 104.

24 Ibid., 103–4.

25 Tosh, *Manliness and Masculinities in Nineteenth-Century Britain,* 63–4.

26 'Mammon and Suicide', *Glasgow Saturday Post* and *Paisley and Renfrewshire Reformer,* 5 November 1864: 1.

27 'Betting and Gambling', *Sunderland Daily Echo,* 1 September 1890: 3; 'Gambling and Suicide', *St. James's Gazette,* 25 August 1890: 8; 'Gambling and Suicide', *The Tamworth Herald,* 30 August 1890: 2.

28 Samuel Smiles, *Self-Help: With Illustrations of Character, Conduct, and Perseverance* (London: John Murray, 1868), 297.

29 George Gissing, *The Whirlpool* (London: Hogarth Press, 1984), 68.

30 George Robb, *White-Collar Crime in Modern England: Financial Fraud and Business Morality, 1845–1929* (Cambridge, UK; New York, NY: Cambridge University Press, 1992), 3; James Taylor, 'Company Fraud in Victorian Britain: The Royal British Bank Scandal of 1856', *The English Historical Review* 122, no. 497 (2007): 700.

31 Claudia C. Klaver, *A/Moral Economics: Classical Political Economy and Cultural Authority in Nineteenth-Century England* (Columbus, OH: Ohio State University Press, 2003), xii.

32 Boyd Hilton, *The Age of Atonement: The Influence of Evangelicalism on Social and Economic Thought, 1785–1865* (Oxford: Clarendon Press, 1991), 146–52; Klaver, *A/Moral Economics,* xii; Emma Rothschild, 'Political Economy', in *The Cambridge History of Nineteenth-Century Political Thought,* ed. Gareth Stedman Jones and Gregory Claeys, The Cambridge History of Political Thought (Cambridge; New York, NY: Cambridge University Press, 2011), 774.

33 Robb, *White-Collar Crime in Modern England,* 3, 11; James Taylor, *Boardroom Scandal: The Criminalization of Company Fraud in Nineteenth-Century Britain* (Oxford: Oxford University Press, 2013), 2; Guest, 'The Subject of Money: Late-Victorian Melodrama's Crisis of Masculinity', 636.

34 Davidoff and Hall, *Family Fortunes,* rev. edn, 74; Tosh, *A Man's Place: Masculinity and the Middle-Class Home in Victorian England,* chap. 2; John Tosh, 'Masculinities in an

Industrializing Society: Britain, 1800–1914', *Journal of British Studies* 44, no. 2 (2005): 333; John Tosh, 'Home and Away: The Flight from Domesticity in Late-Nineteenth-Century England Re-Visited', *Gender & History* 27, no. 3 (1 November 2015): 561–2.

35 Tosh, *A Man's Place: Masculinity and the Middle-Class Home in Victorian England*, 30.

36 Klaver, *A/Moral Economics*, 83.

37 Mary Poovey, *Genres of the Credit Economy: Mediating Value in Eighteenth- and Nineteenth-Century Britain* (Chicago, IL: University of Chicago Press, 2008), 230; Hilton, *The Age of Atonement*, 133; Taylor, 'Company Fraud in Victorian Britain: The Royal British Bank Scandal of 1856', 713; Robb, *White-Collar Crime in Modern England*, 147.

38 Paul Johnson, *Making the Market: Victorian Origins of Corporate Capitalism*, Cambridge Studies in Economic History (Cambridge; New York, NY: Cambridge University Press, 2010), 27.

39 The importance of self-regulation to masculine identity is threaded throughout James Eli Adams, *Dandies and Desert Saints: Styles of Victorian Masculinity* (Ithaca, NY: Cornell University Press, 1995).

40 James Cowles Prichard, *On the Different Forms of Insanity, in Relation to Jurisprudence, Designed for the Use of Persons Concerned in Legal Questions Regarding Unsoundness of Mind* (London: Hippolyte Baillière, 1842), 135.

41 Forbes Winslow, *The Anatomy of Suicide* (London: Henry Renshaw, 1840), 45–6.

42 Brent Shannon, '"The Terrible Mälestrom of Debt": Credit, Consumption, and Masculinity in Oxbridge Fiction, 1841–1911', *Victorian Literature and Culture* 44, no. 2 (2016): 386–7.

43 Benjamin Gregory, *The Thorough Business Man: Memoirs of Walter Powell, Merchant, Melbourne and London*, 2nd edn (London: Strahan & Co., 1872), 271.

44 Ibid.; Paul Johnson, 'Civilizing Mammon: Laws, Morals, and the City in Nineteenth-Century England', in *Civil Histories: Essays Presented to Sir Keith Thomas*, ed. Peter Burke, Brian Howard Harrison and Paul Slack (Oxford; New York, NY: Oxford University Press, 2000), 304.

45 Hilton, *The Age of Atonement*, 133.

46 Ibid., 136, 162.

47 Nancy Henry, '"Rushing into Eternity": Suicide and Finance in Victorian Fiction', in *Victorian Investments: New Perspectives on Finance and Culture*, ed. Nancy Henry and Cannon Schmitt (Bloomington, IN: Indiana University Press, 2009), 162.

48 Weiss, *The Hell of the English*, 21–2.

49 Tamara S. Wagner, 'Speculators at Home in the Victorian Novel: Making Stock-Market Villains and New Paper Fictions', *Victorian Literature and Culture* 36, no. 1 (2008): 36.

50 John Galbraith, quoted in Henry, '"Rushing into Eternity": Suicide and Finance in Victorian Fiction', 161.

51 Ibid.

52 For example, 'Death of Mr. Abraham Goldsmid', *Evening Mail*, 1 October 1810: 3; 'Attempt At Suicide In High Life', *The Morning Post*, 16 April 1819: 3; 'Forgery and Suicide By A Banker!', *Saunders's News-Letter*, 26 March 1828: 2; 'SUICIDE', *The Leicester Chronicle; or, Commercial and Agricultural Advertiser*, 17 September 1831; 'Railway Gambling, Bankruptcy, And Suicide', *The Morning Chronicle*, 22 December 1845; 'Court Of Bankruptcy.—Saturday', *John Bull*, 27 December 1845.

53 'Death of Mr. Abraham Goldsmid', *Evening Mail*, 1 October 1810: 3; 'The Late Mr. Goldsmid', *The Morning Chronicle*, 1 October 1810: 3; 'Death of Mr. Abraham Goldsmid', *The Hampshire Chronicle*, 1 October 1810: 4; 'Death of Mr. Abraham Goldsmid', *Leicester Journal*, 5 October 1810: 2; 'Death of Mr. A. Goldsmid', *Bristol Mirror*, 6 October 1810: 4; 'Death Of Mr. Abraham Goldsmid', *Oxford University and City Herald*, 6 October 1810: 4; 'Death of Mr. Goldsmid', *Manchester Mercury*, 9 October 1810: 2.

54 'Death of Mr. Abraham Goldsmid', *The Hampshire Chronicle*, 1 October 1810: 4.

55 'Death of Mr. Goldsmid', *Manchester Mercury*, 9 October 1810: 2.

56 'The Late Mr. Goldsmid', *The Morning Chronicle*, 1 October 1810: 3.

57 'Death of Mr. Abraham Goldsmid', *The Hampshire Chronicle*; 'Death of Mr. Abraham Goldsmid', *Leicester Journal*, 5 October 1810: 2; 'Death of Mr, A. Goldsmid', *Bristol Mirror*, 6 October 1810: 4; 'Death of Mr. Abraham Goldsmid', *Oxford University and City Herald*, 6 October 1810: 4.

58 Hilton, *The Age of Atonement*, 146.

59 Leeann Hunter, 'Communities Built from Ruins: Social Economics in Victorian Novels of Bankruptcy', *Women's Studies Quarterly* 39, no. 3/4 (2011): 141.

60 Henry, '"Rushing into Eternity": Suicide and Finance in Victorian Fiction', 126, 163; Tamara S. Wagner, *Financial Speculation in Victorian Fiction: Plotting Money and the Novel Genre, 1815–1901* (Columbus, OH: Ohio State University Press, 2010), 26; Weiss, *The Hell of the English*, 22.

61 Dickens, *Dombey and Son*, 682.

62 Anthony Trollope, *The Prime Minister* (Oxford; New York, NY: Oxford University Press, 2011), 460.

63 Olive Anderson, *Suicide in Victorian and Edwardian England* (Oxford: Clarendon Press, 1987), 196–7.

64 Wagner, 'Speculators at Home in the Victorian Novel: Making Stock-Market Villains and New Paper Fictions'; Wagner, *Financial Speculation in Victorian Fiction*, 1–3 (quote from 3).

65 Sadleir had also been MP for Carlow 1847–53, 'The Suicide of Mr. Sadleir, M.P.', *Daily News*, 20 February 1856; 'Suicide of Mr. John Sadleir, M.P.', *The Tyrone Constitution*, 22 February 1856: 2.

66 Gates, *Victorian Suicide*, 40; John R. Reed, 'A Friend to Mammon: Speculation in Victorian Literature', *Victorian Studies* 27, no. 2 (1984): 185 n.14; Henry, '"Rushing into Eternity": Suicide and Finance in Victorian Fiction', 167; Norman Russell, *The Novelist and Mammon: Literary Responses to the World of Commerce in the*

Nineteenth Century (Oxford; New York, NY: Clarendon Press; Oxford University Press, 1986), 131–48.

67 Hilton, *The Age of Atonement*, 123; Taylor, *Boardroom Scandal*, 3, 104–8, 113; Robb, *White-Collar Crime in Modern England*, 61–2; some effort towards an analysis of how Sadleir's suicide fits into the wider narrative has been made by Barbara Gates Gates, *Victorian Suicide*, 63–7.

68 'The Inquest on Mr Sadleir, M.P.', *Saunders's* Newsletter, 21 February 1856: 1.

69 'The Suicide of Mr. Sadleir, M.P.', *Daily News*, 20 February 1856.

70 Ibid.; 'Suicide of Mr. John Sadleir, M.P.', *The Tyrone Constitution*.

71 'Suicide of Mr. John Sadleir, M.P.', *The Tyrone Constitution*.

72 'The Suicide of Mr. Sadleir, M.P.', *Daily News*; 'Suicide of Mr. John Sadleir, M.P.', *The Tyrone Constitution*.

73 James O'Shea, *Prince of Swindlers: John Sadleir, M.P. 1813–1856* (Dublin: Geography Publications, 1999), 415.

74 'Melancholy Suicide of Mr. John Sadleir, M.P. for Sligo', *The Belfast News-Letter*, 20 February 1856: 2.

75 'Suicide of Mr. John Sadleir, M.P.', *The Standard*, 18 February 1856: 3.

76 'Weekly Summary', *Leicester Journal*, 22 February 1856: 8.

77 'Suicide of Mr. John Sadleir, M.P.', *The Standard*, 18 February 1856: 3.

78 'The Suicide of Mr. Sadleir, M.P.', *The Standard*, 19 February 1856: 1.

79 'Suicide of Mr. John Sadleir, M.P.', *The Times*, 19 February 1856: 9.

80 'Death of Mr. Sadleir, M.P.', *The Freeman's Journal*, 19 February 1856: 2.

81 'Reverse of fortune' was listed as the third largest cause of suicide for both men and women after poverty and 'Domestic grief' in the London Medical and Surgical Journal, listed in Winslow, *The Anatomy of Suicide*, 50; Charles Mercier, *Sanity and Insanity* (London: Walter Scott, 1890), 267–8; George Mann Burrows, *Commentaries on the Causes, Forms, Symptoms, and Treatment, Moral and Medical, of Insanity* (London: Thomas and George Underwood, 1828), 15–16.

82 'Suicide of Mr. A. Grant', *The Age*, 24 January 1841: 30; 'Attempted Suicide From the Failure of Theatrical Speculation', *The Morning Post*, 21 October 1845: 11; 'Another Suicide From Unfortunate Share Speculations', *The Manchester Courier* and *Lancashire General Advertiser*, 22 November 1845: 7; 'Awful Suicide in Clonmel', *The Glasgow Citizen*, 20 December 1845: 3; 'Suicide From Railway Speculation', *The Perthshire Advertiser*, 15 January 1846: 2; 'Suicide from Railway Speculations', *The Perthshire Courier*, 29 January 1846: 2; 'Suicide From Railway Speculation', *The Newry Telegraph*, 16 September 1847: 4.

83 'Miscellaneous News', *The Somerset County Gazette*, 27 July 1839: 4.

84 Winslow, *The Anatomy of Suicide*, 79.

85 Burrows, *Commentaries on the Causes, Forms, Symptoms, and Treatment, Moral and Medical, of Insanity*, 16.

86 Henry Maudsley, *The Physiology and Pathology of the Mind* (London: Macmillan, 1867), 205.

87   Trollope, *The Way We Live Now*, 562.

88   'Money Market and City News', *The Morning Chronicle*, 13 February 1856: 7.

89   'Monetary and Commercial', *The Evening Freeman*, 13 February 1856: 3; 'The Money Market', *The Morning Advertiser*, 14 February 1856: 6; 'The Tipperary Joint Stock Bank', *The Carlow Post*, 16 February 1856: 2.

90   'Commercial Intelligence', *The Evening Freeman*, 18 February 1856: 3; 'Tipperary Joint-Stock Bank', *The Constitution; or, Cork Advertiser*, 19 February 1856: 2; 'IRELAND', *The Evening Mail*, 20 February 1856: 2; 'The Tipperary Bank', *The Tralee Chronicle*, 22 February 1856: 4.

91   'Royal Swedish Railway Company', *The Morning Chronicle*, 21 February 1856; 'Money Market and City Intelligence', *The London Evening Standard*, 21 February 1856: 2.

92   'Money Market and City News', *The Morning Chronicle*, 20 February 1856: 3; 'Suicide of Mr. Sadleir, M.P.', *Freeman's Journal*, 21 February 1856: 3; 'The Late Mr. Sadleir, M.P.', *The Waterford Mail*, 21 February 1856: 1.

93   'Mr. John Sadleir. M.P.—The Late Astounding Disclosures', *The Morning Advertiser*, 23 February 1856: 4. It should be noted that the *Carlisle Journal* of 22 February 1856, reports that 'The *Morning Advertiser* asserts that there is every reason to believe that the amount of frauds and forgeries of which Mr. Sadleir has been guilty will not be much under one million.' However, I have been unable to find any reference to Sadleir's frauds in the *Morning Advertiser* previous to 23 February, and no mention of his frauds in the British Newspaper Archive previous to the *Carlisle Journal*'s article of 22 February, bar a reference to the depreciation of Royal Swedish Railway Company shares, since Sadleir's death 'in consequence of very prejudicial rumours in reference to surreptitiously issues bonds' which proved to be true. 'Money Market', *The Morning Advertiser*, 22 February 1856: 5.

94   'Mr. John Sadleir. M.P.—The Late Astounding Disclosures', *The Morning Advertiser*, 23 February 1856: 4.

95   Ibid.

96   'The Suicide of Mr. Sadleir, M.P.', *The Standard*, 25 February 1856: 2.

97   'The Suicide of Mr. Sadleir', *The Morning Advertiser*, 26 February 1856: 5; 'The Suicide of Mr. Sadleir, M.P.', *The Standard*, 25 February 1856: 2.

98   'The Suicide of Mr. Sadleir, M.P.', *The Standard*, 25 February 1856: 2; 'The Suicide of Mr. Sadleir', *The Morning Advertiser*, 26 February 1856: 5.

99   'The Suicide of Mr. Sadleir', *The Morning Advertiser*, 26 February 1856: 5; 'The Suicide of Mr. Sadleir, M.P.', *The Standard*, 25 February 1856: 2.

100 'The Suicide of Mr. Sadleir', *The Morning Advertiser*, 26 February 1856: 5.

101 'Mr. Sadleir's Frauds, &c.', *Reynolds's Newspaper*, 9 March 1856: 7.

102 'The Case of The Late Mr Sadleir, M.P.', *The Era*, 2 March 1856: 14.

103 David Mourier Evans, *Facts, Failure, and Frauds: Revelations, Financial, Mercantile, Criminal* (London: Groombridge & Sons, 1859), 108.

104 Taylor, *Boardroom Scandal*, 103.

105 'Mr. John Sadleir. M.P.—The Late Astounding Disclosures', *The Morning Advertiser*, 23 February 1856: 4.

106 'The Suicide and Startling Frauds of Mr. Sadleir, M.P.', *The Leeds Times*, 1 March 1856: 7.

107 'The Suicide of The Late Mr. John Sadleir, M.P.', *The Standard*, 11 March 1856: 2.

108 'The Late Mr. Sadleir, M.P.', *The Globe*, 11 March 1856: 2.

109 'The Suicide of The Late Mr. John Sadleir, M.P.', *The Standard*, 11 March 1856: 2.

110 'The Late Mr. Sadleir, M.P.', *The Globe*, 11 March 1856: 2; 'The Suicide of The Late Mr. John Sadleir, M.P.', *The Standard*, 11 March 1856: 2.

111 Gates, *Victorian Suicide*, 38.

112 'The Suicide of The Late Mr. John Sadleir, M.P.', *The Standard*, 11 March 1856: 2.

113 Ibid., 64.

114 Ibid., 63.

115 Ibid., 64.

116 'Suicide of A Bank Manager', *The Teesdale Mercury*, 26 October 1864: 3.

117 'Suicide in Kensington Gardens', *St. James's Gazette*, 21 August 1897: 10; 'Speculation and Suicide', *The Liverpool Mercury*, 21 August 1897: 5; 'A Speculator's Suicide', *The Sheffield Daily Telegraph*, 21 August 1897: 8.

118 'The Suicide of Mr. Sadleir, M.P.', *Daily News*, 20 February 1856.

119 'Sadleirism in Scotland', *The Falkirk Herald*, 28 May 1857: 3.

120 'Suicide of Mr. Henry Salmon, Sen.', *The Falkirk Herald*, 4 June 1857: 3.

121 'Bank Defalcation At Falkirk', *The York Herald*, 30 May 1857: 11; 'The Suicide of Mr Salmon', *The Elgin and Morayshire Courier*, 12 June 1857: 4.

122 Taylor, *Boardroom Scandal*, 125.

123 Ibid., 128–30 (quote on 130).

124 Ibid., 139.

125 Collini, *Public Moralists*, 105–6 (quote from 106).

126 R. A. Houston, *Punishing the Dead?: Suicide, Lordship, and Community in Britain, 1500–1830* (Oxford; New York, NY: Oxford University Press, 2010), 375; Lisa J. Nicoletti, 'Resuscitating Ophelia: Images of Suicide and Suicidal Insanity in Nineteenth-Century England' (Madison, WI: University of Wisconcin, 1999), 139; Gates, *Victorian Suicide*, 14, 16; Olive Anderson even goes as far as to suggest that different 'genres' of suicide were each associated with certain 'stock character types'. Anderson, *Suicide in Victorian and Edwardian England*.

127 Winslow, *The Anatomy of Suicide*, 36, 81, 87.

128 Society for the Promotion of Christian Knowledge, 'Suicide; Its Guilt and Punishment. Earnestly Addressed to All Classes, Particularly Those in Humble

Life', in *Religious Tracts Circulated by the Society for Promoting Christian Knowledge*, vol. 3 (London: Printed for the Society for Promoting Christian Knowledge, 1836), 5.

129   'Felo De Se', *The Ulsterman*, 12 March 1856: 2.

130   'The Inquest on the Body of John Sadleir', *The Evening Packet*, 13 March 1856: 2.

131   'Historic Doubts Concerning the Suicide of John Sadleir', *The Nation*, 29 March 1856: 10.

132   Reed, 'A Friend to Mammon: Speculation in Victorian Literature', 190; Weiss, *The Hell of the English*, 21.

133   Russell, *The Novelist and Mammon*, 135–7.

134   Dickens, *Little Dorrit*, 670.

135   'The Late Mr. Sadleir, M.P.', *The Faversham Gazette, and Whitstable, Sittingbourne, & Milton Journal*, 1 March 1856: 3.

136   'Sadleirism in Banking', *Glasgow Herald*, 19 March 1856: 2.

137   Hilton, *The Age of Atonement*, 123.

138   'The Late Mr. Sadleir, M.P.', *The Faversham Gazette, and Whitstable, Sittingbourne, & Milton Journal*.

139   Finn, *The Character of Credit*, 18–19.

140   Ibid., 10, 21, 320.

141   Evans, *Facts, Failure, and Frauds: Revelations, Financial, Mercantile, Criminal*, 228.

142   O'Shea, *Prince of Swindlers*, 401.

143   Evans, *Facts, Failure, and Frauds: Revelations, Financial, Mercantile, Criminal*, 227.

144   'Melancholy Suicide of Mr. John Sadleir, M.P. for Sligo', *The Belfast News-Letter*, 20 February 1856: 2.

145   'Suicide of Mr. John Sadleir, M.P.', *The Standard*, 18 February 1856: 3.

146   'Death of Mr. John Sadleir, M.P. For Sligo', *The Times*, 18 February 1856: 12.

147   'London, Wednesday, Feb. 27, 1856', *The Morning Post*, 27 February 1856: 4.

148   Finn, *The Character of Credit*, 10.

149   'London, Wednesday, Feb. 27, 1856', *The Morning Post*, 4.

150   Poovey, *Genres of the Credit Economy*, 6, 62.

151   Klaver, *A/Moral Economics*, 79, 82 (quote on 79).

152   Ibid., 98.

153   Roger L. Slakey, 'Melmotte's Death: A Prism of Meaning in the Way We Live Now', *ELH* 34, no. 2 (1967): 253–4.

154   Evans, *Facts, Failure, and Frauds: Revelations, Financial, Mercantile, Criminal*, 235.

155   Hilton, *The Age of Atonement*, 13.

Military trauma and dishonour

The features were in perfect repose, as if he had quietly determined to give himself a soldier's death without going through the violent mental struggle that so often prefaces a painful and self-inflicted end.
– "Fighting Mac", *Northern Daily Telegraph*,
26 March 1903: 2

The above description of Major-General Sir Hector Macdonald's suicide as 'a soldier's death' might come as a surprise, especially given that the condemnation of suicide as a desertion of duty and a cowardly act would seem particularly fitting in the military context.[1] But connotations of cowardice did not appear to be common in reports of nineteenth-century soldier suicides. Neither have I found much to suggest that the suicides of these soldiers were understood as a result of trauma experienced in battle. Instead, the narratives of military suicides in this chapter appear to be more concerned with a preservation of honour in light of aspersions on their conduct.

Suicide rates amongst the British Army in the nineteenth century were high and became the subject of sustained interest as early as the first public report on army medical statistics.[2] This was also picked up by Durkheim, whose study of suicide revealed a significantly higher rate of suicide amongst armies throughout Europe and the US, with English soldiers being 2.6 times more likely to commit suicide compared with civilians of the same age for the period 1876–90.[3] Janet Padiak has documented the various reasons attributed to this, ranging from the practicalities of easy access to firearms, to excessive alcohol consumption and the conditions of military life. Also noticeable was that in the latter half of the century, the risk of suicide increased with age and length of service. Padiak's study also suggests that some regimental surgeons recognized psychological conditions, such as 'mania, melancholia, amentia, and hysteria' amongst soldiers.[4] Reports of suicide in the press, however, make limited mention of psychological conditions amongst the suicides of soldiers and veterans, nor do they always explicitly relate these conditions to their military experience. Some allusions were made to vague psychological issues and, given the understanding of post-traumatic stress disorder (PTSD) and suicide amongst soldiers and veterans today, it would be tempting to read these as narratives of trauma and suicide. Whilst I will briefly discuss the subtle hints some reports provide towards the psychological impact of war, they provide insufficient evidence to support this narrative interpretation, and I argue that it would be ahistorical to write them as clear narratives of military trauma and suicide.

For Durkheim, the higher suicide rates of soldiers was particularly surprising given the increased social cohesion and communal life provided in the military, which were factors he had identified as providing protection against suicide.[5] In an attempt to explain this anomaly, Durkheim instead attributed the higher rate of suicides amongst soldiers to altruism – an excessive integration of an individual into society whereby one sacrifices themselves out of obedience or love of something bigger than themselves.[6] Harold Braswell and Harold Kushner have challenged this Durkheimian assumption that high military suicide rates were a product of altruism, which they believe has prevented investigations on the impact of military culture on suicidal behaviour. Instead, they propose that military suicides should be classified as fatalistic – a category Durkheim addressed only very briefly – pointing out that deaths (sacrifices) in combat would not be classified as suicides anyway.[7] In the fatalistic category, the suicide occurs as a result of integration into an overly constraining social group, or, to quote Durkheim, 'from an excess of regulation, the one committed by those whose future is pitilessly confined and whose passions violently constrained by oppressive discipline'.[8] Braswell and Kushner believe that Durkheim's theory of fatalism maps particularly well onto military life, especially considering the nature of military masculine culture, which they term 'masculine fatalism'. This theory of masculine fatalism revolves around the idea that a 'cult of masculinity' is the 'cementing principle' of military life, whereby soldiers are taught to master external situations by controlling their emotions and 'emotional or situational flexibility is discouraged'. Such a culture encourages internalization of frustration and anger, and encourages individuals to see failure as the result of personal shortcomings.[9] Whilst Holly Furneaux has rightly drawn attention to the importance of the military man of feeling in Victorian culture, I suggest that the concept of masculine fatalism is still visible in the narratives of honour surrounding the military suicides in this chapter.

The principle of death before dishonour in military suicides has been around since antiquity. Brutus and Cassius committed suicide rather than submit after being defeated by Mark Anthony's army at the Battle of Philippi; Vulteuis encouraged his men to commit suicide 'rather than suffer the humiliation of being taken prisoner' during Caesar's civil war; and Cato the Younger also committed suicide after Caesar's victory as 'his loyalty to the defeated republican values forbids him to live under Caesar's autocracy' and because 'accepting life under tyranny' would have 'impaired his freedom to make the honourable moral choices'.[10] The central themes amongst these ancient suicides, and of suicide in antiquity more generally, were, as Elise Garrison has shown, honour and shame, which played an important part in determining responses to suicide.[11] Garrison highlights the range of responses to suicide in Ancient Greece. Whilst suicide out of 'laziness or cowardice' was condemned, self-sacrifice to save others was virtuous, suicidal obedience in battle was praised, suicide as a response to shame and guilt was commendable and suicide to restore honour was 'embraced approvingly'.[12] Nowhere is the code of honour more present than the military. This, according to Kwame Appiah, is attributed to the need to regulate the army and the difficulty of doing so through other means, such as the law, which require extensive surveillance. As he suggests, 'when battle is hardest, everything is obscured by the fog of war'. Honour codes, by contrast, are grounded in each soldier's individual sense of honour, and all those who adhere to it and belong to the 'honor world' become effective enforcers of it.[13] The masculine fatalism, then, presents itself through the way in which honour is closely monitored and highly valued in the military.

There are various ways to describe honour. As Alexander Welsh has pointed out, its meaning has changed over the course of the last century or so.[14] Before the First World War, Welsh identifies a form of honour that can be defined as 'a kind of moral imperative', whereby honour was a 'compelling motive' to act (or not act).[15] This conception of an internal sense of honour was supported by the Evangelical values of middle-class masculinity that came to ascendancy in the mid-century, as discussed in the previous chapter. This is distinct from an honour that is conceived as a measure of status or fame, which Welsh sees as more common today. The former concept of honour is described as horizontal honour, based on mutual respect amongst peers, while the latter, described as vertical honour, is graded and competitive.[16] But whilst these are two distinct categories, Welsh points out how they tend to exist in conjunction with one another, with vertical honour operating within a horizontal honour group.[17] In looking at the narratives of military suicide from dishonour, I conceive of the military as a horizontal honour group that regulates the honour of soldiers and shames those found lacking.

These themes of honour and shame show themselves in the suicides of military men throughout the nineteenth century. Drawing on the suicides of three officers, Sir George Ralph Collier, Lieutenant-Colonel John King and Sir Hector Archibald Macdonald, this chapter looks at how honour was central to policing masculinity, particularly in a military context. These three cases, which happened at different periods across the century and under differing circumstances, attest to the permanence of a military code of honour despite nuanced changes in expectations of masculine behaviour. They show how suicide became a recourse to restore a soldier's honour when it was cast into doubt. It is in this way that the suicide of Sir Hector Macdonald could be seen as a 'soldier's death', as reports described it. I also suggest that, these suicides attest to the performative nature of honour, which was heightened in the late-Victorian period with the onslaught of New Imperialism and a new masculinity with an emphasis on competition.

Trauma

In light of the current concern around military suicide rates, and the lack of historical literature on the subject, it would be an oversight to look at military suicides in the nineteenth century without discussing trauma. Given our experience of military suicides in the present day and recent past, it would be easy to assume that historical suicides amongst active soldiers and veterans must inevitably be the product of the traumas and stresses of warfare and military life. From a presentist point of view, it is easy to assume that post-traumatic stress has always been part of the experience of soldiering. Studies have located symptoms akin to PTSD in ancient texts such as Lucretius' *De Natura Rerum* or Pliny the Younger's account of the eruption of Vesuvius in 79 CE, in Samuel Pepys' recollections of the Great Fire of London, the works of Shakespeare, clinical notes of Napoleonic military surgeon's and Florence Nightingale's biography.[18] Some have even gone as far as suggesting that soldiers have 'always collapsed in battle' and they 'have done so in precisely the same ways that they do today'.[19] But such histories of PTSD have been accused by others – who see PTSD as a 'culture-derived' diagnosis' – of exhibiting a '"Whiggish" tendency' to see PTSD as a modern form of older war syndromes, moving 'in a steady progression from ignorance to post *DSM-III* enlightenment'.[20]

Turning to the more recent past, and using broader terms such as 'war syndromes', 'psychiatric battle casualties' and battle fatigue, medical historian Edgar Jones and psychiatrist Simon Wessely have looked at the prevalence of health issues experienced by soldiers such as Da Costa's Syndrome or Disordered Action of the Heart (DAH), rheumatism, shell-shock and other 'functional syndromes' with 'medically unexplained symptoms'. Their findings show that the latter half of the nineteenth century saw a rise in unexplained heart disorders amongst soldiers. Jones and Wessely note that investigations into the cause of these heart disorders repeatedly tried to find the cause in a 'mechanical pathology', despite what they see as clear links to combat. The connection between DAH and battle fatigue or constant exposure to combat was not made until the publication of a report on medical arrangements during the South African War by Sir W. D. Wilson in 1904. The report noted that once soldiers had 'succumbed' to DAH, symptoms were recurring, and tended to worsen with extra exertion or 'the excitement or nervousness of going under fire'.[21] Rheumatism had similarly proved a problem during the Boer War, but few veterans who had been pensioned for the disease showed any objective signs within a few years of discharge.[22] This is something that Anthony Bowlby had found when treating soldiers in South Africa. Bowlby noted that out of fifteen cases of rheumatism treated, eleven manifested in 'consistent pain in the legs without swelling of the joints', most often myalgic in character and 'indefinite as to localisation, but … very real to the patient'. 'Of true rheumatic fever', Bowlby noted, 'we saw no example except one on the ship coming home'.[23]

Symptoms of sunstroke and rheumatic fever were often noted in reports of military suicides during the nineteenth century. When Lance-Sergeant Walter James shot himself at Southsea in November 1890, several witnesses deposed that he had suffered from rheumatism and regularly complained of pains in his arms and legs.[24] Similarly, at the inquest on John Millichamp of the Royal Marine Artillery, who shot himself in May 1868, it was noted that he had been sent to the hospital 'complaining of what appeared to be rheumatic pains'.[25] Sunstroke was another ailment noted in the suicides of military and ex-military men, one which was a known cause of insanity, especially amongst soldiers who had seen foreign service. Thomas Muzzard, an army pensioner, committed suicide in July 1900 at the age of sixty-five. Muzzard had seen much foreign service, serving two years in the Crimea, where he had participated in some of the worst battles – Alma, Balaclava, Inkerman and Sebastopol – for which he had been given medals and clasps, the Cape of Good Hope for six and a half years, and Cabul for another six and a half. Throughout his service he had shown exemplary character, receiving four good conduct badges, which the coroner commented 'was very rare'. His daughter deposed that nothing had been preying on his mind, but he had suffered sunstroke three times whilst a soldier and had occasionally complained of 'pains in his head'. Another witness, a private in the Royal Marines who was home on furlough, said he had seen Muzzard every day for a month, and he had not seemed depressed or complained much about his head. After the coroner summed up, the Foreman commented on Muzzard's sunstroke, suggesting that it had 'probably affected the man's mind'.[26]

Although Wessely and Jones have shown that acknowledgement of the mental toll that combat could take on soldiers was limited, some connection between mental disorder and military service was being made. Kingsmill Jones remarked in a 1903 article in *The Dublin Journal of Medical Science*, that insanity could emerge 'after a very long and trying campaign'.[27] Bowlby's account of mental disorders witnessed in soldiers in South Africa, for example, stressed that, 'considering the extremely harassing nature of the military operations, it is rather remarkable that we did not see more of such cases'. He continued:

> Outpost duty in the face of a watchful enemy is of itself sufficiently wearying, especially to officers, but it is still more so when it involves want of sleep, which it usually does. One of us saw a sergeant at Modder River, who was evidently suffering from delusions of persecution, but he was the only one in our experience who was certifiably insane. We, however, heard of at least three officers who committed suicide.[28]

Press reports of military suicides also reveal how causal connections were occasionally made between experiences in service and mental states. Colonel Whitehead, a retired officer who had 'served a considerable time as captain in India', was found dead at his lodgings on 9 February 1884, having shot himself through the head with a pistol.[29] At the inquest his son deposed that his father's health had been deteriorating, and that he had frequently threatened to commit suicide. Following questions from the coroner, he revealed that he believed his mind had also been affected and had seemed depressed, expressing that 'he was tired of life, and would like to be in Heaven, where he wished to join a recently deceased friend'.[30] *Lloyd's Weekly Newspaper* commented that it was 'supposed that his services in India had affected the deceased's head'.[31] Similarly, when Staff-sergeant M'Culloch committed suicide later the same year, *The St. James's Gazette* concluded its report of the tragedy by stating that 'He had seen much foreign service, which it is supposed had affected his mind'.[32] Sergeant-Major Cheer, an Officer who had seen service in the Crimea, was found dead at his home after shooting himself in the head in 1873 (although some believed it had been an accident whilst cleaning his guns). The *Western Mail* commented that although he had been in usual health until the incident, he had been long suffering from pains in the head, which were supposedly 'caused by the hardships he endured during the Crimean War'.[33] As will be seen later, even seemingly heroic soldiers felt the mental toll of service and were described as having been broken down by the war. Whilst many reports of suicide that referred to service abroad were often linking the act (explicitly or implicitly) to organic illnesses, such as sunstroke, as an explanation for insanity, they demonstrate some level of understanding that military service could take a toll on a soldier's mental health. The fact that field doctors were reporting cases of physical illnesses such as DAH or rheumatism without any organic symptoms – suggesting instead that the cause was psychosomatic – shows that at some level the mental strain of service was acknowledged. There is, however, little to suggest a widespread understanding that the experience of war could negatively affect soldiers' mental health.

One thing that might be telling, however, is the prevalence of alcohol in military suicide narratives throughout the nineteenth century. Whilst Anthony Bowlby recorded that alcohol was not part of the diet on active service, and 'almost total abstinence was the rule' throughout the campaigns in South Africa,[34] drunkenness and apparent alcoholism were prevalent throughout the century, amongst both active soldiers and veterans and was frequently implicated as a cause of suicide. Today the relationship between trauma and alcohol abuse is widely acknowledged.[35] This relationship between trauma and alcohol was not totally alien in the nineteenth century, as Emma Butcher has shown. Butcher notes how the early writings of Charlotte and Branwell Brontë demonstrated an 'understanding of contemporary conceptions of war trauma that were present within the publications of the period' and suggests their work was a 'vicarious response to the psychological impact of battle, and the damaging substance abuse used to curb and relieve that impact'.[36] This, as Butcher notes, supports Jones and Wessely's conclusion that despite the lack of a formal, medical, categorization of battle trauma, there was an 'underlying recognition of its effects within medical spheres'.[37]

But whilst Butcher sees evidence of direct links between alcohol abuse and battle trauma in memoirs that use emotive language and recognize changes in behaviour linked to specific events, this is almost absent in press reports of military suicides. William Hawkins, a Waterloo soldier, committed suicide at the age of forty-seven in February 1839, and had served throughout the whole Peninsular War where he had been 'repeatedly wounded'. He had been discharged ten years earlier, with a year's pay and had since turned to shoemaking and drank heavily. He had, on more than one occasion, attempted to commit suicide during 'fits of drunkenness' before, but each time had been prevented. The verdict returned was temporary insanity.[38] No direct connection is made between Hawkins' habitual heavy drinking and his service during the Peninsular War. Another case in point was that of Sergeant Robinson, of the Grenadier Company of the Connaught Rangers, who was also reported to have committed suicide through drink at camp in Sebastopol, November 1855. He had 'seen long service' with his regiment, and had 'several times been conspicuous for bravery'. He had been drinking heavily for some days previous, which it was reported had produced an 'artificial horror'.[39] The modern reader might be quick to identify alcoholism among nineteenth-century soldiers as the product of traumatic experiences in warfare. Whilst Butcher reads an understanding of the use of alcohol to deal with traumatic experiences of war in the Brontës' writings, such associations are absent in reports of military suicides. There is acknowledgement of heavy drinking throughout military life, and of the role of alcohol in producing a suicidal state, but seldom is an explicit connection made between experiences of war and the turn to drink.

Honour

Rather than seeing suicide as the product of trauma, or an act of cowardice, reports of military suicides throughout the nineteenth century suggest that they were perceived within the context of an honour code that regulated soldiers' behaviour. On the morning of 24 March 1824, Sir George Ralph Collier was found weltering in a pool of blood, having cut his throat at his home in Soho Square. Collier was born into a prominent naval family[40] and became a captain in the Royal Navy, serving in the French Revolutionary Wars – for which he had been noted for his 'perseverance and bravery' whilst in command of the *Victor* – the Napoleonic Wars and the War of 1812. During peacetime he had been involved in the suppression of the slave trade, and was warmly commended for his service by the government.[41] He had been 'universally esteemed' by those who had known him in his private life, and as a Naval officer was highly regarded for his zeal and gallantry.[42] The *Caledonian Mercury* described him as 'an honour to his country and an ornament to society', and a fellow Naval Officer spoke of him as 'a man of the strictest integrity, the mildest manners, and most genuine worth … Ever foremost as the champion of his country's good'.[43]

During the three months preceding Collier's suicide, friends had noticed a distinct change in his state of mind, fixating on a paragraph published in *James's Naval History* which contained 'severe strictures' on his conduct aboard the *HMS Leander* during the war with America. The passage in question had thrown 'a slur upon his character' by insinuating that he had allowed an American frigate, the *Constitution*, to escape his squadron during the war.[44] At the inquest John Dyer, Esq., chief clerk at the Admiralty, deposed that Collier had travelled down to London because of the passage in the *Naval History*, which he had not yet read but was anxious to see. Having a copy on him, Dyer handed it to Collier, who after reading it appeared 'agitated and hurt'. Both Dyer and Sir Edward Hamilton – who had 'incautiously' told Collier about the passage and was present at the meeting – attempted to reason Collier out of his irritation and ease his mind. Returning again the next morning, Collier was described as being 'anxious to see some of the Members of the Board, to see if the publication had excited any unpleasant feelings in them about him', particularly wishing to meet Vice Admiral Sir George Cockburn. Cockburn reassured him that 'nothing any person could say or write, would alter the high opinion he entertained of his character and conduct as an officer'. He then became anxious about Lord Melville and was advised to write a letter asking him to 'state his opinion of him, that he might lay it before his brother officers for their satisfaction'. Collier's search for reassurance that his reputation had not been damaged in the eyes of his peers is testament to the importance of the horizontal honour among peer groups that Welsh describes, and to its fragility.

Following Dyer, Sir Edward Hamilton gave evidence that Collier believed 'some enemy' had given false information to Mr James, and suspecting he knew the person, asked Hamilton 'whether it would not be right to call him out and shoot him through the head' – a clear reference to the use of the duel to defend one's honour.[45] Hamilton advised him that this would not change the statement and proposed an alternative course of action, a 'paper war', for which Collier expressed his dislike.[46] Collier had served in the Navy during a time in which the pistol duel was in decline and was being replaced with a duel of words, as tolerance of public violence waned and conceptions of masculinity shifted.[47] But as Shoemaker and Margery Masterson attest, the duel had continued cultural relevance particularly for martial masculinity. Shoemaker observes that throughout this period those in the military – especially officers – were under great pressure to defend their honour when it was challenged because their courage needed to be 'beyond question'.[48] As late as 1862, Masterson identifies a pressure amongst the military for soldiers to 'issue a challenge' following disputes.[49] This, according to N. A. M. Rodger, had been felt especially in the Navy, where, unlike the army, many officers had 'obscure if not disreputable' backgrounds. The code of honour thus acted as a code to live by, stronger than religion and Christian morality.[50] Officers were encouraged, and almost *required* to defend their honour, to the death if necessary. Rodger demonstrates this with reference to the proceedings following a fatal duel between two captains in 1750. When the surviving officer was convicted of murder and sentenced to death, the First Lord of the Admiralty appealed for pardon on the basis that, had he not 'resented the repeated & outrageous provocations', his military career would have, inevitably, been ruined.[51]

Although Rodger suggests that the 'personal, interested, egotistical service of one's king and one's honour' was gradually infiltrated by a more 'disinterested duty to God, the Crown, and the good of the Service', examples of suicide such as Collier's, which persisted throughout the nineteenth century, provide clear examples of the enduring importance of honour as a military code to live by.[52] Instead of defending his honour in a duel as Collier had initially wanted, he sought instead to defend it with his own death, conforming to the principle of death before dishonour that had been prevalent in militaries since antiquity. Hamilton concluded his deposition by reaffirming Collier's character and his martial masculinity. In the thirty-five years that Hamilton had known him, he assured the jury that Collier had always been 'a most exemplary officer' and proposed that 'such a charge as that may as well be placed against the immortal Nelson, or any other exalted character in the navy'. This statement was met with 'a sensation of applause'. Owing to the concern of his friends and family, every effort had been made to prevent Collier doing harm to himself and his brother had ordered his razors to be removed from his hotel. It appeared, however, that he had managed to conceal one about his person, with which he committed the fatal deed. After hearing the evidence, the jury found that Collier had committed suicide 'whilst in a state of temporary derangement'.[53] He had, the *Caledonian Mercury* reported, fallen 'victim to those feelings which a constitution already broken in the service of his country rendered insupportable'.[54] Although witnesses recognized Collier's seemingly deteriorating mental state, they did not connect this to his military service; but remarks such as this suggest some level of understanding that war could affect a man's mind.

Just over twenty-five years later, Lieutenant-Colonel John Wallace King, who had served in the Second Anglo-Sikh War, committed suicide under similar circumstances on 6 July 1850. King had been commanding the 14th Light Dragoons at the disastrous battle of Chillianwallah, on 13 January 1849.[55]

Advancing through thick jungle, the regiment fell into confusion and apparently heard orders to retreat; following the battle reports accused the regiment of running away, describing the retreat as the result of 'fearful and horrible panic'.[56] At a review of the regiment at Lahore in December 1849, Sir Charles Napier – then Commander in Chief – referred to the accusations of cowardice launched at the regiment but assured the regiment that he believed none of them. He then remarked that although Colonel King had described the men as young and their swords not as sharp as their enemy's, he saw 'fine broad-shouldered fellows' and hoped to see them test the sharpness of their swords, apparently concluding that 'you only require leading'.[57]

According to reports, Napier's remark resulted in a feeling of unease between Colonel King and his men. Six months later one private soldier had 'publicly charged Colonel King with cowardice', and was sentenced to flogging by a Court-Martial. However, having somehow managed to consume a 'large quantity of spirits' unnoticed, he underwent his flogging whilst intoxicated. After his punishment, having been 'stung to madness by pain while under the influence of liquor', he rushed up to the Colonel and, in front of the whole regiment, repeated his accusation. He was then brought before another Court-Martial, and sentenced to seven years' transportation. Charles Napier protested the sentence, on the grounds that the Assistant Surgeon and Adjutant had allowed the prisoner to undergo punishment whilst drunk, adding that 'all this took place in the presence of Colonel King, the Commanding Officer of the Regiment', adding a further insult to King's character. Napier failed to persuade the Court to change the sentence and instead issued a pardon of the soldier. As the *Dover Telegraph* remarked, the soldier 'being permitted to return to his ranks after such a public outrage upon his commanding officer, could not but be felt as an insult and an indignity by Colonel King, while it held out an inducement to insubordination among the men'.[58]

Accusations of cowardice were powerful insults to the reputations of military men; as *John Bull* remarked, the reputation of a regiment is as sensitive to a slight as a woman's, 'a breath suffices to sully its purity, and it cannot endure a doubt'.[59] So powerful were notions of cowardice and honour as regulatory tools that men would rather commit suicide than be thought of as cowards. Writing on the trauma of Confederate soldiers, Dianne Sommerville has linked 'the burden of anxiety about manly and honourable performance' to suicide, which she argues could become a more appealing alternative to being revealed as a coward. In this way, Sommerville demonstrates that in the battle environment, a man's self-worth and personal identity was dependent upon the opinions of his peers and acts of cowardice 'might dog a man long after the guns had silenced'.[60] Reports acknowledged that King had been in a desponding state for some time, owing to the insubordinate conduct of some men in the regiment, namely of the private who had initially accused him of cowardice. In a letter to Charles Napier, King apparently blamed him for his suicide. Napier's speech, he believed, had lowered him in the eyes of his regiment and resulted in insubordination and personal accusations of cowardice. He also complained of Napier's conduct towards him personally, all of which 'so preyed upon his mind, that he felt life was nothing further to him'.

Many reports firmly laid the blame for King's suicide on Charles Napier, believing that no one who knew the circumstances of the 'melancholy affair' could doubt 'that it was the language and conduct of Sir Charles Napier that drove Colonel King to commit suicide' and others believed Napier had 'goaded' King into the act.[61] Whilst not all reports found fault with Napier's conduct, King's suicide is clearly represented as a result from lost honour. And it appears that this was not the first time such a thing had happened. Reporting King's suicide, the *South Eastern Gazette* reminded readers of a Major Parker, of the 78th Highlanders, who committed suicide six years earlier 'after having received a severe, and it was alleged, unmerited rebuke from Sir C. Napier'.[62] The blame, again, seems to fall on Napier, and there was no suggestion that King had acted rashly or inappropriately in his suicide.

The article went on to describe Colonel King's character with adulation. He was noted for a 'winning gentleness of manner, and unaffected frankness of disposition', and appeared to be a kind and benevolent officer to his men. Much like the military men of feeling whom Holly Furneaux has written about, King was represented as a benevolent and kind officer, concerned with the well-being of his men. Looking at the Crimean War, Furneaux has noted 'an increasing emphasis on an officer's care for the well-being of their men', as exemplified by mid-century military conduct books, such as J. H. Stocqueler's *The British Officer, His Positions, Duties, Emoluments and Privileges* (1851) which she describes as advocating 'a capacity for feeling and pleasure combined with disciplined restraint, prioritizing courtesy, justice, and honour as well as a capacity for well-placed fellow feeling'.[63] King appears to fit much of this. He had a 'kindly regard' for the feelings of others, an 'innate amiability of a disposition generous, frank, and forgiving', a 'sweetness of temper, which nothing could ruffle or provoke to anger' and '[n]o case of real distress ever came before him unrelieved or was left unsoothed by his sympathy'.[64] Similarly, in an attempt to rescue King's memory, Sir Joseph Thackwell appended a vindication of his character to his *Narrative of the Second Sikh War in 1848–49* (1851). In this, Thackwell included a letter received from a private who had served under King in the 14th Dragoons, who attested to King's 'gallantry in the field' and 'kindness in quarters'.[65] This portrayal of Colonel King is a prequel to that of Captain Taunton, of Dickens' 'Seven Poor Travellers' (1854), who responds with 'sympathy and fellow feeling' to the emotions of his men.[66]

Although traditional gallantry was still an integral part of honourable soldiering, the celebration of King's kind and benevolent treatment of his men is a testament to the fact that 'acts of battlefield care' were coming to be seen as the best examples of chivalry and heroism, rather than in 'heroics of violence'.[67] It is clear that a value was placed on an officer's empathy and kindness in the way the article equates his amiability with his admiration: 'As he was one of the most amiable, so was he one of the most admirable.'[68] The value placed on the gentle soldier has, as Holly Furneaux notes, been overlooked and overshadowed by the enduring stereotype of the British stiff upper lip, as well as the perception of Victorian men as strong, silent and enduring hardship with stoic reticence.[69] Yet, whilst the soldier who had a 'particular capacity for feeling' was the most applauded military figure and in line with narratives of the Crimean period,[70] it was not without problems. It was this very attribute that made King vulnerable to the words of others. Being 'possessed of such refined feelings, and of so sensitive a nature', the *Glasgow Herald* suggested that King 'could not brook the base interpretations of evil men, and the conduct of one from whom he had expected, and ought to have received, support'.[71] Whilst there is nothing to suggest that his fine feelings – or his suicide – made him any less soldierly, King is the only one of the three case studies in this chapter whose suicide was not enveloped in a somewhat heroic rhetoric. George Collier had been placed among the great Naval heroes such as Nelson, but his constitution had been broken in the war, and, as I will show, Hector Macdonald's suicide was seen to be perfectly in keeping with a 'soldier's death'.

Hector Macdonald, the youngest son of a Scottish crofter,[72] grew up in the aftermath of the Crimean War and the Indian Rebellion, a time in which attitudes towards the British army and a military career were undergoing an important shift. Throughout the first half of the nineteenth century the British army had been viewed with 'suspicion and distaste' on account of the poor education and moral character of rank-and-file recruits, prone to drinking and their use as a tool of government oppression in preventing and controlling working-class protests. In addition, soldiers received a meagre wage of 1s a day (out of which they had to pay for their rations, laundry, soap and other personal necessities, and any damages to equipment or the barracks, often leaving them with only 1*d*), and thus usually relied on the poorest of the working classes for recruits. By the end of the century, however, the army had transformed from 'vicious' to 'virtuous' and the imperial soldier had become the ideal national hero.[73] This shift in public opinion has largely been located in the Crimean War, when William Howard Russell's reports of appalling conditions and incompetent management generated public sympathy for the plight of the soldier. Heather Streets has expanded this turning point to include the Indian Rebellion of 1857 in which, she argues, British (and loyal native) soldiers were turned into 'saviours' of the British women and children in India whose lives were in danger, and propelled the image of the British soldier into that of a brave and noble hero.[74]

Macdonald had shown a penchant for soldiering at a young age and enlisted in the famous Gordon Highlanders (then the 92nd Highlanders) at the age of only seventeen.[75] He was quickly promoted to corporal in 1872 and excelled through the ranks, becoming sergeant in 1873 and colour-sergeant in 1874. His service in the Second Anglo-Afghan War earned him widespread renown and promotion to second lieutenant in 1880, becoming full lieutenant only a year later.[76] The zenith of his career came at the Battle of Omdurman in 1896, during the Sudan campaign, where he had been appointed to command the Sudanese brigade with a local rank of Brigadier-General. It was thought that the battle had been won, and British forces were about to advance when ten thousand of the Khalifa's men charged on Macdonald's troops from both the front and the rear. Ordered to retire Macdonald reportedly exclaimed 'Retire! I'll not do it. I'll see them damned first. We maun just fight!'. Luckily for Macdonald, the two attacks were not synchronized, war correspondent Bennet Burnleigh reported the battle thus:

> Steady as a gladiator, with what to some of us looked like inevitable disaster staring him in the face, Macdonald fought his brigade for all it was worth. He moved quickly upon the best available ground, formed up, wheeled about, and stood to die or win. He won practically unaided.

Men were 'delirious in his praise' and Macdonald was praised as the real hero of Omdurman.[77] He was called to take command of the Highland Brigade in South Africa, following the death of General Wauchope, and was injured in battle at Paardeberg. He returned to England in 1901, where he was knighted, and proceeded to take up command of troops in Ceylon. This would prove to be his last position.[78] Two years later, on 25 March 1903, Sir Hector Macdonald was found dead in his hotel room at the Hotel Regina, Paris, having blown his brains out.

In late February 1903, British newspapers reported that 'Fighting Mac', as he had been nicknamed, was on his way back to England from Ceylon after being summoned by the War Office. Speculation began on the reason for Macdonald's 'sudden summons' and rumours 'placed him theoretically in most of the posts now vacant at home'[79] – some believed he was to take up 'an important command at home under the new army corps system', others suggested he might be appointed as the new Quartermaster-General, and further still it was thought he might have been summoned to give evidence at the War Commission.[80] A Dublin paper suggested that he was being dispatched to Somaliland, where 'a strong man' was wanted for an expedition against Mullah, noting how his 'great experience on the Upper Nile would be of distinct advantage at this time'.[81] The War Office, however, released an official statement announcing that Macdonald had not been 'summoned' and was merely home on leave, his visit not being connected with any new command.[82] Macdonald arrived in England on 17 March and, to the disappointment of his Scottish fans, after little more than twenty-four hours, left for the continent.[83]

On 20 March, Sir Hector checked into the Hotel Regina, Paris, taking only a small, simple room and apparently going about unrecognized. He led a relatively quiet life at the hotel: he rose at an early hour and took lunch outside of the hotel, he often returned in the afternoon but always dined out in the evenings, returning and retiring to sleep at an early hour. After his breakfast on 25 March, Macdonald was observed perusing the morning's papers in the hotel reading room, when 'Suddenly, he was seen to start, and the paper he was reading fell from his hand'. He remained apparently frozen for a moment, before picking up the paper and reading 'with great deliberation'.[84] According to some reports 'he actually burst into tears'.[85] He then turned to the other papers available, reading them through one after another. He appeared to 'remain in deep thought' for a short time, before 'slowly folding the newspaper', rising from his seat and pacing slowly up and down the room, 'his left hand the while stroking his moustache'. Then, after seeming to have 'an inspiration' Macdonald lit a cigar and quietly proceeded up to his room, his face being visibly more relaxed.[86] At around two o'clock Sir Hector Macdonald was found lying on the floor of his chamber having blown his brains out.

The papers that Macdonald had been reading so avidly on the morning of his death contained details of 'grave charges' that had been brought against him in Ceylon.[87] The French paper, *Le Matin*, had reported that Sir Hector had been accused of 'unnatural acts with native youths',[88] and whilst the British papers only ever referred euphemistically to the 'grave charges', as Trevor Royle suggests, there was no one in London who would have misunderstood its meaning.[89] Such offences did not come under the scope of Ceylon law but Macdonald returned to England to seek advice from his friends and superiors on how to proceed. On his short visit to London, he met with Commander-in-Chief Lord Roberts, who, after hearing 'a full statement of the facts' from Macdonald, told him it was 'his duty' to return to Ceylon and demand a trial by court-martial.[90] When he departed for the Continent, it was expected that he would continue to Marseilles and from there sail on a Steamer back to the East.[91] Some reports suggested that, after several days of Macdonald remaining in Paris, the War Office sent a letter 'instructing him to return to Ceylon without another moment's delay', which he received on the morning of his suicide.[92] It was this, some papers believed, that prompted Macdonald's rash act. The *Dundee Evening Telegraph* believed that it was 'perfectly clear' that the shock Macdonald had received at seeing the charges against him made public had prompted 'the fell deed', and that, 'scarcely had he read what was said about him than he resolved to take his own life, and walking upstairs to his chamber, seized the revolver and fired the fatal shot'.[93] Another suggested that he must have become 'considerably affected by seeing that the story of his return to Ceylon to be court-martialled had become public property'.[94] In this way, the newspapers represent Macdonald's suicide as a response to dishonour.

Honour had been an important component of masculinity throughout the nineteenth century, but as Bradely Deane has shown, it took a turn in the latter decades which accompanied the rise of the New Imperialism.[95] This new system of honour was based on competition, and the judgement and discipline of male peers, rather than the morality, inner self-scrutiny and discipline of the mid-nineteenth century.[96] The way in which Sir Hector Macdonald's actions were reported fits into this dynamic well – the choice of phrase 'to face his accusers', and the comments that 'though *he was not deficient in courage*' (emphasis added) this had been something that he 'could not face', serve to reinforce Sir Hector's masculine image in light of what could have been read as an act of cowardice.[97] But commenting on the suicide, it was reported that 'an old comrade' in the Gordon Highlanders even believed he had 'done the right thing' and one rumour suggested that Macdonald had been 'instigated to commit suicide by a third person'.[98] Despite the popular rhetoric of suicide as a cowardly act that circulated throughout the nineteenth century and beyond, most notably in sermons, but also in editorial newspaper articles and the official opinion of the military,[99] his suicide was described in several papers as 'a soldier's death'. The *Dundee Evening Telegraph* recounted the 'mystery' that clouded the later years of his career and his lack of promotion to a high command, sparking rumours that Sir Hector might not be in full health. 'And now the end', the article continues, 'A soldier's death but not in war'.[100] Similarly, describing the body, the *Northern Daily Telegraph* described his features as being 'in perfect repose, as if he had quietly determined to give himself a soldier's death without going through the violent mental struggle that so often prefaces a painful and self-inflicted end'.[101] This statement possibly stems from the use of firearms (the most popular method of suicide amongst military personnel), but such a redemptive description was not afforded to other soldiers in the reports of military suicides I have found.[102] It adds a touch of heroism to a death that was perhaps not fitting for a national hero whose career had been defined by gallantry and marred by controversy at the last.

Sir Hector's suicide was presented as a matter of death before dishonour – a sentiment echoed by some of his fellow soldiers, who expressed their opinion that it was 'Better [to] die thus than face dishonour'.[103] In the new rhetoric of masculinity and manliness enshrined in the New Imperialism, where instinct and impulse were valued as markers of authentic masculinity, this kind of act could be hailed as an appropriate response to dishonour or defeat.[104] In the mid-1880s, during the Northwest Uprising of Metis and First Nation Cree-Assiniboine against the Canadian Government, Matthew Barrett has shown how in the face of military defeat, the Métis general, Gabriel Dumont, fled to the US. But instead of this being branded as an act of cowardice, his escape was lauded and Dumont was presented as 'a fearless individual who would rather die than submit'.[105] In the context of late-nineteenth-century masculinity, acts that could be framed as cowardly now became heroic. Similarly, Christian Goeschel has also found that suicide could be conceptualized as an honourable death in Nazi Germany. Amongst both the Nazis and the resistance, suicide could provide an honourable death for those who were captured, and in some cases it was expected of German soldiers who had been captured by the Soviets. During the downfall of the regime, Nazi leaders like Joseph Goebbels drew on images of Cato to frame their suicides as an honourable alternative to defeat.[106]

The commitment to the narrative of heroism is reflected in the way Macdonald's final moments were narrated. The timing of Sir Hector's last movements varied from report to report, stating that Macdonald had left the reading room anywhere between eleven and twelve and the finding of the body between one and two, leaving a not-insignificant lapse of time between his leaving the reading room and his death (the official time of death was given as being between one and two). The reading room was the last time Macdonald was seen alive and no one could have known what took place once he entered his room, yet most describe the suicide as an impulsive reaction to his reading the news, an act committed immediately on returning to his room. Macdonald was a paragon of New Imperialism, and his death was no different. His suicide was a 'bold symbolic stroke', one that fit New Imperialism's fixation on prestige, and the 'performative' and 'theatrical' elements of power.[107]

The decline of the duel, and indeed the decline of interpersonal violence, is often attributed to the emergence of the an Evangelical masculinity that emphasized self-restraint and transformed honour into 'an internal Christian value' defended by words rather than weapons.[108] This oversimplifies what historians like Tosh and Masterson have acknowledged is a far more nuanced picture, in which elements of older concepts of honour and manliness, as externally proved and validated, persisted.[109] The masculinity that was characteristic of New Imperialism attests to this. Honour once again became performative and often turned to violence, only this time it was legitimated in the theatre of war. Macdonald's return to Ceylon was couched in terms of battle and honour – he was to return 'to face his accusers', to defend not only his own honour, but that of the entire British Army.[110] In Macdonald's suicide, however, the violence came outside the battlefield and was turned on the self. In some ways this evidences a persistence of the internalization of honour that historians note in accounting for the decline of duelling. So here we see a form of honour that is both a resurgence or hangover of early modern concepts, and a product of the internalization of the mid-nineteenth century.

No inquest was held on the body, but the police report stated that Sir Hector Macdonald had killed himself 'in a condition of temporary insanity'.[111] Some newspapers, however, took it upon themselves to make their own inquiries. Some reported an interview with Dr John Robertson, an old friend of the General, which revealed that his health had been ailing for some time. When he saw him during Sir Hector's last visit to England (apparently the only social visit the General made), Robertson remarked that the Boer War had 'told very much on his constitution': he had 'aged considerably', his hair had changed colour within the last few years, his eyesight had been deteriorating for some time. He had also observed that he had looked wretched at this last visit, he seemed very much depressed and the doctor believed that Macdonald's mind was much affected. A general officer who knew him well described the state of Sir Hector's health in greater detail, describing him as 'a victim of the war'. He had suffered from dysentery and sunstroke, and despite his 'robust' appearance, suffered from nervous ailments which had been intensified during his time in

South Africa. Since suffering sunstroke at Paardeberg, he had been 'always more or less ailing and desponding' and a leg wound he had received in 1901 was refusing to heal. Ceylon appeared to be the final blow to his health, which grew continually worse, and 'depression marked him for her own'. According to his own friends, it was said that he was to be invalided from the service due to his failing health. It was even suggested that there had been fears about Macdonald's sanity for some time, with many circumstances leading others to believe that his brain, 'once so clear and vigorous and manly, had become overclouded'.[112] Whilst, as discussed earlier, few made the direct connection between war and psychological trauma in the same way that we understand PTSD today, these descriptions of the effect of war on Macdonald's mental state do demonstrate some awareness of the damaging effects of war on the human mind.

Sir Hector Macdonald had been a British, and even more so a Scottish, hero, and one of the most famous soldiers of his time, whose career had been well documented in the British press throughout his service. In the wake of his suicide, the story of his life that was eulogized in papers over and over again on the pages of the press throughout Britain and presented Macdonald as an imperial soldier par excellence and the epitome of New Imperial masculinity. Soldiering was in Macdonald's blood and even in his youngest days had indicated a 'tendency towards soldiering'.[113] Whilst at school, it was said, the young Hector Macdonald divided his time between lessons and 'the conduct of that petty warfare which raged between the "armies" of his own school—himself being the "general"—and its rivals in the neighbourhood'.[114] Working on the farm, it was remarked that he had once been found 'riding barebacked round the farm lands with all the vigour and dash that the future general was later to exhibit under circumstances more exciting'.[115] In response to his developing passion for soldiering, his parents, who disapproved of an army career, apprenticed him to a drapery business in Inverness in the hope that this would cool his military ardour. The plan failed and his yearnings for a military career were stimulated further by his fellow lodger and old soldier who, at Macdonald's request, would drill him in the early hours before commencing work at the drapers.[116] As the *Yorkshire Post* put it, 'frosty mornings, early drill, and all the charms of the drapery business were hardly likely to turn from his purpose a youth who, even at 17, had the square-cut head and determined jaw of Hector Macdonald'.[117] A popular anecdote appearing in the papers was that Macdonald regularly drilled his fellow apprentices after a day's work, and returning to the warehouse unexpectedly one afternoon, the master draper found the shop empty and on further investigation found Macdonald drilling the other assistants, using yard measures for rifles.[118] After two years as a draper's assistant, and without his master's knowledge, Macdonald enlisted in the Gordon Highlanders.[119]

This story of Sir Hector's early life indubitably painted him as a natural born soldier and not only appealed to late-Victorian masculine ideals, but also fed into the popular ideology of 'martial races', which had surrounded the Gordon Highlanders. Whilst 'martial races' ideology has traditionally focused primarily on the Indian context – looking at the Punjabi Sikhs and Nepalese Gurkhas of the British Army in India – Heather Streets has also added the Gordon Highlanders to the list. This ideology, as Streets describes it, was the 'belief that some groups of men are biologically or culturally disposed to the arts of war; and can be used to explain why the Highlanders, Sikhs and Gurkhas were seen as the Empire's "fiercest, most manly soldiers"'.[120] References to Macdonald's striking, soldierly appearance, then, feed into this narrative of a natural military predisposition of Scots. The *Yorkshire Post*'s reference to Macdonald's 'square-cut head and determined jaw' as a sign that he was destined for military service reflects attitudes of biological determinism and social Darwinism that were also becoming popular during the late nineteenth century. The previously noted descriptions of Macdonald's physique contrast starkly to Lord Macaulay's infamous description of Bengali effeminacy:

> The physical organization of the Bengalee is feeble even to effeminacy. He lives in a constant vapour bath. His pursuits are sedentary, his limbs delicate, his movements languid. During many ages he has been trampled upon by men of bolder and more hardy breeds. Courage, independence, veracity are qualities to which his constitution and his situation are equally unfavourable.[121]

Just as Macaulay interpreted Bengalis' apparent feebleness of body and mind as proof that they were destined to be 'trampled on', so too did newspapers interpret Macdonald's physical stature as proof the he was destined to military heroism.

But recent work on imperial masculinity, including Streets and Bradley Deane, has begun to see masculinity, in its raw or 'savage' form, as usurping race as the 'imaginative site' upon which global-imperial politics was manipulated and controlled.[122] Moreover, as Heather Streets points out, the Sikhs, Punjabis and Highlanders were not 'races', they were a diverse group of people. Instead, the martial race ideology, in the British context at least, acted as an 'inspirational tool'; anyone could 'become' a Highlander.[123] Hector Macdonald's career after his enlistment is further proof of this. Reflecting on Sir Hector's career in 1899, the *Aberdeen Journal* remarked how rare it was for a rank and file soldier to rise to a position above the 'average sergeant or non-com'; to do so, it was believed, the soldier must have been either 'aided by some mysterious and powerful personal interest or influence, or he has been fortunate enough to render his country some unique service that does not fall to the lot of one man in a thousand'. Such a career as his then, became 'peculiarly interesting' and guaranteed 'a thrilling story of conspicuous bravery and gallantry'.[124] Having been a working-class Scottish boy who had risen on merit, without going through the traditional 'training ground of Imperial adventures' such as the public schools and military academies, Macdonald was held up as an example to others that it was possible to rise on merit alone. However, many contemporaries and some biographers believed that it was precisely his working-class roots that led to his downfall and, ultimately, his suicide.

Despite his innate talent for soldiering, Sir Hector did not always fit comfortably within the officer class. His manners were often rough around the edges, he had criticized Lord Kitchener's strategies in the Boer War and had mixed freely with all classes and communities in Ceylon. He also frequently shunned the company of Colonial officials and British expatriates, instead preferring the company of mixed-race Burgher families, which, at a time when British racial feeling had reached its peak under Lord Curzon's viceroyalty, could only have made Macdonald more unfavourable.[125] Macdonald's close friendship with the de Saram family became an especial cause of suspicion, particularly his perceived intimacy with their two teenage sons, to whom he apparently gave gifts of affection.[126] As Robert Aldrich notes in his account of the scandal, the actual details of Macdonald's case are unclear and archival documents have either been lost or destroyed.[127] Various speculations have been made as to the exact accusation, but all remains vague: one suggestion was that he had 'tampered with' several boys, another that he had exposed himself to seventy schoolboys on a train and another that he was engaged in 'habitual misbehaviour' with schoolboys. At worst, Trevor Royle believes, the 'habitual crime' was likely to have been mutual masturbation.[128] But it appears that there had been some suspicion of sexual misconduct for some years, with similar rumours circulating about his behaviour in South Africa and India, one suggesting that he had engaged in homosexual relations with a Boer prisoner whilst in South Africa.[129]

Work on sexuality and empire has suggested that the colonies were, for many, an attractive alternative to a '"normal" married life' at home that, in the words of Edward Said, provided 'sexual promise (and threat), untiring sensuality' and 'unlimited desire'.[130] Although Said's focus was on heterosexual behaviour and the Oriental woman, his point is equally applicable to homosexual desire, as those such as Joseph Boone, Christopher Lane and Robert Aldrich have pointed out.[131] Certainly, many parts of the Empire were less repressive about sexuality as British moral discourse, with homosexuality (or, perhaps more accurately, sodomy) not being punishable under criminal law in many places, including Ceylon. But although those such as Ronald Hyam – whose analysis of the role of sex in Empire building is deeply problematic – suggest that sexual opportunity made the Empire appealing, it also engendered anxieties about masculinity.[132] Philippa Levine has suggested how sex 'was something that needed regulating and managing', too much sex, or 'deviant' sex, threatened to undermine British racial superiority based on rationality and moderation.

Irregular sexual desires, in whatever form they might take, were a particularly gendered concern; with men being seen as 'more directly sexual', there was concern that 'the sensuality of the colonial environment might unhinge him from the British path of civilized moderation'.[133] But the anxieties about masculinity in the empire ran deeper than this. In *The Underworld of India* (1933), Lieutenant-General Sir George MacMunn described the prevalence of homosexuality in (British) India, noting particularly how it subverted expected gender norms: 'While in the West homosexuality or pederasty is the sign of the degenerate or mentally unstable, and accompanies the disappearance of manliness and self-respect, in Asia, it is often the vice of the most resolute characters.'[134] The unease with this subversion and indeterminacy is clear in MacMunn's suggestion that because 'the most in other respects reputable of Eastern friends and conferencers may be so inclined', there was a hidden barrier friendship between Eastern and Western men. He urged that 'The East would do well … to purge itself ruthlessly of this canker and relegate it from the category of a tolerated practice to that of a condemned vice.'[135]

As Revathi Krishnaswamy suggests, this subversive masculinity injected 'a fearful indeterminacy into the economy of colonial desire' and presented 'the colonizing male imagination with strange possibilities and unknown dangers'.[136] Hector Macdonald presents exactly this kind of subversion that the British found so unsettling. In adhering to the prevailing heroic masculinity that was used to justify colonial rule, but acting on homosexual desires, Macdonald threatened not only Western 'assumptions about male sexual desire, masculinity, and heterosexuality' but also imperial power.[137] Moreover, it was thought that homosexuality posed a threat to military discipline and strength.[138] This might suggest why Hector Macdonald's behaviour met with a zero-tolerance attitude on the part of the War Office, who demanded he face a court-martial. As many – both then and now – have pointed out, however, there had been many before him, and have been many since, who were given far more leniency. A newspaper article sent to Joseph West Ridgeway, Governor of Ceylon, reminded readers that 'the law has moved very slowly against these offences on more than one occasion'. They named Robert Eyton (Canon of Westminster), who had been 'allowed to go'; he resigned his canonry under the guise that 'his health has completely broken down under mental strain', which he had apparently been suffering for a while, but the news still came as a shock to many.[139] The article also suggested that there were 'several officers whom we could name' who were 'offenders in this respect' and were 'allowed to travel eastwards in search of military employment', as well as a 'preminent (sic) member of the Upper House and a personal friend of royalty' who had been allowed to stay in the country 'after a scandal which laid bare years of prurient conduct'.[140] Ronald Hyam also notes General Gordon and two field marshals in the mid-twentieth century who were all 'protected by the absolute loyalty of their staff'.[141] (Although he also acknowledges that Gordon never acted on his homosexual desires – his 'sexual aim' was limited to '[s]eeing the naked body of a boy'[142] – and does not appear to have been the subject of a scandal.) Adding even more resentment to Macdonald's treatment, the article also asserted that 'Quite a number of the members of the House of Lords ... are addicted to it', claiming that 'Nobody would have taken any notice of the matter had it not been that Macdonald was hustled, so well is the practice known in "Society" circles.'[143] Similar remarks were made elsewhere. It seemed to some that the General's 'plebeian origin' became 'a serious drawback' in facing the charges, and suggested that if he had 'had aristocratic influence at his back the scandal would have been hushed up'.[144]

But Sir Hector Macdonald was not part of the 'Society' circles. As a ranker of working-class origins Macdonald was an outsider and, as has been noted, he did not always get along with his fellow officers. Many refused to believe the allegations against Hector, insisting that the 'suggestions' of his crimes were made out of 'vulgar feelings of spite and jealousy' for his success in rising through the ranks, and felt that Macdonald had been 'cruelly assassinated by vile and slandering tongues'.[145] A telegram to the editor of the *Dundee Advertiser* had suggested that he had been the victim of 'Blackmail, malice, and official jealousy' which had 'saddled him with circumstantial evidence which he was too poor to fight'.[146] As Aldrich suggests, whether Macdonald was guilty or not – whether the charges were true or not – such allegations 'provided a way to discredit a figure who was perhaps not quite of the "right sort"'.[147] It certainly seems plausible that there was a political element to Macdonald's treatment, and the case, like those of Collier and King, is a testament to the power of shame as a powerful controlling force of masculinity. Macdonald's case reflects Revathi Krishnaswamy's reading of Flora Annie Steel's *On the Face of Waters* (1896) in which the Gissings, described as 'crass and vulgar merchants', prefer living in India where they can be 'rich and respectable members of white society'. In the end, however, they die at the hands of Indians, a death 'that indirectly serves as punishment for low-class waywardness, economic as well as sexual'. Imperial masculinity was class-specific.[148] During war-time Macdonald had been a classic national hero – full of bravery, ready to fight and refusing to give up – but in peacetime his abrasive nature and open dislike of official company made him a stone in the establishment's shoe. Macdonald had displayed all the characteristics of New Imperialist masculinity but masculinity depended on more than just actions. Class was clearly a crucial element in the Macdonald scandal. It seems plausible, considering the cases before and since involving members of the 'right' society, that if Macdonald had had friends in higher places, and the weight of 'proper' birth behind him, he would have survived the scandal.

Conclusion

Throughout the nineteenth century honour remained a consistent part of military masculinity, used not only to police behaviour appropriate to gender, but also, as Macdonald's case shows, class and sexuality. The ways in which this masculine code of honour presented itself varied throughout the century, and much has been said of the turn away from the public show of the duel, to the battle of words and the rise of a quiet, internalized honour brought about with the rise of Evangelicalism. But for military men the violence of the duel remained part of this code of honour throughout, performed in subtly different ways.

With the Indian rebellion of 1857, this masculine honour was used in calls to arms to fight to defend Britain, raising the status of the army from disreputable to respectable. In this way, and in stark contrast to the traditional interpretation of mid-century honour, the old violence of the duel was legitimated in the theatre of war. But suicide, too, carried over this violence. Rather than turning one's pistol on another, honour could be defended by turning it against oneself. As the reports of Macdonald's suicide show, by the end of the century this course of action had come to be accepted, and even expected. Whilst the suicides of Collier and King lacked the glory of explicit references to honour in the same way as Macdonald, their actions still represent its power in ensuring proper masculine conduct. To be accused of incompetence or cowardice was to place men outside of an accepted standard of military masculinity. To kill oneself over such accusations was to conform to the code of death before dishonour, and reassert one's masculinity.

In an age that has inherited an understanding of war from two world wars, where men not in khaki were given white feathers, and where stories proliferate of men suffering from shell-shock being accused of malingering and cowardice, it is easy to assume that the suicide of a soldier would always have been understood as a cowardly act. One might also expect to be able to find evidence of what we now understand as PTSD, which went unrecognized by a less enlightened society. We would, however, be mistaken. To read these cases, with a modern understanding to psychology and psychiatry, as narratives of trauma and suicide would be ahistorical. Instead, we find that suicide was not always the cowardly way out. In cases where a soldier's honour was threatened, suicide could be a 'soldier's death' as much as losing one's life in battle, and perfectly in accord with masculine codes of honour throughout the century.

Notes

1   This was particularly prominent in religious rhetoric against suicide. For example, Rev. J. Gurnhill, *The Morals of Suicide* (London: Longmans, Green, and Co., 1900), 7–8, 69–70; Society for the Promotion of Christian Knowledge, 'Suicide; Its Guilt and Punishment. Earnestly Addressed to All Classes, Particularly Those in Humble Life', in *Religious Tracts Circulated by the Society for Promoting Christian Knowledge*, vol. 3 (11 vols, London: Printed for the Society for Promoting Christian Knowledge, 1836); Joseph Lathrop, *Two Sermons on the Atrocity of Suicide: And on the Causes Which Lead to It* (Springfield, MA: Brewer, 1805), 11; even some medical texts decried suicide as cowardice, Charles Moore, *A Full Inquiry into the Subject of Suicide*, vol. 2 (London: J. F. and C. Rivington, 1790), 57; Forbes Winslow, *The Anatomy of Suicide* (London: Henry Renshaw, 1840), 42. Suicide was sometimes explicitly compared to a soldier abandoning his post. For example, 'On Suicide', *The Examiner*, 18 October 1818: 14 and 'The Sands of Thought', *Caledonian Mercury*, 8 February 1856: 4.

2   Janet Padiak, 'Death by Suicide in the British Army, 1830–1900', in *Histories of Suicide: International Perspectives on Self-Destruction in the Modern World*, ed. John C. Weaver and David Wright (Toronto: University of Toronto Press, 2009), 119, 128–9.

3   Emile Durkheim, *Suicide : A Study in Sociology* (London: Routledge & Kegan Paul, 1970), 248.

4   Padiak, 'Death by Suicide in the British Army, 1830–1900', 127–8.

5   Émile Durkheim, *On Suicide*, trans. Robin Buss, Penguin classics (London: Penguin, 2006), 247–8. For his theory on social cohesion, see Book 2, chaps 2 and 3.

6   Ibid., 258.

7   Harold Braswell and Howard I. Kushner, 'Suicide, Social Integration, and Masculinity in the U.S. Military', *Social Science & Medicine* 74, no. 4 (2012): 532.

8   Durkheim, *On Suicide*, n. 305.

9   Braswell and Kushner, 'Suicide, Social Integration, and Masculinity in the U.S. Military', 531–3.

10 Alan H. Marks, 'Historical Suicide', in *Handbook of Death and Dying*, ed. Clifton D. Bryant (California: Sage, 2003), 311; Alexei V. Zadorojnyi, 'Cato's Suicide in Plutarch', *The Classical Quarterly* 57, no. 1 (2007): 216; Catharine Edwards, 'Modelling Roman Suicide? The Afterlife of Cato', *Economy and Society* 34, no. 2 (1 May 2005): 204.

11 Elise P. Garrison, 'Attitudes toward Suicide in Ancient Greece', *Transactions of the American Philological Association* 121 (1991): 2.

12 Ibid., 4.

13 Anthony Appiah, *The Honor Code: How Moral Revolutions Happen*, 1st edn (New York, NY: W.W. Norton, 2010), 192–3.

14 Alexander Welsh, *What Is Honor? A Question of Moral Imperatives* (New Haven, CT: Yale University Press, 2008), ix.

15 Ibid., ix, 1.

16 Appiah, *The Honor Code*, 14; Frank Henderson Stewart, *Honor* (Chicago, IL: University of Chicago Press, 1994), 59; Bradley Deane, *Masculinity and the New Imperialism: Rewriting Manhood in British Popular Literature, 1870–1914* (New York, NY: Cambridge University Press, 2017), 36.

17 For example, Alexander Welsh argues that even within vertical or hierarchic honour, the terms of the competition must be equal at the start, if one competitor was to have an advantage over another (e.g. through cheating) then there would be no honour in winning. As such, each 'competitor' is part of one horizontal honour group, and thus Walsh concludes that, 'scholars who assert, at least in passing, that honor is hierarchic must be confusing the relation with fame'. For the full discussion, see Welsh, *What Is Honor?*, 12–15.

18 Philippe Birmes et al., 'Early Historical Literature for Post-Traumatic Symptomatology', *Stress and Health* 19, no. 1 (2003): 19–23; R. J. Daly, 'Samuel Pepys and Post-Traumatic Stress Disorder', *British Journal of Psychiatry* 143, no. 1 (1983): 64–6.

19 Richard A. Gabriel, *No More Heroes: Madness & Psychiatry in War*, 1st edn (New York, NY: Hill and Wang, 1987), 6.

20 Edgar Jones et al., 'Flashbacks and Post-Traumatic Stress Disorder: The Genesis of a 20th-Century Diagnosis', *The British Journal of Psychiatry* 182, no. 2 (2003): 158;

Edgar Jones and Simon Wessely, 'War Syndromes: The Impact of Culture on Medically Unexplained Symptoms', *Medical History* 49, no. 1 (2005): 57; see also Derek Summerfield, 'The Invention of Post-Traumatic Stress Disorder and the Social Usefulness of a Psychiatric Category', *British Medical Journal* 322, no. 7278 (13 January 2001): 95–8; Allan Young, *The Harmony of Illusions: Inventing Post-Traumatic Stress Disorder* (Princeton, NJ: Princeton University Press, 2001), 5.

21   Jones and Wessely, 'War Syndromes: The Impact of Culture on Medically Unexplained Symptoms' (W. D. Wilson quoted on 65); Edgar Jones and Simon Wessely, 'Psychiatric Battle Casualties: An Intra- and Interwar Comparison', *British Journal of Psychiatry* 178, no. 3 (March 2001): 242–7.

22   Jones and Wessely, 'War Syndromes: The Impact of Culture on Medically Unexplained Symptoms', 66–7.

23   Anthony Bowlby et al., *A Civilian War Hospital: Being an Account of the Work of the Portland Hospital, and of Experience of Wounds and Sickness in South Africa, 1900* (London: John Murray, 1901), 126–7.

24   'A Soldier's Suicide at Southsea', *The Portsmouth Evening News*, 11 November 1890: 3.

25   'Frightful Suicide of a Soldier at Lumps Fort', *Portsmouth Times and Naval Gazette*, 16 May 1868: 5.

26   'Suicide of a Crimean Veteran', *Middlesex and Buckinghamshire Advertiser, Uxbridge, Harrow and Watford Journal*, 28 July 1900: 7.

27   Kingsmill Williams Jones, 'Delirium in Febrile Conditions', *Dublin Journal of Medical Science (1872–1920)* 115, no. 6 (1 June 1903): 420.

28   Bowlby et al., *A Civilian War Hospital*, 130.

29   'Suicide of a Military Officer', *Lloyd's Weekly Newspaper*, 10 February 1884: 7.

30   'Suicide of Colonel F. G. Whitehead', *The Essex Standard*, 16 February 1884: 2; 'The Suicide In Pall-Mall', *The Standard*, 14 February 1884: 3.

31   'Suicide of a Military Officer', *Lloyd's Weekly Newspaper,* 10 February 1884: 7.

32   'Suicide of a Soldier', *St. James's Gazette*, 30 June 1884: 12.

33   'Shocking Suicide of a Cavalry Officer', *Western Mail*, 10 February 1873: 3.

34   Bowlby et al., *A Civilian War Hospital*, 127.

35   Edgar Jones and Nicola T. Fear, 'Alcohol Use and Misuse in the Military: A Review', *International Review of Psychiatry* 23 (2011): 166.

36   Emma Butcher, 'War Trauma and Alcoholism in the Early Writings of Charlotte and Branwell Brontë', *Journal of Victorian Culture* 22, no. 4 (2017): 465–6.

37   Butcher, 'War Trauma and Alcoholism', 469.

38   'Suicide from Drunkenness', *The Globe*, 12 February 1839: 4.

39   'The War', *Caledonian Mercury*, 26 November 1855: 2; 'Fearful Suicide in The Crimea', *The Falkirk Herald*, 29 November 1855: 4.

40   Several contemporary reports of his suicide stated that he was the son of Admiral Collier, which was incorrect. He was the son of Ralph Collier, chief Clerk at the

Royal Navy's Victualling department. John Marshall, *Royal Naval Biography*, vol. II, Part II (London: Longman, Rees, Orme, Brown & Green, 1825), 518.

41 'Melancholy Suicide', *The Morning Chronicle*, 25 March 1824: 3; 'Melancholy Suicide', *The Morning Post*, 26 March 1824: 3; 'Melancholy Suicide of Sir George Ralph Collier', *Caledonian Mercury*, 29 March 1824: 2; 'Melancholy Suicide', *Oxford Journal*, 27 March 1824: 2.

42 'Melancholy Suicide of Sir George Ralph Collier', *Caledonian Mercury*, 29 March 1824: 2; 'Melancholy Suicide', *Leicester Chronicle*, 3 April 1824: 1.

43 'Melancholy Suicide of Sir George Ralph Collier', *Caledonian Mercury*; 'Melancholy Suicide', *The Royal Cornwall Gazette*, 3 April 1824: 4.

44 'Melancholy Suicide', *The Morning Post*; 'Admiral Sir G. R. Collier', *Cambridge Chronicle and Journal*, 2 April 1824: 4. The passage referred to can be found in William James, *The Naval History of Great Britain*, vol. V (London: Baldwin, Craddock, and Joy, 1824), 547–50. It was also printed in *The Morning Post*'s article on Collier's suicide.

45 'Melancholy Suicide', *The Morning Post*.

46 Ibid.

47 Robert B. Shoemaker, 'The Taming of the Duel: Masculinity, Honour and Ritual Violence in London, 1660–1800', *The Historical Journal* 45, no. 3 (2002): 544.

48 Ibid., 540.

49 Margery Masterson, 'Dueling, Conflicting Masculinities, and the Victorian Gentleman', *Journal of British Studies* 56, no. 3 (2017): 617.

50 N. A. M. Rodger, 'Honour and Duty at Sea, 1660–1815', *Historical Research* 75, no. 190 (16 December 2002): 435–6.

51 Quoted in ibid., 436.

52 Rodger does acknowledge the resonance honour still has to the military, even today. Ibid., 446.

53 'Melancholy Suicide', *The Morning Post*.

54 'Melancholy Suicide of Sir George Ralph Collier', *Caledonian Mercury*.

55 Commenting on the battle, *The Morning Chronicle* remarked that, if their account had failed to convey to their readers 'a clear and intelligible picture of the fray', they 'must remind them 'that no truth-loving historian can give a methodical form to operations characterised by an utter absence of method, or describe with distinctness and precision a series of military operations, which, in point of strategic science, appear to have been on a par with a faction fight at an Irish fair'. 'The Morning Chronicle', *The Morning Chronicle*, 6 March 1849: 4; 'The Battle of Chillianwallah', *Hampshire Telegraph*, 10 March 1849: 2.

56 'The Cavalry Affair at The Battle On The Jhelum', *The Globe*, 9 April 1849: 1; 'The Indian Brevet and The Fourteenth Dragoons', *John Bull*, 11 June 1849: 357; 'Suicide of Colonel King', *Dover Telegraph and Cinque Ports General Advertiser*, 7 September

1850: 4; 'London, Wednesday, Sept. 4, 1850', *The Morning Post*, 4 September 1850: 2; 'Sir Charles Napier and The Late Colonel King', *The Glasgow Gazette*, 7 September 1850: 2.

57   In the wake of King's suicide, Napier's actual words became a matter of controversy, with some denying he had made the remark about needing to be led, others suggested that his actual words were that they 'would go anywhere if properly led'. One report about Napier's address before King's suicide also reported that Napier had suggested he said that there was no regiment he would rather lead. 'The 14th Dragoons', *South Eastern Gazette*, 12 February 1850: 4; 'India', *Norfolk Chronicle*, 16 February 1850: 2; 'The Late Colonel King of The 14th Light Dragoons', *Dundee, Perth, and Cupar Advertiser*, 8 October 1850: 1; 'Colonial', *John Bull*, 9 September 1850: 564; 'Bombay, July 25', *The Morning Chronicle*, 2 September 1850: 6. Napier's brother vehemently defended him and denied he had uttered the words in a letter to the editor of *The Times* and widely printed across the British press. 'To The Editor of The Times', *The Times*, 13 September 1850: 5; 'Sir Charles Napier and The Tragedy At Lahore', *Westmorland Gazette*, 21 September 1850: 2; 'Sir Charles Napier and The Late Colonel King', *Glasgow Gazette*, 21 September 1850: 2.

58   'Suicide of Colonel King', *Dover Telegraph and Cinque Ports General Advertiser*, 7 September 1850: 4; 'London, Wednesday, Sept. 4, 1850', *The Morning Post*.

59   'The Indian Brevet and The Fourteenth Dragoons', *John Bull*, 11 1849: 357.

60   Diane Miller Sommerville, '"A Burden Too Heavy to Bear": War Trauma, Suicide, and Confederate Soldiers', *Civil War History* 59, no. 4 (2013): 462–3.

61   'The Fourteenth Light Dragoons', *Maidstone Journal and Kentish Advertiser*, 10 September 1850: 4; 'The Late Colonel King', *Glasgow Herald*, 23 September 1850: 2.

62   'Suicide Of Lieut-Col. King', *The South Eastern Gazette*, 10 September 1850: 2. Reports of Parker's suicide in the press did not mention Sir Charles Napier, and simply said he shot himself 'whilst under the influence of fever, and was supposed to be delirious'. 'India And China', *Londonderry Standard*, 10 January 1844: 1; 'India and China', *Bell's Weekly Messenger*, 8 January 1844: 3.

63   Holly Furneaux, *Military Men of Feeling: Emotion, Touch, and Masculinity in the Crimean War* (Oxford: Oxford University Press, 2016), 38.

64   'The Late Colonel King', *Glasgow Herald*.

65   J. Thackwell, *Narrative of the Second Sikh War in 1848–49. With a Detailed Account of the Battles of Ramnugger, the Passage of the Chenab, Chillianwallah, Goojerat, &c.*, 2nd edn (London: Richard Bentley, 1851), 298–303 (quote on 303).

66   Furneaux, *Military Men of Feeling*, 56.

67   Ibid., 9.

68   'The Late Colonel King', *Glasgow Herald*.

69   Furneaux, *Military Men of Feeling*, 11–15.

70   Ibid., 34.

71   'The Late Colonel King', *Glasgow Herald*.

72 Kenneth I. E. Macleod, *The Ranker: The Story of Sir Hector Macdonald's Death* (Cortland, NY: the author, 1976), vii.

73 J. A. Mangan, 'Duty unto Death: English Masculinity and Militarism in the Age of the New Imperialism', *The International Journal of the History of Sport* 27, no. 1–2 (1 January 2010): 129; Heather Streets, *Martial Races: The Military, Race and Masculinity in British Imperial Culture, 1857–1914* (Manchester; New York, NY: Manchester University Press, 2004), 20–1; Olive Anderson, 'The Growth of Christian Militarism in Mid-Victorian Britain', *The English Historical Review* 86, no. 338 (1971): 46–7.

74 Streets, *Martial Races*, 24.

75 'Sir Hector Macdonald', *The London Daily News*, 25 March 1903: 7; 'Suicide of Sir Hector Macdonald', *The Dundee Evening Telegraph*, 26 March 1903: 4.

76 'Sir Hector Macdonald', *The London Daily News*; 'Suicide of Sir Hector Macdonald', *The Dundee Evening Telegraph*; Roger T. Stearn, 'Macdonald, Sir Hector Archibald (1853–1903), Army Officer and Popular Hero', *Oxford Dictionary of National Biography*, 22 September 2011, https://www.oxforddnb.com/view/10.1093/ ref:odnb/9780198614128.001.0001/odnb-9780198614128-e-34702 (accessed 22 November 2021).

77 'Suicide of Sir Hector Macdonald', *The Dundee Evening Telegraph*.

78 Ibid.; 'Suicide Of "Fighting Mac"', *The Yorkshire Evening Post*, 26 March 1903: 4.

79 'Lord Kitchener and Sir Hector Macdonald', *Lincolnshire Echo*, 21 February 1903: 3.

80 'Sir Hector Macdonald', *The Daily Telegraph*, 21 February 1903: 6; 'Sir Hector Macdonald's Return', *Bournemouth Daily Echo*, 21 February 1903: 2;

81 'Sir Hector Macdonald for Somaliland', *Dublin Daily Express*, 20 February 1903: 5; 'Our London Letter', *Exeter and Plymouth Gazette*, 21 February 1903: 3.

82 'Sir Hector Macdonald's Return', *Dundee Evening Post*, 21 February 1903: 7; 'Sir Hector Macdonald's Return', *St. James's Gazette*, 21 February 1903: 10; '"Fighting Mac's" Return', *Northern Daily Telegraph*, 21 February 1903: 2.

83 'The Suicide Of Sir Hector Macdonald', *The Newry Reporter*, 28 March 1903: 4.

84 'Suicide of "Fighting Mac"', *The Yorkshire Evening Post*, 26 March 1903: 4; 'Sir Hector Macdonald', *The Worcester Chronicle*, 28 March 1903: 1; 'The Suicide of Sir Hector Macdonald', *The Belfast Evening Telegraph*, 26 March 1903: 4.

85 'Suicide of "Fighting Mac"', *The Yorkshire Evening Post*, 4; 'Sir H. Macdonald', *Aberdeen Daily Journal*, 26 March 1903: 5.

86 'Suicide of "Fighting Mac"', *The Yorkshire Evening Post*, 4; 'Sir Hector Macdonald', *The Worcester Chronicle*, 28 March 1903: 1; 'The Suicide of Sir Hector Macdonald', *The Belfast Evening Telegraph*, 4.

87 'Grave Charges Against Sir Hector Macdonald', *The Edinburgh Evening News*, 25 March 1903: 6; 'Sir Hector Macdonald', *The Citizen*, 25 March 1903: 3; 'Sir Hector Macdonald', *The London Daily News*, 25 March 1903: 7; 'Suicide Of "Fighting Mac"', *The Yorkshire Evening Post*, 4.

88   'Il est accusé aujourd'hui d'avoir commis, à Ceylan, des actes contre nature avec de jeunes indigènes.' 'Le Cas Du Général Macdonald', *Le Matin*, 25 March 1903: 3.

89   Trevor Royle, *Death Before Dishonour: The True Story of Fighting Mac* (Edinburgh: Mainstream, 1982), 158.

90   'Grave Charges Against Sir Hector Macdonald', *The Edinburgh Evening News*; 'Sir Hector Macdonald', *The Citizen*.

91   'The Late Sir Hector Macdonald', *Edinburgh Evening News*, 27 March 1903: 4.

92   'The Suicide of Sir Hector Macdonald', *The Newry Reporter*, 28 March 1903: 4.

93   'Suicide of Sir Hector Macdonald', *The Dundee Evening Telegraph*, 26 March 1903: 4.

94   'Macdonald Case', *The Yorkshire Telegraph and Star*, 26 March 1903: 4.

95   See the Introduction in Bradley Deane, *Masculinity and the New Imperialism: Rewriting Manhood in British Popular Literature, 1870–1914* (New York, NY: Cambridge University Press, 2017).

96   Ibid., 7.

97   'Suicide of "Fighting Mac"', *The Yorkshire Evening Post*, 4.

98   Ibid.

99   Patricia E. Prestwich, 'Suicide and French Soldiers of the First World War: Differing Perspectives, 1914–1939', in *Histories of Suicide: International Perspectives on Self-Destruction in the Modern World*, ed. Weaver and Wright, 135.

100   'Suicide of Sir Hector Macdonald', *The Dundee Evening Telegraph*.

101   '"Fighting Mac"', *Northern Daily Telegraph*.

102   W. H. Millar, 'Statistics of Death by Suicide among Her Majesty's British Troops Serving at Home and Abroad During the Ten Years 1862–71', *Journal of the Statistical Society of London* 37, no. 2 (1874): 189; William Ogle also observed the link between profession and suicide method, whereby the soldier chose the gun, the chemist or doctor chose something 'in his poison chest'. William Ogle, 'Suicides in England and Wales in Relation to Age, Sex, Season, and Occupation', *Journal of the Statistical Society of London* 49, no. 1 (1886): 110. The term 'a soldier's death' was not used in any other articles I have come across.

103   'Suicide of Sir Hector Macdonald', *The Chard and Ilminster News*, 28 March 1903: 3.

104   Deane, *Masculinity and the New Imperialism*, 7.

105   Matthew Barrett, '"Hero of the Half-Breed Rebellion": Gabriel Dumont and Late Victorian Military Masculinity', *Journal of Canadian Studies/Revue d'études Canadiennes* 48, no. 3 (2014): 82.

106   Christian Goeschel, *Suicide in Nazi Germany* (Oxford; New York, NY: Oxford University Press, 2009), particularly 140–3, 154–5.

107   Deane, *Masculinity and the New Imperialism*, 9.

108   Shoemaker, 'The Taming of the Duel: Masculinity, Honour and Ritual Violence in London, 1660–1800', 542; John Tosh, 'Masculinities in an Industrializing Society: Britain, 1800–1914', *Journal of British Studies* 44, no. 2 (2005): 333–4.

109 See Masterson, 'Dueling, Conflicting Masculinities, and the Victorian Gentleman';
     Tosh, 'Masculinities in an Industrializing Society: Britain, 1800–1914', 335.

110 'Grave Charges Against Sir Hector Macdonald', *The Lancashire Daily Post*, 25
     March 1903: 2; 'Suicide of Sir Hector Macdonald', *Totnes Times* and *Devon News*,
     26 March 1903: 6.

111 'Macdonald Case', *The Yorkshire Telegraph and Star*, 26 March 1903: 4.

112 'Suicide of Sir Hector Macdonald', *The Dundee Evening Telegraph*.

113 'Sir Hector Macdonald', *The Preston Herald*, 28 March 1903: 8.

114 'Suicide of General Hector Macdonald', *The Yorkshire Post*, 26 March 1903: 7;
     'Tragic Death of Sir Hector Macdonald', *The Shields Daily News*, 26 March 1903: 4.

115 'Sir Hector Macdonald', *The Preston Herald*.

116 'Hector Macdonald', *The London Daily News*, 26 March 1903: 12; 'Suicide of
     General Hector Macdonald', *The Yorkshire Post*, 26 March 1903: 7.

117 'Suicide of General Hector Macdonald', *The Yorkshire Post*.

118 Some accounts state that this happened during a morning. 'Tragic Death of Sir
     Hector Macdonald', *The Shields Daily News*, 26 March 1903: 4; 'Suicide of General
     Hector Macdonald', *The Gloucester Citizen*, 26 March 1903: 3; 'Macdonald Case',
     The Yorkshire Telegraph and Star, 26 March 1903: 4.

119 'Hector Macdonald', *The London Daily News*, 26 March 1903: 12.

120 Streets, *Martial Races*, 1.

121 Macaulay quoted in Mrinalini Sinha, *Colonial Masculinity: The 'manly
     Englishman' and the 'Effeminate Bengali' in the Late Nineteenth Century*, Studies
     in Imperialism (Manchester; New York, NY: Manchester University Press, 1995),
     16–17.

122 Streets, *Martial Races*, 1; Deane, *Masculinity and the New Imperialism*, 16–17.

123 Streets, *Martial Races*, 9–10.

124 'Colonel Hector Macdonald', *The Aberdeen Journal*, 12 May 1899: 8.

125 Kenneth Ballhatchet, *Race, Sex, and Class under the Raj: Imperial Attitudes and
     Policies and Their Critics, 1793–1905* (London: Weidenfeld and Nicolson, 1980), 6.

126 Robert Aldrich, *Colonialism and Homosexuality* (London; New York, NY:
     Routledge, 2003), 187–8; Macleod, *The Ranker: The Story of Sir Hector
     Macdonald's Death*, 12, 17; Royle, *Death before Dishonour*, 160; Ronald Hyam,
     Empire and Sexuality: The British Experience (Manchester: Manchester University
     Press, 1998), 34.

127 Aldrich, *Colonialism and Homosexuality*, 188; the fact that no documents can
     be found which detail the exact circumstances of the charges against Hector
     Macdonald and his subsequent suicide has been a matter of suspicion; see
     Macleod, *The Ranker: The Story of Sir Hector Macdonald's Death*, 8–9; Royle,
     Death before Dishonour, 125–6.

128 Aldrich, *Colonialism and Homosexuality*, 188; Royle, *Death before Dishonour*, 125–6.

129 Aldrich, *Colonialism and Homosexuality*, 188; Macleod, *The Ranker: The Story of Sir Hector Macdonald's Death*, 11–12.

130 Aldrich, *Colonialism and Homosexuality*, 1; Edward W. Said, *Orientalism* (New Delhi: Penguin Books, 1995), 188.

131 Joseph Allen Boone, *The Homoerotics of Orientalism* (New York, NY: Columbia University Press, 2014); Joseph A. Boone, 'Vacation Cruises; Or, the Homoerotics of Orientalism', *PMLA* 110, no. 1 (1995): 89–107; Christopher Lane, *The Ruling Passion: British Colonial Allegory and the Paradox of Homosexual Desire* (Durham: Duke University Press, 1995); Aldrich, *Colonialism and Homosexuality*.

132 Hyam, *Empire and Sexuality*, 88.

133 Philippa Levine, 'Sexuality, Gender, and Empire', in *Gender and Empire*, ed. Philippa Levine (Oxford; New York, NY: Oxford University Press, 2004), 134–7.

134 Sir George MacMunn, *The Underworld of India* (London: Jarrolds, 1933), 202.

135 Ibid.

136 Revathi Krishnaswamy, *Effeminism: The Economy of Colonial Desire* (Ann Arbor, MI: University of Michigan Press, 1998), 32.

137 Boone, 'Vacation Cruises; Or, the Homoerotics of Orientalism', 90.

138 Ballhatchet, *Race, Sex, and Class under the Raj*, 10; Joane Nagel, 'Masculinity and Nationalism: Gender and Sexuality in the Making of Nations', *Ethnic and Racial Studies* 21, no. 2 (1 January 1998): 257.

139 I have been unable to locate the newspaper from which the article was taken, it is attached to correspondence between Governor Ridgeway and Lord Roberts. Letter from Governor Joseph West Ridgeway to Lord Roberts, 17 May 1903, Roberts Papers, CO 7101/23/46 f. 114, National Army Museum; 'Ecclesiastical Intelligence', *The Times*, 13 January 1899: 9; 'Resignation of Canon Eyton', *The Nottingham Evening Post*, 14 January 1899: 4.

140 Ridgeway to Roberts, Roberts Papers, CO 7101/23/46 f. 114.

141 Hyam, *Empire and Sexuality*, 33.

142 Ibid., 15.

143 Ridgeway to Roberts, Roberts Papers, CO 7101/23/46 f. 114.

144 'Gen. Hector Macdonald', *The Daily News*, 27 March 1903: 7.

145 'The Late Sir Hector Macdonald', *The Aberdeen Daily Journal*, 25 September 1903: 7.

146 'The Late Sir Hector Macdonald', *Sheffield Daily Telegraph*, 1 April 1903: 5.

147 Ibid., 33.

148 Revathi Krishnaswamy, *Effeminism: The Economy of Colonial Desire* (Ann Arbor, MI: University of Michigan Press, 1998), 70.

Conclusion

Reports of suicides in the nineteenth-century press were more than simply the bland, factual accounts that those such as Matthew MacDonald and Michel Foucault believed them to be. Whether an accurate account of an inquest, or a journalistic summary of events, they are reconstructions of lives made in order to make sense of the world and mediated through experience. They are stories. In some cases, like that of the unidentified labourer and those of other 'ordinary' people, who have not otherwise made their mark on our histories or been subject to biography, these stories might be the only ones we have. For the most part they are stories told about people by others, rarely do we hear the voice of the suicide himself, and in this way they are part of the historical process itself, purposely presenting a narrative to a broader audience. Following Kali Israel's and Carolyn Steedman's approaches to writing lives of historical actors in his most recent book, Matt Houlbrook outlines how he uses the lives and stories of Netley Lucas as a guide to the Britain of the 1920s and 1930s, and attests to 'the power of his stories to both evoke and unsettle the world in which he told them'.[1] Here I have endeavoured to do the same with the recorded deaths of historical subjects. Just as the stories Lucas made for himself were 'evocative of a time and of a place', so too were the narratives people told of suicides.[2] For relatives, friends, witnesses, the press and their audience, the narratives constructed around a suicide's life and motives were a meaning-making exercise, helping them to understand the why of self-destruction. For the historian, they prove more useful in understanding the attitudes and values of a distant time and place.

Suicide narratives show us how people made sense of the events of another's life, and in doing so reveal the attitudes that guided them. The narrative types outlined here were common frames of reference people used to understand suicide; the heartbroken and the jealous; the unemployed; the fraudster and bankrupt; and the soldier who chose death before dishonour. All of these narratives were shaped by personal experience, literature, other reports of suicide, but also gendered and class-based expectations of behaviour. The end product is the making of a life (or death) for someone, historically and contextually situated but recognizable to the reader.[3] Whilst, at its core, this is a history of nineteenth-century suicide, it is ultimately a history of nineteenth-century moral values and attitudes towards masculinity.

The proliferation of digitized newspaper archives in the last decade has allowed me to access the deaths (and lives) of hundreds of 'ordinary' men. Men like Frank Taylor, George Saville, George William Short, John Sheppard, James Sproston and countless others, who might have otherwise escaped notice. As a result, I have been able to move away from traditional canons of nineteenth-century masculinities, and towards a more nuanced study of 'everyday' masculinity. This is, in part, due to the expansive (and continually expanding) range of papers available in these digital archives. Andrew Hobbs' 2013 article lamented the overuse of *The Times* and London dailies, even with the advent of the *Times Digital Archive* and *19th Century British Library Newspapers*.[4] In the years since the publication of Hobbs' article the number of newspapers digitally available has grown exponentially, with the *British Newspaper Archive* now hosting over forty million pages, compared to the four million at its launch.[5] The London dailies have undoubtedly featured prominently throughout my research, but I have also been able to make use of regional and provincial papers, which provide greater access to local events like suicide. Whilst this methodology has allowed me to access the lives and deaths of more diverse and representative historical subjects, I am also aware that those made available to me in any full detail are the result of journalistic and editorial decisions, and have been guided by considerations of sensationalism, popular attitudes, ideas about gender and class and, ultimately, what sells. Whilst they have given me greater access to the voices of everyday people in reporting inquest proceedings, there is no denying that it is, ultimately, the voice of the press that has spoken the most. This does not make these narratives any less real. With the proliferation of newspapers during the nineteenth century, the press became, in Aled Jones' words, 'an essential reference point in the daily lives of millions', which not only reflected opinion, but also helped shape it.[6] The narratives of suicide that I have looked at through this work were part of a discourse that aided people in making sense of suicide, and in this way informed the narratives told as much as reported them.

Much like many microhistories, these stories are an example of the 'exceptional "normal"' in history. Suicide, although an inevitable part of society, is not a 'normal' death, and in many cases it is an extraordinary event in otherwise ordinary lives. To add to the methodological challenge, they are also representations of why men killed themselves, constructed by inquest witnesses, and then mediated through the press. It begs the question, then, how representative are they of the past and of past experience? This question will always be up for debate.[7] But suicide is embedded in cultural and social contexts. Whilst these are assumptions about what motivated someone to a suicide, as construed by other people, they are still guided by beliefs and attitudes about why men killed themselves and about the bounds of 'normal' or acceptable behaviour. Whilst I believe these narratives provide insight into the experiences of these suicidal men, I accept that they are just that. Narratives of lives that, as Edouard Levé suggested, have been 'rewritten' in light of their extraordinary deaths.[8] They are not able to capture the lived experiences of the men who chose to take their own life, neither can I claim that these were the true motives behind the act. That does not make them less useful to the historian for understanding past society. These narratives reveal what was thought to be important enough to push a man to take his own life and, in commenting on their behaviour and character, provide insight into important ideas about masculinity.

Inevitably, the approach I have taken also turned up many 'extraordinary' cases, by virtue either of their notable lives or the circumstances of their deaths, which have been given far more attention by the press. Some of these men are not unfamiliar. Both John Sadleir and Hector Macdonald have been subjects of biography, and some of the lesser-known cases have cropped up in other research.[9] The approach I have taken here, however, has turned up new information and taken new perspectives. John Sadleir's biography primarily serves to document the rise and fall of one of the century's greatest fraudsters, and works on white-collar crime give little attention to his suicide. Not only has my primary focus been on Sadleir's death, rather than his life, the quick return of information that the digital archives offer has enabled me to demonstrate the relationship between new media and coroners' courts, and the impact the press could have. For Hector Macdonald, previous biographies have often attempted to posthumously clear him of the charges brought against him, but here I have instead been concerned with how the reaction to his death and the stories recounted of his life demonstrate how suicide was incorporated into a code of honour inscribed in military masculinity. In the Novelli murder-suicide, the keyword-searchable digital archives have allowed me to trace the family history of suicide and insanity across a century and directly compare the evidence that lead to juries' verdicts across cases.

Contrary to previous histories of suicide, I have shown that the act of killing oneself was not necessarily gendered 'feminine' throughout the nineteenth century. Whilst the trope of the love-mad or fallen woman's suicide was undoubtedly popular amongst Victorians, this work has made it evident that this was one among many. It was clear to those who studied suicide and insanity, to those who collected the statistics and to those who frequently read the newspapers, that men made up the majority of suicides. Love-mad men were common in reports of suicide, as were the fraudsters, the dishonoured soldiers and most of all the underemployed men of the working classes. However, the narratives and stories told about male suicide were guided by judgements based on gendered expectations of men, and what it meant to be a man.

These expectations were far more nuanced than simple gendered binaries of masculinity and femininity. In the early nineteenth century, the men who killed themselves for love could be held up as examples of a Wertherian masculinity associated with eighteenth-century sensibility and Europe. Whilst Werther's sensibility has previously been interpreted as a sign of femininity, few of the romantic, Wetherian suicides reported in the press were branded in this way. Instead of being branded as feminine, their Wertherism was contrasted against the expectations of an English brand of masculinity that rejected the dramatic and valued stoicism. Their behaviour was seen as un-English and unmanly rather than distinctly feminine. For the military men of chapter 4, suicide was encompassed in a masculine code of honour which had been prefigured by the duel. In the cases outlined here, honour was defended not by turning their pistols towards their opponent, but towards themselves. For men like Collier and King, accusations of incompetence and cowardice were felt so acutely that the support of others was insufficient to temper the slight against their honour. For others, like Macdonald, the concept of honour was used to police both behaviour and social class. In the military context, suicide was not seen as an unmanly act of cowardice, but as an act in line with honourable military masculinity. Suicide was not, as some have previously suggested, always seen as a feminine, or even unmanly, act.

Character was another element that was key in measuring masculinity. Much as in criminal trials, judgements were often made on suicides based on their character and previous life. John Sadleir's case in chapter 3, and the coroner's pronouncement of the verdict, provides a clear example of this. Whilst he was believed to be a man of respectable character, much of which was guided by the assumptions of social class, the coroner had no doubts that he had been insane at the time. However, by the time Sadleir's extended series of frauds had been made clear, the coroner was willing to group him amongst the worst criminals and he was found *felo de se*. For men of the working classes, the narratives told about their suicides measured their masculinity against a Smilesian 'self-help' ethos and individualism that blamed poverty on the victims of systemic problems. These men's lives were examined for evidence of respectability, hard work and independence that was held up as an idealized working-class masculinity, as Frank Taylor's did. For others, like John Sheppard, their failure to live up to these expectations often resulted in harsh judgement. For professional, middle-class men whose lives had been exemplary or without fault, like Alexander Novelli, evidence was sought for insanity in their weakly character. It seems that most coroners' juries of the nineteenth century were willing to find cause to return verdicts of insanity, but if it transpired that the character of a suicide failed to measure up, judgements could be harsh and, as in the cases of John Sadleir and John Sheppard, a verdict of *felo de se* could be used as a rare, but decisive, punishment.

What has been made clear from the lives and deaths of these men is that masculinity was nuanced in ways that move beyond gendered binaries. Masculinity was, and is, a multifaceted experience. There were no clear cut categories of attributes, or actions that would guarantee a verdict of insanity or *felo de se*, and judgements on masculine character were not always made explicitly through verdicts, but subtly through the construction of narratives of suicide. Measures of masculinity were made based on an otherness that encompassed class, profession, sexuality and the time and place. The discussion of male suicide that has emerged in popular discourse over the past decade has been a step in acknowledging this, and highlighting the dangers of a rigid masculinity. The form of masculinity that has been opened up to renewed criticism today can find origins in the nineteenth-century turn towards the stoicism, emotional strength and quiet honour of the Evangelical movement, and then the bravado, physical strength and heroism of the New Imperialism. But it would be misguided to assume that these were the only models of masculinity available for men to perform and adopt.

There have been many stories I have been unable to tell, of lives cut short by their own devices. Alongside the narrative of the unemployed labourer existed that of the overworked professional, one that offers an interesting class dynamic to a larger narrative of suicide related to work. Alannah Tomkins has made some inroads with her work on doctor's suicides but there is room for further discussion into suicides from overwork. The narratives of military suicides in the final chapter barely touched the surface of what is a promising field of research. Some recent interest in suicides during the American Civil War has begun to make inroads into a somewhat untouched area,[10] but little has been done on the suicide of men during the two world wars. The case of Hector Macdonald also brought up issues of sexuality, and in researching this work, I have found traces of evidence that make the tentative beginnings of a queer history of suicide. It is also perhaps time to revisit the trope of the love-mad or fallen woman's suicide. Although my focus has been primarily on men, I have, unsurprisingly, found the same variety of narratives surrounding women's suicides, and stories that need to be told. Desertion and love are undoubtedly popular narratives for women's suicide, but so were poverty and religious delusion. These stories are at once personal, public and often political.

As we have moved through the twentieth and into the twenty-first century, these narratives of suicide have been hidden by media guidelines, which dictate that suicide be presented as an individual pathology in an effort to reduce the possibility of copycat acts. But suicide is multifaceted and complex, and reducing it to individual pathology ignores many of the social issues that lead men to take their own lives. Such pathologizing also denies a suicide's agency, and whilst the same can be (and has been)[11] said of insanity verdicts of the nineteenth century, the public narratives told about suicide throughout the century invariably encompassed social, as well as psychological, causes. These narratives offer vital social context to the drastic actions people take. Whether these contexts are rigid expectations of masculinity, damaging welfare policies or cultures of shame and honour, they offer us a greater understanding of both the act of suicide and the society in which it takes place.

Notes

1 Matt Houlbrook, *Prince of Tricksters: The Incredible True Story of Netley Lucas, Gentleman Crook* (Chicago, IL ; London: University of Chicago Press, 2016), 2, 16–17.

2 Ibid., 3.

3 Carolyn Steedman, 'On Not Writing Biography', *New Formations* 67, no. 67 (1 June 2009): 17; Houlbrook, *Prince of Tricksters*, 16.

4 Andrew Hobbs, 'The Deleterious Dominance of *The Times* in Nineteenth-Century Scholarship', *Journal of Victorian Culture* 18, no. 4 (December 2013): 472–97.

5 Amy, 'The British Newspaper Archive – Launch Press Release (29/11/2012, 00:01)', https://blog.britishnewspaperarchive.co.uk/2011/11/29/the-british-newspaper-archive-launch-press-release-29112012-0001/ (accessed 22 July 2019); 'Home | Search the Archive | British Newspaper Archive', https://www.britishnewspaperarchive.co.uk/ (accessed 22 July 2019).

6   Aled Jones, *Powers of the Press: Newspapers, Power and the Public in Nineteenth-Century England*, The Nineteenth Century (Aldershot, England: Brookfield, VT, USA: Scolar Press; Ashgate Pub. Co, 1996), 1–4 (quote on 2).

7   On debates about historical truths and methodological limits, see Richard D. Brown, 'Microhistory and the Post-Modern Challenge', *Journal of the Early Republic* 23, no. 1 (2003): 1–20; similarly, on debates around the methodological challenges in studying suicide, Bailey's summary is particularly useful. Victor Bailey, *This Rash Act: Suicide Across the Life Cycle in the Victorian City* (Stanford, CA: Stanford University Press, 1998), chap. 1.

8   Edouard Levé, *Suicide*, trans. Jan H. Steyn, 1st edn (Champaign, IL: Dalkey Archive Press, 2011), 29.

9   For example, Shani D'Cruze has discussed the Novelli case in relation to domestic voilence. Shani D'Cruze, 'The Eloquent Corpse: Gender, Probity, and Bodily Integrity in Victorian Domestic Murder', in *Criminal Converstions: Victorian Crimes, Social Panic, and Moral Outrage*, ed. Judith Rowbotham and Kim Stevenson (Columbus, OH: Ohio State University Press, 2005).

10 Diane Miller Sommerville, '"A Burden Too Heavy to Bear": War Trauma, Suicide, and Confederate Soldiers', *Civil War History* 59, no. 4 (2013): 453–91; Diane Miller Sommerville, *Aberration of Mind: Suicide and Suffering in the Civil War-Era South* (Chapel Hill, NC: University of North Carolina Press, 2018); David Silkenat, *Moments of Despair: Suicide, Divorce, & Debt in Civil War Era North Carolina* (Chapel Hill, NC: University of North Carolina Press, 2011).

11 Emma Liggins, for example, has suggested that verdicts of temporary insanity removed agency in women's suicide, an interpretation that is equally applicable to male suicide. Emma Liggins, 'Her Resolution to Die: "Wayward Women" and Constructions of Suicide in Wilkie Collins's Crime Fiction', *Wilkie Collins Society Journal* 4 (2001): 2; Ian Hacking observes that the pathological turn came on the back of the trend for statistics, which allowed for 'massive enumerations' and categorizations of deviancy. Ian Hacking, *The Taming of Chance*, Ideas in Context (Cambridge; New York, NY: Cambridge University Press, 1990), chaps 1 and 7; Ian Hacking, 'The Suicide Weapon', *Critical Inquiry* 35, no. 1 (1 September 2008): 1–32; see also Zohreh Bayatrizi, *Life Sentences: The Modern Ordering of Mortality* (Toronto; Buffalo: University of Toronto Press, 2008), chap. 3.

Bibliography

Archival material

The National Archives

Alleged libel on Governor Ridgeway, CO 537/411.
Lunacy Patients Admission Registers', 1850, MH94/8.
Note of Macdonald's return to England, CO 537/410.
Personal Files of Hector Macdonald, WO 138/24.
Will of Lewis Novelli, Merchant of Manchester, Lancashire, PROB 11/2083/326.
Will of Philip Novelli of Dulwich Wood House, Surrey, PROB 11/2163/122.

The National Army Museum Archives

Four letters from RSM John Dobson White, 1st Buckinghamshire Yeomanry to his
    mother. Accession no. 2002-11-732.
Letter to Lord Roberts from Ridgeway. April 20 1903. Accession no. 7101-23-46-133.
Photocopies of documents relating to Gen Sir Hector MacDonald and the controversy
    surrounding his court-martial and death. Accession no. 1973-09-59.
Transcripts of thirty-four letters written by James Wymondham Hughes-Hallett
    (1852–1927). Accession no. 1985-11-13.

Newspapers

Aberdeen Press and Journal (1903)
Bath Chronicle and Weekly Gazette (1839)
Belfast Evening Telegraph (1903)
Belfast News-Letter (1856–95)
Bell's Life in London and Sporting Chronicle (1825–85)
Bell's Weekly Messenger (1844)
Bristol Mercury (1895)
Bristol Mirror (1810)
Bury and Norwich Post (1822–85)
Caledonian Mercury (1824–55)
Cambridge Chronicle and Journal (1822–4)

Canterbury Journal, Kentish Times and Famers' Gazette (1839)

Carlisle Journal (1839)

Cheshire Observer (1855)

Daily Gazette for Middlesbrough (1886–94)

Dublin Weekly Register (1839)

Dundee Advertiser (1863)

Dundee Courier (1898)

Dundee Evening Post (1903)

Dundee Evening Telegraph (1893–1903)

Dundee, Perth, and Cupar Advertiser (1850)

Dunfermline Saturday Press (1863)

Edinburgh Evening News (1886–1903)

Evening Mail (1810–56)

Exeter and Plymouth Gazette (1903)

Exeter Flying Post (1883)

Faversham Gazette, and Whitstable, Sittingbourne, & Milton Journal (1856)

Glasgow Evening Post (1893)

Grantham Journal (1898)

Hampshire Advertiser (1892)

Hampshire Telegraph (1800–49)

Hereford Journal (1822)

Hull Daily Mail (1898)

John Bull (1822–50)

La Belle Assemblée; or, Bell's Court and Fashionable Magazine (1812)

Lancashire Evening Post (1891)

Le Matin (1903)

Leeds Intelligencer (1822)

Leicester Chronicle (1810)

Leicester Daily Post (1892)

Leicester Journal (1810–56)

Lincolnshire Echo (1903)

Liverpool Mercury (1855–97)

Lloyd's Weekly Paper (1850–84)

London Daily News (1847–1903)

London Evening Standard (1839–95)

Maidstone Journal and Kentish Advertiser (1850)

Manchester Times (1836)

Middlesex and Buckinghamshire Advertiser (1900)

Morpeth Herald (1859)

North Devon Gazette (1898)

Northern Daily Telegraph (1898–1903)

Nottingham Evening Post (1893–9)
Nottinghamshire Guardian (1893)
Pateley Bridge & Nidderdale Herald (1898)
Perthshire Advertiser (1846)
Portsmouth Evening News (1890)
Portsmouth Times and Naval Gazette (1868)
Reynolds's Newspaper (1856–95)
Saunders's News-Letter (1810–56)
Sheffield Daily Telegraph (1897–1903)
Sheffield Independent (1878–95)
Sherborne Post (1859)
Shields Daily Gazette (1882)
Soulby's Ulverston Advertiser (1851)
South London Chronicle (1869)
South Wales Daily News (1872–99)
St. James's Gazette (1884–1903)
Sussex Agricultural Express (1892)
Taunton Courier, and Western Advertiser (1839)
The Age (1841)
The Berkshire Chronicle (1839–86)
The Birmingham Daily Post (1871–95)
The Blackburn Standard (1893–4)
The Bolton Chronicle (1836)
The Bournemouth Daily Echo (1903)
The Bradford Daily Telegraph (1886)
The Bridport News (1893)
The Cardiff Times (1893)
The Carlisle Patriot (1886)
The Carlow Post (1856)
The Chard and Ilminster News (1903)
The Chelmsford Chronicle (1833)
The Cheltenham Chronicle (1892)
The Citizen (1882–1903)
The Cork Constitution (1856)
The Devizes and Wiltshire Gazette (1822)
The Dover Telegraph and Cinque Ports General Advertiser (1850)
The Drogheda Argus (1837)
The Dublin Evening Packet and Correspondent (1856)
The Dublin Weekly Nation (1856)
The Eastern Evening News (1884)
The Elgin Courier (1857)

The Era (1856)
The Essex Standard (1884)
The Evening Freeman (1856)
The Evening News (1895)
The Examiner (1839–76)
The Falkirk Herald (1855–97)
The Freeman's Journal (1856)
The Gentleman's Magazine (1784)
The Glasgow Citizen (1845)
The Glasgow Gazette (1849–50)
The Glasgow Herald (1822–50)
The Globe (1839–81)
The Gloucester Citizen (1895)
The Hampshire Chronicle (1810–22)
The Horsham Advertiser (1880)
The Huddersfield Chronicle (1882–93)
The Hull Advertiser and Exchange Gazette (1822)
The Hull Packet and East Riding Times (1850)
The Illustrated London News (1846–95)
The Ipswich Journal (1857)
The Kent and Sussex Courier (1880)
The Ladies Journal (1896)
The Lancashire Daily Post (1895–1903)
The Leeds Mercury (1872)
The Leeds Times (1856–9)
The Leighton Buzzard Observer (1893)
The Lincolnshire Chronicle (1893)
The Liverpool Echo (1892)
The London Dispatch (1839)
The Manchester Courier and Lancashire General Advertiser (1845–1905)
The Manchester Guardian (1850)
The Manchester Mercury (1810)
The Manchester Weekly Times (1898)
The Morning Advertiser (1818–65)
The Morning Chronicle (1810–59)
The Morning Post (1808–99)
The Newry Reporter (1903)
The Newry Telegraph (1847)
The Norfolk Chronicle (1850)
The North Wales Chronicle (1892)
The Northern Daily Telegraph (1903)

The Northern Whig (1833–95)

The Nuneaton Advertiser (1893)

The Oxford Times (1876)

The Oxford University and City Herald (1810–22)

The Pall Mall Gazette (1872)

The Preston Chronicle (1872)

The Preston Herald (1903)

The Public Ledger and Daily Advertiser (1822)

The Royal Cornwall Gazette (1824–90)

The Scotsman (1822–92)

The Shields Daily News (1893–1903)

The Somerset County Gazette (1839)

The South Eastern Gazette (1850)

The South London Press (1889)

The South Wales Echo (1886–93)

The Staffordshire Advertiser (1839)

The Standard (1856–95)

The Star (1822)

The Sunderland Daily Echo and Shipping Gazette (1890)

The Tamworth Herald (1882–90)

The Teesdale Mercury (1864)

The Telegraph (1872–1903)

The Times (1850–99)

The Tralee Chronicle (1856)

The Tyrone Constitution (1856)

The Ulsterman (1856)

The Waterford Mail (1856)

The Wellington Journal (1893)

The Western Daily Press (1859)

The Western Gazette (1894)

The Whitney Express ((1880)

The Whitney Gazette (1888)

The Whitstable Times and Herne Bay Herald (1900)

The Wolverhampton Chronicle (1833)

The Worcestershire Chronicle (1893–1903)

The York Herald (1857–95)

The Yorkshire Post (1903)

Totnes Weekly Times (1903)

West Kent Guardian (1839)

Western Mail (1873)

Westmorland Gazette (1839–50)

Worcester Journal (1822–45)

Yorkshire Evening Post (1893–1903)
Yorkshire Gazette (1821)
Yorkshire Telegraph and Star (1903)
Young Folks Paper (1888)

Published material

Adams, James Eli. *Dandies and Desert Saints: Styles of Victorian Masculinity*. Ithaca, NY: Cornell University Press, 1995.

Aldrich, Robert. *Colonialism and Homosexuality*. London; New York, NY: Routledge, 2003.

Alker, Zoe, and Christopher Donaldson. 'Workflow'. *Journal of Victorian Culture* 22, no. 2 (1 June 2017): 222–3.

Alvarez, Al. *The Savage God: A Study of Suicide*. London: Bloomsbury, 2002.

Amy. 'The British Newspaper Archive – Launch Press Release (29/11/2012, 00:01)'. https://blog.britishnewspaperarchive.co.uk/2011/11/29/the-british-newspaper-archive-launch-press-release-29112012-0001/ (accessed 22 July 2019).

Anderson, Olive. 'The Growth of Christian Militarism in Mid-Victorian Britain'. *The English Historical Review* 86, no. 338 (1971): 46–72.

Anderson, Olive. *Suicide in Victorian and Edwardian England*. Oxford: Clarendon Press, 1987.

Appiah, Anthony. *The Honor Code: How Moral Revolutions Happen*. 1st edn. New York, NY: W.W. Norton, 2010.

Bailey, Joanne. '"A Very Sensible Man": Imagining Fatherhood in England c.1750–1830'. *History* 95, no. 3 (319) (2010): 267–92.

Bailey, Joanne. 'Masculinity and Fatherhood in England c. 1760–830'. In *What Is Masculinity?: Historical Dynamics from Antiquity to the Contemporary World*, edited by John Arnold and Sean Brady, 167–86. Genders and Sexualities in History. Houndmills, Basingstoke, Hampshire; New York, NY: Palgrave Macmillan, 2011.

Bailey, Victor. *This Rash Act: Suicide Across the Life Cycle in the Victorian City*. Stanford, CA: Stanford University Press, 1998.

Ballhatchet, Kenneth. *Race, Sex, and Class under the Raj: Imperial Attitudes and Policies and Their Critics, 1793–1905*. London: Weidenfeld and Nicolson, 1980.

Barrett, Matthew. '"Hero of the Half-Breed Rebellion": Gabriel Dumont and Late Victorian Military Masculinity'. *Journal of Canadian Studies/Revue d'études Canadiennes* 48, no. 3 (2014): 79–107.

Barrie, David G. 'Naming and Shaming: Trial by Media in Nineteenth-Century Scotland'. *Journal of British Studies* 54, no. 2 (2015): 349–76.

Baudelot, Christian, and Roger Establet. *Suicide: The Hidden Side of Modernity*. Cambridge, UK; Malden, MA: Polity Press, 2008.

Bayatrizi, Zohreh. *Life Sentences: The Modern Ordering of Mortality*. Toronto; Buffalo: University of Toronto Press, 2008.

Beer, Gillian. *Darwin's Plots: Evolutionary Narrative in Darwin, George Eliot, and Nineteenth-Century Fiction*. 2nd edn. Cambridge, UK; New York, NY: Cambridge University Press, 2000.

Bell, David A. 'Total History and Microhistory: The French and Italian Paradigms'. In *A Companion to Western Historical Thought*, edited by Lloyd Kramer and Sarah Maza, 262–76. Malden, MA: Blackwell Publishers, 2002.

Biddle, Jennifer. 'Shame'. In *Emotions: A Cultural Studies Reader*, edited by Jennifer Harding and E. Deidre Pribram, 1st edn, 113–25. Oxford; New York, NY: Routledge, 2009.

Birmes, Philippe, Leah Hatton, Alain Brunet and Laurent Schmitt. 'Early Historical Literature for Post-Traumatic Symptomatology'. *Stress and Health* 19, no. 1 (2003): 17–26.

Bonser, Thomas Owen. *The Right to Die*. London: Freethought Publishing Company, 1885.

Boone, Joseph Allen. 'Vacation Cruises; Or, the Homoerotics of Orientalism'. *PMLA* 110, no. 1 (1995): 89–107.

Boone, Joseph Allen. *The Homoerotics of Orientalism*. New York: Columbia University Press, 2014.

Booth, Charles. 'The Inhabitants of Tower Hamlets (School Board Division), Their Condition and Occupations'. *Journal of the Royal Statistical Society* 50, no. 2 (1887).

Bowlby, Anthony, Howard H. Tooth, Cuthbert Wallace, John E. Calverly and Charles R. Kilkelly. *A Civilian War Hospital: Being an Account of the Work of the Portland Hospital, and of Experience of Wounds and Sickness in South Africa, 1900*. London: John Murray, 1901.

Bradstock, Andrew, Sue Morgan, Sean Gill and Anne Hogan, eds. *Masculinity and Spirituality in Victorian Culture*. Basingstoke: Macmillan, 2000.

Brake, Laurel, Marysa Demoor, Margaret Beetham, Gowan Dawson, Odin Dekkers and Ian Haywood, eds. *Dictionary of Nineteenth-Century Journalism in Great Britain and Ireland*. Gent: Academia Press, 2009.

Braswell, Harold, and Howard I. Kushner. 'Suicide, Social Integration, and Masculinity in the U.S. Military'. *Social Science & Medicine* 74, no. 4 (2012): 530–6.

Breitenberg, Mark. *Anxious Masculinity in Early Modern England*. Cambridge Studies in Renaissance Literature and Culture 10. Cambridge; New York, NY: Cambridge University Press, 1996.

British Newspaper Archive. 'Home | Search the Archive | British Newspaper Archive'. https://www.britishnewspaperarchive.co.uk/ (accessed 22 July 2019).

Brodey, Inger Sigrun. 'Masculinity, Sensibility, and the "Man of Feeling": The Gendered Ethics of Goethe's Werther'. *Papers on Language and Literature* 35, no. 2 (March 1999): 115–40.

Bronstein, Jamie L. *Caught in the Machinery: Workplace Accidents and Injured Workers in Nineteenth-Century Britain*. Stanford, CA: Stanford University Press, 2008.

Brown, Richard D. 'Microhistory and the Post-Modern Challenge'. *Journal of the Early Republic* 23, no. 1 (2003): 1–20.

Burnett, John. *Idle Hands: The Experience of Unemployment, 1790–1990*. London; New York, NY: Routledge, 1994.

Burrows, George Mann. *Commentaries on the Causes, Forms, Symptoms, and Treatment, Moral and Medical, of Insanity*. London: Thomas and George Underwood, 1828.

Burrows, George Mann. 'Observations on the Comparative Mortality of Paris and London'. In *The History of Suicide in England, 1650–1850*, edited by Daryl Lee, vol. 7, 117–50. London: Pickering & Chatto, 2013.

Butler, Judith. *Gender Trouble: Feminism and the Subversion of Identity*. Routledge Classics. New York, NY: Routledge, 2006.

Campaign Against Living Miserably. 'What Is CALM?'. https://www.thecalmzone.net/about-calm/what-is-calm/ (accessed 9 May 2019).

Canetto, Silvia Sara. 'She Died for Love and He For Glory: Gender Myths of Suicidal Behaviour'. *Omega: Journal of Death and Dying* 26, no. 1 (1993): 1–17.

Claeys, Gregory. 'Malthus and Godwin: Rights, Utility and Productivity'. In *New Perspectives on Malthus*, edited by Robert J. Mayhew, 52–73. Cambridge, United Kingdom: Cambridge University Press, 2016.

Clark, Anna. 'The Rhetoric of Chartist Domesticity: Gender, Language, and Class in the 1830s and 1840s'. *Journal of British Studies* 31, no. 1 (1992): 62–88.

Clark, Anna. *The Struggle for the Breeches: Gender and the Making of the British Working Class*. Studies on the History of Society and Culture 23. Berkeley, CA: University of California Press, 1995.

Cleary, Anne. *The Gendered Landscape of Suicide: Masculinities, Emotions, and Culture*. Houndmills, Basingstoke, Hampshire; New York, NY: Palgrave Macmillan, 2019.

Cohen, Michèle. *Fashioning Masculinity: National Identity and Language in the Eighteenth Century*. London; New York, NY: Routledge, 1996.

Cohen, Michèle. 'Manliness, Effeminacy and the French: Gender and the Construction of National Character in Eighteenth-Century England'. In *English Masculinities, 1660–1800*, edited by Tim Hitchcock and Michèle Cohen, 44–62. Women and Men in History. New York, NY: Addison Wesley, 1999.

Coleman, Daniel, Mark S. Kaplan and John T. Casey. 'The Social Nature of Male Suicide: A New Analytic Model'. *International Journal of Men's Health* 10, no. 3 (1 October 2011): 240–52.

Collini, Stefan. *Public Moralists: Political Thought and Intellectual Life in Britain*. Oxford: Clarendon, 1991.

Connell, R. W. *Masculinities*. Cambridge: Polity Press, 1995.

Cox, Catherine. *Negotiating Insanity in the Southeast of Ireland, 1820–1900*. Oxford: Oxford University Press, 2018.

Daly, R. J. 'Samuel Pepys and Post-Traumatic Stress Disorder'. *British Journal of Psychiatry* 143, no. 1 (1983): 64–8.

Danahay, Martin A. *Gender at Work in Victorian Culture: Literature, Art and Masculinity*. The Nineteenth Century Series. Aldershot; Burlington: Ashgate, 2005.

Davidoff, Leonore, and Catherine Hall. *Family Fortunes*. Rev. edn. London; New York, NY: Routledge, 2002.

D'Cruze, Shani. 'The Eloquent Corpse: Gender, Probity, and Bodily Integrity in Victorian Domestic Murder'. In *Criminal Conversations: Victorian Crimes, Social Panic, and Moral Outrage*, edited by Judith Rowbotham and Kim Stevenson, 181–97. Columbus: Ohio State University Press, 2005.

Deane, Bradley. *Masculinity and the New Imperialism: Rewriting Manhood in British Popular Literature, 1870–1914*. New York, NY: Cambridge University Press, 2017.

Dickens, Charles. *Dombey and Son*. Hertfordshire: Wordsworth Editions, 1995.

Dickens, Charles. *Little Dorrit*. Hertfordshire: Wordsworth Editions, 2002.

Doolittle, Megan. 'Fatherhood and Family Shame: Masculinity, Welfare and the Workhouse in Late Nineteenth-Century England'. In *The Politics of Domestic Authority in Britain Since 1800*, edited by Lucy Delap, Ben Griffin and Abigail Wills, 84–108. Basingstoke, Hampshire; New York, NY: Palgrave Macmillan, 2009.

Douglas, Jack Daniel. *The Social Meanings of Suicide*. 2nd edn. Princeton Paperbacks. Princeton, NJ: Princeton Univ. Press, 1973.

Dowling, Linda. *Hellenism and Homosexuality in Victorian Oxford*. Ithaca, NY: Cornell University Press, 1994.

Durkheim, Émile. *Suicide: A Study in Sociology*. London: Routledge & Kegan Paul, 1970.

Durkheim, Émile. *On Suicide*. Translated by Robin Buss. Penguin classics. London: Penguin, 2006.

Edwards, Catharine. 'Modelling Roman Suicide? The Afterlife of Cato'. *Economy and Society* 34, no. 2 (1 May 2005): 200–22.

Englander, David. *Poverty and Poor Law Reform in Britain: From Chadwick to Booth, 1834–1914*. London: Routledge, 1998.

Esquirol, Jean-Étienne. *Mental Maladies. A Treatise on Insanity*. Translated by E. K. Hunt, M.D. Philadelphia, PA: Lea and Blanchard, 1845.

Evans, David Mourier. *Facts, Failure, and Frauds: Revelations, Financial, Mercantile, Criminal*. London: Groombridge & Sons, 1859.

Finn, Margot C. *The Character of Credit: Personal Debt in English* Culture, *1740–1914*. Cambridge Social and Cultural Histories 1. Cambridge; New York, NY: Cambridge University Press, 2003.

Fox, Pamela. *Class Fictions: Shame and Resistance in the British Working-Class Novel, 1890–1945*. Durham: Duke University Press, 1994.

Furneaux, Holly. *Military Men of Feeling: Emotion, Touch, and Masculinity in the Crimean War*. Oxford: Oxford University Press, 2016.

Gabriel, Richard A. *No More Heroes: Madness & Psychiatry in War*. 1st edn. New York, NY: Hill and Wang, 1987.

Garrison, Elise P. 'Attitudes toward Suicide in Ancient Greece'. *Transactions of the American Philological Association* 121 (1991): 1–34.

Gates, Barbara T. *Victorian Suicide: Mad Crimes and Sad Histories*. Princeton, NJ: Princeton University Press, 1988.

Gavin, Mike, and Anne Rogers. 'Narratives of Suicide in Psychological Autopsy: Bringing Lay Knowledge Back In'. *Journal of Mental Health* 15, no. 2 (January 2006): 135–44.

Ginzburg, Carlo. 'Microhistory: Two or Three Things That I Know about It'. Translated by John Tedeschi and Anne C. Tedeschi. *Critical Inquiry* 20, no. 1 (1993): 10–35.

Gissing, George. *The Whirlpool*. London: Hogarth Press, 1984.

Goc, Nicolá. *Women, Infanticide, and the Press, 1822–1922: News Narratives in England and Australia*. London: Routledge, 2016.

Goeschel, Christian. *Suicide in Nazi Germany*. Oxford; New York, NY: Oxford University Press, 2009.

Grandy, Christine. 'Cultural History's Absent Audience'. *Cultural and Social History* 16, no. 5 (20 October 2019): 643–63.

Gregory, Benjamin. *The Thorough Business Man: Memoirs of Walter Powell, Merchant, Melbourne and London*. 2nd edn. London: Strahan & Co., 1872.

Gregory, Brad S. 'Is Small Beautiful? Microhistory and the History of Everyday Life'. Edited by Alf Lüdtke, William Templer and Jacques Revel. *History and Theory* 38, no. 1 (1999): 100–10.

Gregory, George. *A Sermon on Suicide*. London: J. Nichols; and sold by C. Dilly, Messrs. F. and C. Rivington, J. Johnson and J. Hookham, 1797.

Guest, Kristen. 'The Subject of Money: Late-Victorian Melodrama's Crisis of Masculinity'. *Victorian Studies* 49, no. 4 (2007): 635–57.

Gurnhill, Rev. J. *The Morals of Suicide*. London: Longmans, Green, and Co., 1900.

Hacking, Ian. *The Taming of Chance*. Ideas in Context. Cambridge; New York, NY: Cambridge University Press, 1990.

Hacking, Ian. 'The Suicide Weapon'. *Critical Inquiry* 35, no. 1 (1 September 2008): 1–32.

Hall, Donald E., ed. *Muscular Christianity: Embodying the Victorian Age*. Cambridge Studies in Nineteenth-Century Literature and Culture 2. Cambridge; New York, NY: Cambridge University Press, 1994.

Hardy, Thomas. *Jude the Obscure*. London: Penguin, 1998.

Henry, Nancy. '"Rushing into Eternity": Suicide and Finance in Victorian Fiction'. In *Victorian Investments: New Perspectives on Finance and Culture*, edited by Nancy Henry and Cannon Schmitt, 161–81. Bloomington, IN: Indiana University Press, 2009.

Higonnet, Margaret. 'Suicide: Representations of the Feminine in the Nineteenth Century'. *Poetics Today* 6, no. 1/2 (1985): 103–18.

Higonnet, Margaret. 'Speaking Silences: Women's Suicide'. In *The Female Body in Western Culture: Contemporary Perspectives*, edited by Susan Rubin Suleiman, 68–83. Cambridge, MA: Harvard University Press, 1986.

Hilton, Boyd. *The Age of Atonement: The Influence of Evangelicalism on Social and Economic Thought, 1785–1865*. Oxford: Clarendon Press, 1991.

Hitchcock, Tim, and Michèle Cohen, eds. *English Masculinities, 1660–1800*. Women and Men in History. New York: Addison Wesley, 1999.

Hittner, James B. 'How Robust Is the Werther Effect? A Re-Examination of the Suggestion-Imitation Model of Suicide'. *Mortality* 10, no. 3 (1 August 2005): 193–200.

Hobbs, Andrew. 'The Deleterious Dominance of *The Times* in Nineteenth-Century Scholarship'. *Journal of Victorian Culture* 18, no. 4 (December 2013): 472–97.

Houlbrook, Matt. *Prince of Tricksters: The Incredible True Story of Netley Lucas, Gentleman Crook*. Chicago, IL; London: University of Chicago Press, 2016.

Houston, R. A. *Punishing the Dead?: Suicide, Lordship, and Community in Britain, 1500–1830*. Oxford; New York, NY: Oxford University Press, 2010.

Houston, R. A. 'Fact, Truth, and the Limits of Sympathy: Newspaper Reporting of Suicide in the North of England, circa 1750–1830'. *Studies in the Literary Imagination* 44, no. 2 (2011): 93–108.

Houston, R. A. 'Explanations for Death by Suicide in Northern Britain during the Long Eighteenth Century'. *History of Psychiatry* 23, no. 1 (1 March 2012): 52–64.

Hunter, Leeann. 'Communities Built from Ruins: Social Economics in Victorian Novels of Bankruptcy'. *Women's Studies Quarterly* 39, no. 3/4 (2011): 137–52.

Hyam, Ronald. *Empire and Sexuality: The British Experience*. Manchester: Manchester University Press, 1998.

Iemmi, Valentina, Jason Bantjes, Ernestina Coast, Kerrie Channer, Tiziana Leone, David McDaid, Alexis Palfreyman, Bevan Stephens and Crick Lund. 'Suicide and Poverty in Low-Income and Middle-Income Countries: A Systematic Review'. *The Lancet Psychiatry* 3, no. 8 (1 August 2016): 774–83.

Israel, Kali. *Names and Stories: Emilia Dilke and Victorian Culture*. New York, NY: Oxford University Press, 1999.

Ittmann, Karl. *Work, Gender and Family in Victorian England*. Basingstoke: Macmillan, 1995.

James, William. *The Naval History of Great Britain*. Vol. V. London: Baldwin, Craddock, and Joy, 1824.

Jaworski, Katrina. *The Gender of Suicide: Knowledge Production, Theory and Suicidology*. Farnham, Surrey: Ashgate, 2014.

Johnson, Paul. 'Civilizing Mammon: Laws, Morals, and the City in Nineteenth-Century England'. In *Civil Histories: Essays Presented to Sir Keith Thomas*, edited by Peter Burke, Brian Howard Harrison and Paul Slack, 301–20. Oxford; New York, NY: Oxford University Press, 2000.

Johnson, Paul. *Making the Market: Victorian Origins of Corporate Capitalism*. Cambridge Studies in Economic History. Cambridge; New York, NY: Cambridge University Press, 2010.

Jonas, Klaus. 'Modelling and Suicide: A Test of the Werther Effect'. *British Journal of Social Psychology* 31, no. 4 (1 December 1992): 295–306.

Jones, Aled. *Powers of the Press: Newspapers, Power and the Public in Nineteenth-Century England*. The Nineteenth Century. Aldershot, England: Brookfield, VT: Scolar Press; Ashgate, 1996.

Jones, Edgar, and Simon Wessely. 'Psychiatric Battle Casualties: An Intra- and Interwar Comparison'. *British Journal of Psychiatry* 178, no. 3 (March 2001): 242–7.

Jones, Edgar, and Simon Wessely. 'War Syndromes: The Impact of Culture on Medically Unexplained Symptoms'. *Medical History* 49, no. 1 (2005): 55–78.

Jones, Edgar, Robert Hodgins Vermaas, Helen McCartney, Charlotte Beech, Ian Palmer, Kenneth Hyams and Simon Wessely. 'Flashbacks and Post-Traumatic Stress Disorder: The Genesis of a 20th-Century Diagnosis.' *The British Journal of Psychiatry* 182, no. 2 (2003): 158–63.

Jones, Joanne. '"She Resisted with All Her Might": Sexual Violence against Women in Late Nineteenth-Century Manchester Press.' In *Everyday Violence in Britain, 1850–1950: Gender and Class*, edited by Shani D'Cruze, 104–18. Women and Men in History. Harlow, England; New York, NY: Longman, 2000.

Jones, Kingsmill Williams. 'Delirium in Febrile Conditions.' *Dublin Journal of Medical Science (1872–1920)* 115, no. 6 (1 June 1903): 420–2.

Jones, Owen. 'Suicide and Silence: Why Depressed Men Are Dying for Somebody to Talk To.' *The Guardian*, 15 August 2014.

Kelly, Linda. *The Marvellous Boy: The Life and Myth of Thomas Chatterton*. London: Faber and Faber, 2008.

Kerr, William C., Mark S. Kaplan, Nathalie Huguet, Raul Caetano, Norman Giesbrecht and Bentson H. McFarland. 'Economic Recession, Alcohol, and Suicide Rates: Comparative Effects of Poverty, Foreclosure, and Job Loss.' *American Journal of Preventive Medicine* 52, no. 4 (1 April 2017): 469–75.

Kilday, Anne-Marie, and David Nash. *Shame and Modernity in Britain: 1890 to the Present*. London: Palgrave Macmillan, 2017.

Klaver, Claudia C. *A/Moral Economics: Classical Political Economy and Cultural Authority in Nineteenth-Century England*. Columbus, OH: Ohio State University Press, 2003.

Kopelson, Kevin. 'Saint-Saëns's Samson.' In *Masculinity in Opera*, edited by Philip Purvis, 105–20. New York: Routledge, 2013.

Krishnaswamy, Revathi. *Effeminism: The Economy of Colonial Desire*. Ann Arbor, MI: University of Michigan Press, 1998.

Kuruvilla, A., and K. S. Jacob. 'Poverty, Social Stress & Mental Health.' *Indian Journal of Medical Research* 126, no. 4 (2007): 273–8.

Kushner, Howard I. 'Women and Suicide in Historical Perspective.' *Signs* 10, no. 3 (Spring 1985): 537–52.

Kushner, Tony. 'Oral History at the Extremes of Human Experience: Holocaust Testimony in a Museum Setting.' *Oral History* 29, no. 2 (2001): 83–94.

Lane, Christopher. *The Ruling Passion: British Colonial Allegory and the Paradox of Homosexual Desire*. Durham: Duke University Press, 1995.

Laragy, Georgina. '"A Peculiar Species of Felony": Suicide, Medicine, and the Law in Victorian Britain and Ireland.' *Journal of Social History* 46, no. 3 (1 March 2013): 732–43.

Lathrop, Joseph. *Two Sermons on the Atrocity of Suicide: And on the Causes Which Lead to It*. Springfield, IL: Brewer, 1805.

Leaver, Kristen. 'Victorian Melodrama and the Performance of Poverty.' *Victorian Literature and Culture* 27, no. 2 (1999): 443–56.

Lemire, Beverly. *The Business of Everyday Life: Gender, Practice and Social Politics in England, c.1600–1900*. Gender in History. Manchester: Manchester University Press, 2005.

Lester, David, John F. Gunn III and Paul Quinnett, eds. *Suicide in Men: How Men Differ from Women in Expressing Their Distress*. Springfield, IL: Charles C. Thomas, Publisher, Ltd, 2014.

Levé, Edouard. *Suicide*. Translated by Jan H. Steyn. 1st edn. Champaign, IL: Dalkey Archive Press, 2011.

Levine, Philippa. 'Sexuality, Gender, and Empire'. In *Gender and Empire*, edited by Philippa Levine, 134–55. Oxford; New York, NY: Oxford University Press, 2004.

Levine-Clark, Marjorie. '"Embarrassed Circumstances": Gender, Poverty, and Insanity in the West Riding of England in the Early-Victorian Years'. In *Sex and Seclusion, Class and Custody: Perspectives on Gender and Class in the History of British and Irish Psychiatry*, edited by Johnathan Andrews and Anne Digby, 123–48. Amsterdam: Rodopi, 2004.

Levine-Clark, Marjorie. *Unemployment, Welfare, and Masculine Citizenship: 'So Much Honest Poverty' in Britain, 1870–1930*. Basingstoke: Palgrave Macmillan, 2015.

Liggins, Emma. 'Her Resolution to Die: "Wayward Women" and Constructions of Suicide in Wilkie Collins's Crime Fiction'. *Wilkie Collins Society Journal* 4 (2001).

Long, Orie W. 'English Translations of Goethe's Werther'. *The Journal of English and Germanic Philology* 14, no. 2 (1915): 169–203.

MacDonald, Michael. 'Suicide and the Rise of the Popular Press in England'. *Representations*, no. 22 (1988): 36–55.

MacDonald, Michael. 'The Medicalization of Suicide in England: Laymen, Physicians, and Cultural Change, 1500–1870'. *The Milbank Quarterly* 67 (1989): 69–91.

Macleod, Kenneth I. E. *The Ranker: The Story of Sir Hector Macdonald's Death*. Cortland, NY: the author, 1976.

MacMunn, Sir George. *The Underworld of India*. London: Jarrolds, 1933.

Malthus, Thomas. *An Essay on the Principle of Population: Or. A View of Its Past and Present Effects on Human Happiness*. 2nd edn. London: J. Johnson, 1803.

Malthus, Thomas. *An Essay on the Principle of Population: Or. A View of Its Past and Present Effects on Human Happiness*. Vol. 1. 4th edn. London: J. Johnson, 1807.

Mandler, Peter, ed. *Liberty and Authority in Victorian Britain*. Oxford: Oxford University Press, 2006.

Mangan, J. A. 'Duty unto Death: English Masculinity and Militarism in the Age of the New Imperialism'. *The International Journal of the History of Sport* 27, no. 1–2 (1 January 2010): 124–49.

Marcus. *On the Possibility of Limiting Populousness*. London: John Hill, 1838.

Marks, Alan H. 'Historical Suicide'. In *Handbook of Death and Dying*, edited by Clifton D Bryant, vol. 1, 309–18. California: Sage, 2003.

Marsh, Ian. *Suicide: Foucault, History and Truth*. Cambridge: Cambridge University Press, 2010.

Marshall, Alfred. *Principles of Economics*. Vol. 1. London; New York, NY: Macmillan, 1890.

Marshall, John. *Royal Naval Biography*. Vol II. Part II. London: Longman, Rees, Orme, Brown & Green, 1825.

Masterson, Margery. 'Dueling, Conflicting Masculinities, and the Victorian Gentleman'. *Journal of British Studies* 56, no. 3 (2017): 605–28.

Maudsley, Henry. *The Physiology and Pathology of the Mind*. London: Macmillan, 1867.

Mayer, David. 'Encountering Melodrama'. In *The Cambridge Companion to Victorian and Edwardian Theatre*, edited by Kerry Powell, 145–63. Cambridge Companions to Literature. Cambridge, UK; New York, NY: Cambridge University Press, 2004.

Mayhew, Henry. *London Labour and the London Poor: The Condition and Earnings of Those That Will Work, Cannot Work, and Will Not Work*. Vol. 1. 4 vols. London: George Woodfall and Son, 1851.

McDonagh, Josephine. *Child Murder and British Culture, 1720–1900*. Cambridge: Cambridge University Press, 2003.

McGuire, Kelly. 'True Crime: Contagion, Print Culture, and Herbert Croft's *Love and Madness; or, A Story Too True*'. *Eighteenth-Century Fiction* 24, no. 1 (2011): 55–75.

McGuire, Kelly. *Dying to Be English: Suicide Narratives and National Identity, 1721–1814*. Gender and Genre 8. London; Brookfield, VT: Pickering & Chatto, 2012.

McWilliam, Rohan. 'Melodrama and the Historians'. *Radical History Review* 2000, no. 78 (2000): 57–84.

McWilliam, Rohan. 'Melodrama'. In *A Companion to Sensation Fiction*, edited by Pamela K. Gilbert, 54–66. Blackwell Companions to Literature and Culture 75. Malden, MA: Wiley-Blackwell, 2011.

Mercier, Charles. *Sanity and Insanity*. London: Walter Scott, 1890.

Millar, W. H. 'Statistics of Death by Suicide among Her Majesty's British Troops Serving at Home and Abroad During the Ten Years 1862–71'. *Journal of the Statistical Society of London* 37, no. 2 (1874).

Miller, Ian. 'Representations of Suicide in Urban North-West England c.1870–1910: The Formative Role of Respectability, Class, Gender and Morality'. *Mortality* 15, no. 3 (August 2010): 191–204.

Mills, China. '"Dead People Don't Claim": A Psychopolitical Autopsy of UK Austerity Suicides'. *Critical Social Policy* 38, no. 2 (17 August 2017): 302–22.

Milne-Smith, Amy. 'Shattered Minds: Madmen on the Railways, 1860–80'. *Journal of Victorian Culture* 21, no. 1 (2 January 2016): 21–39.

Milroy, C.M. 'Homicide Followed by Suicide: Remorse or Revenge?' *Journal of Clinical Forensic Medicine* 5, no. 2 (1 June 1998): 61–4.

Moore, Charles. *A Full Inquiry into the Subject of Suicide*. Vol. 2. London: J. F. and C. Rivington, 1790.

Morrissey, Susan K. *Suicide and the Body Politic in Imperial Russia*. Cambridge Social and Cultural Histories 9. Cambridge, UK; New York, NY: Cambridge University Press, 2006.

Morselli, Enrico Agostino. *Suicide: An Essay on Comparative Moral Statistics*. New York, NY: D. Appleton and Company, 1882.

Munslow, Alun. 'Genre and History/Historying'. *Rethinking History* 19, no. 2 (3 April 2015): 158–76.

Murray, Alexander. *Suicide in the Middle Ages: The Violent against Themselves*. Oxford; New York: Oxford University Press, 1998.

Nagel, Joane. 'Masculinity and Nationalism: Gender and Sexuality in the Making of Nations'. *Ethnic and Racial Studies* 21, no. 2 (1 January 1998): 242–69.

Nash, David, and Anne-Marie Kilday. *Cultures of Shame: Exploring Crime and Morality in Britain 1600–1900*. Houndmills, Basingstoke; New York, NY: Palgrave Macmillan, 2010.

Navickas, Katrina, and Adam Crymble. 'From Chartist Newspaper to Digital Map of Grass-Roots Meetings, 1841–44: Documenting Workflows'. *Journal of Victorian Culture* 22, no. 2 (1 June 2017): 232–47.

Nicoletti, Lisa J. 'Resuscitating Ophelia: Images of Suicide and Suicidal Insanity in Nineteenth-Century England'. Madison, WI: University of Wisconcin, 1999.

Ogle, William. 'Suicides in England and Wales in Relation to Age, Sex, Season, and Occupation'. *Journal of the Statistical Society of London* 49, no. 1 (1886).

Oliffe, John L., Christina S. E. Han, Murray Drummond, Estephanie Sta. Maria, Joan L. Bottorff and Genevieve Creighton. 'Men, Masculinities, and Murder-Suicide'. *American Journal of Men's Health* 9, no. 6 (7 October 2014): 473–85.

O'Shea, James. *Prince of Swindlers: John Sadleir, M.P. 1813–1856*. Dublin: Geography Publications, 1999.

Owens, Christabel, and Helen Lambert. 'Mad, Bad, or Heroic? Gender, Identitty and Accountability in Lay Portrayals of Suicide in Late Twentieth-Century England'. *Culture, Medicine, and Psychiatry* 36 (2012): 348–71.

Paperno, Irina. *Suicide as a Cultural Institution in Dostoevsky's Russia*. Ithaca, NY: Cornell University Press, 1997.

Perceval, Arthur Phillip. *A Clergyman's Defence of Himself, for Refusing to Use the Office for the Burial of the Dead Over One Who Destroyed Himself, Notwithstanding the Coroner's Verdict of Mental Derangement*. London: J. G. Irvington, 1833.

Perkin, Harold James. *The Origins of Modern English Society*. London: Routledge, 2002.

Phillips, David P. 'The Influence of Suggestion on Suicide: Substantive and Theoretical Implications of the Werther Effect'. *American Sociological Review* 39, no. 3 (1974): 340–54.

Poovey, Mary. *Genres of the Credit Economy: Mediating Value in Eighteenth- and Nineteenth-Century Britain*. Chicago, IL: University of Chicago Press, 2008.

Prichard, James Cowles. *On the Different Forms of Insanity, in Relation to Jurisprudence, Designed for the Use of Persons Concerned in Legal Questions Regarding Unsoundness of Mind*. London: Hippolyte Baillière, 1842.

'Probable Suicides 2020'. Edinburgh: National Records of Scotland, 17 August 2021.

Ratcliffe, Barrie M. 'Suicides in the City: Perceptions and Realities of Self-Destruction in Paris in the First Half of the Nineteenth Century'. *Historical Reflections/Réflexions Historiques* 18, no. 1 (1992): 1–70.

Reed, John R. 'A Friend to Mammon: Speculation in Victorian Literature'. *Victorian Studies* 27, no. 2 (1984): 179–202.

'Registrar General Northern Ireland Annual Report 2019'. Belfast: Northern Ireland Statistics and Research Agency, 16 December 2020.

Richmond, Vivienne. *Clothing the Poor in Nineteenth-Century England*. Cambridge; New York, NY: Cambridge University Press, 2013.

Robb, George. *White-Collar Crime in Modern England: Financial Fraud and Business Morality, 1845–1929*. Cambridge, UK; New York, NY: Cambridge University Press, 1992.

Roberts, Robert. *The Classic Slum: Salford Life in the First Quarter of the Century*. Manchester: Manchester University Press, 1971.

Roberts, W. 'Life on a Guinea a Week'. *The Nineteenth Century: A Monthly Review* 23, no. 133 (March 1888): 464–7.

Rodger, N. A. M. 'Honour and Duty at Sea, 1660–1815'. *Historical Research* 75, no. 190 (16 December 2002): 425–47.

Roper, Michael, and John Tosh, eds. *Manful Assertions: Masculinities in Britain since 1800*. London; New York, NY: Routledge, 1991.

Rose, Sonya O. *Limited Livelihoods: Gender and Class in Nineteenth-Century England*. London: Routledge, 1992.

Rothschild, Emma. 'Political Economy'. In *The Cambridge History of Nineteenth-Century Political Thought*, edited by Gareth Stedman Jones and Gregory Claeys, 748–79. The Cambridge History of Political Thought. Cambridge; New York, NY: Cambridge University Press, 2011.

Rowley, William. *A Treatise on Female, Nervous, Hypochondriacal, Bilious, Convulsive Diseases; Apoplexy and Palsy; with Thoughts on Madness, Suicide, &c.* London: C. Nourse, 1788.

Royle, Trevor. *Death Before Dishonour: The True Story of Fighting Mac*. Edinburgh: Mainstream, 1982.

Russell, Norman. *The Novelist and Mammon: Literary Responses to the World of Commerce in the Nineteenth Century*. Oxford; New York, NY: Clarendon Press; Oxford University Press, 1986.

Said, Edward W. *Orientalism*. New Delhi: Penguin Books, 1995.

Scheff, Thomas J. 'Shame and the Social Bond: A Sociological Theory'. *Sociological Theory* 18, no. 1 (1 March 2000): 84–99.

Scherr, Sebastian, and Carsten Reinemann. 'Belief in a Werther Effect: Third-Person Effects in the Perceptions of Suicide Risk for Others and the Moderating Role of Depression'. *Suicide and Life-Threatening Behavior* 41, no. 6 (1 December 2011): 624–34.

Schiffman, Robyn L. 'A Concert of Werthers'. *Eighteenth-Century Studies* 43, no. 2 (2010): 207–22.

Seccombe, Wally. 'Patriarchy Stabilized: The Construction of the Male Breadwinner Wage Norm in Nineteenth-Century Britain'. *Social History* 11, no. 1 (1986): 53–76.

Shannon, Brent. '"The Terrible Mälestrom of Debt": Credit, Consumption, and Masculinity in Oxbridge Fiction, 1841–1911'. *Victorian Literature and Culture* 44, no. 2 (2016): 385–407.

Shenton, Bob. 'Suicide and Surplus People/Value'. *Identities* 18, no. 1 (1 January 2011): 63–8.

Shepherd, Jade. '"One of the Best Fathers until He Went Out of His Mind": Paternal Child-Murder, 1864–1900'. *Journal of Victorian Culture* 18, no. 1 (March 2013): 17–35.

Shoemaker, Robert B. 'The Taming of the Duel: Masculinity, Honour and Ritual Violence in London, 1660–1800'. *The Historical Journal* 45, no. 3 (2002): 525–45.

Silkenat, David. *Moments of Despair: Suicide, Divorce, & Debt in Civil War Era North Carolina.* Chapel Hill, NC: University of North Carolina Press, 2011.

Sinha, Mrinalini. *Colonial Masculinity: The 'manly Englishman' and the 'Effeminate Bengali' in the Late Nineteenth Century.* Studies in Imperialism. Manchester; New York, NY: Manchester University Press, 1995.

Slakey, Roger L. 'Melmotte's Death: A Prism of Meaning in the Way We Live Now'. *ELH* 34, no. 2 (1967): 248–59.

Small, Helen. *Love's Madness: Medicine, the Novel, and Female Insanity, 1800–1865.* Reprinted. Oxford: Clarendon Press, 2007.

Smiles, Samuel. *Self-Help: With Illustrations of Character, Conduct, and Perseverance.* London: John Murray, 1868.

Smith, Sydney. 'On Suicide'. In *Two Volumes of Sermons,* edited by Sydney Smith, vol. 2, 127–42. London: T. Cadell and W. Davies, 1809.

Society for the Promotion of Christian Knowledge. 'Suicide; Its Guilt and Punishment. Earnestly Addressed to All Classes, Particularly Those in Humble Life'. In *Religious Tracts Circulated by the Society for Promoting Christian Knowledge,* Vol. 3. London: Printed for the Society for Promoting Christian Knowledge, 1836.

Sommerville, Diane Miller. '"A Burden Too Heavy to Bear": War Trauma, Suicide, and Confederate Soldiers'. *Civil War History* 59, no. 4 (2013): 453–91.

Sommerville, Diane Miller. *Aberration of Mind: Suicide and Suffering in the Civil War-Era South.* Chapel Hill, NC: University of North Carolina Press, 2018.

'Statistical Bulletin: Suicides in England and Wales: 2020 Registrations'. Office for National Statistics, 7 September 2021. https://www.ons.gov.uk/peoplepopulationandcommunity/birthsdeathsandmarriages/deaths/bulletins/suicidesintheunitedkingdom/2020registrations (accessed 22 November 2021).

'Statistics of Insanity'. *British Medical Journal* s1-9, no. 51 (1845): 739.

Stearn, Roger T. 'Macdonald, Sir Hector Archibald (1853–1903), Army Officer and Popular Hero'. Oxford Dictionary of National Biography, 22 September 2011. https://www.oxforddnb.com/view/10.1093/ref:odnb/9780198614128.001.0001/odnb-9780198614128-e-34702 (accessed 22 November 2021).

Steedman, Carolyn. 'On Not Writing Biography'. *New Formations* 67 (1 June 2009): 15–24.

Steinlight, E. 'Hardy's Unnecessary Lives: The Novel as Surplus'. *Novel: A Forum on Fiction* 47, no. 2 (1 June 2014): 224–41.

Stewart, Frank Henderson. *Honor*. Chicago, IL: University of Chicago Press, 1994.

Stewart, Hugh Grainger. *On Hereditary Insanity*. London: Printed by J. E. Adlard, 1864.

Streets, Heather. *Martial Races: The Military, Race and Masculinity in British Imperial Culture, 1857–1914*. Manchester; New York, NY: Manchester University Press, 2004.

Stuckler, David, and Sanjay Basu. *The Body Economic: Eight Experiments in Economic Recovery, from Iceland to Greece*. London: Penguin Books, 2014.

Summerfield, Derek. 'The Invention of Post-Traumatic Stress Disorder and the Social Usefulness of a Psychiatric Category'. *British Medical Journal* 322, no. 7278 (13 January 2001): 95–8.

Suzuki, Akihito. 'Lunacy and Labouring Men: Narratives of Male Vulnerability in Mid-Victorian London'. In *Medicine, Madness and Social History: Essays in Honour of Roy Porter*, edited by Roberta Bivins and John V. Pickstone, 118–28. Basingstoke: Palgrave Macmillan, 2007.

Taylor, James. 'Company Fraud in Victorian Britain: The Royal British Bank Scandal of 1856'. *The English Historical Review* 122, no. 497 (2007): 700–24.

Taylor, James. *Boardroom Scandal: The Criminalization of Company Fraud in Nineteenth-Century Britain*. Oxford: Oxford University Press, 2013.

Telegraph Men. '"A Crisis of Masculinity": Men Are Struggling to Cope with Life'. *The Telegraph*, 19 November 2014.

Thackwell, J. *Narrative of the Second Sikh War in 1848–49. With a Detailed Account of the Battles of Ramnugger, the Passage of the Chenab, Chillianwallah, Goojerat, &c.* 2nd edn. London: Richard Bentley, 1851.

Thomas, Kyla, and David Gunnell. 'Suicide in England and Wales 1861–2007: A Time-Trends Analysis'. *International Journal of Epidemiology* 39, no. 6 (2 June 2010): 1464–75.

Tosh, John. *A Man's Place: Masculinity and the Middle-Class Home in Victorian England*. New Haven, CT; London: Yale University Press, 1999.

Tosh, John. *Manliness and Masculinities in Nineteenth-Century Britain: Essays on Gender, Family, and* Empire. 1st edn. Women and Men in History. Harlow, England; New York, NY: Pearson Longman, 2005.

Tosh, John. 'Masculinities in an Industrializing Society: Britain, 1800–1914'. *Journal of British Studies* 44, no. 2 (2005): 330–42.

Tosh, John. 'Home and Away: The Flight from Domesticity in Late-Nineteenth-Century England Re-Visited'. *Gender & History* 27, no. 3 (1 November 2015): 561–75.

Trollope, Anthony. *The Way We Live Now*. Hertfordshire: Wordsworth Editions, 1995.

Trollope, Anthony. *The Prime Minister*. Oxford; New York, NY: Oxford University Press, 2011.

Vance, Norman. *The Sinews of the Spirit: The Ideal of Christian Manliness in Victorian Literature and Religious Thought*. Cambridge; New York, NY: Cambridge University Press, 1985.

Vicinus, Martha. "'Helpless and Unfriended': Nineteenth-Century Domestic Melodrama'. *New Literary History* 13, no. 1 (1981): 127–43.

Wagner, Tamara S. 'Speculators at Home in the Victorian Novel: Making Stock-Market Villains and New Paper Fictions'. *Victorian Literature and Culture* 36, no. 1 (2008): 21–40.

Wagner, Tamara S. *Financial Speculation in Victorian Fiction: Plotting Money and the Novel Genre, 1815–1901*. Columbus, OH: Ohio State University Press, 2010.

Waller, John C. 'Ideas of Heredity, Reproduction and Eugenics in Britain, 1800–1875'. *Studies in History and Philosophy of Science Part C: Studies in History and Philosophy of Biological and Biomedical Sciences* 32, no. 3 (1 September 2001): 457–89.

Wasserman, Ira M. 'Imitation and Suicide: A Reexamination of the Werther Effect'. *American Sociological Review* 49, no. 3 (1984): 427–36.

Weaver, John C. *A Sadly Troubled History: The Meanings of Suicide in the Modern Age*. 33. Montréal; Ithaca, NY: McGill-Queen's University Press, 2009.

Weaver, John C. and David Wright, eds, *Histories of Suicide: International Perspectives on Self-Destruction in the Modern World*. Toronto: University of Toronto Press, 2009.

Weber, Max. *The Protestant Ethic and the Spirit of Capitalism*. Routledge Classics. London; New York, NY: Routledge, 2001.

Weiss, Barbara. *The Hell of the English: Bankruptcy and the Victorian Novel*. Lewisburg; London; Cranbury, NJ: Bucknell University Press; Associated University Presses, 1986.

Welsh, Alexander. *What Is Honor? A Question of Moral Imperatives*. New Haven, CT: Yale University Press, 2008.

White, Hayden. 'The Value of Narrativity in the Representation of Reality'. *Critical Inquiry* 7, no. 1 (1980): 5–27.

White, Hayden. 'The Question of Narrative in Contemporary Historical Theory'. *History and Theory* 23, no. 1 (1984): 1–33.

WHO. *Preventing Suicide: A Resource for Media Professionals*. Geneva: WHO, 2000.

WHO. *Preventing Suicide: A Resource for Media Professionals*. Geneva: WHO, 2008.

WHO. *Preventing Suicide: A Resource for Media Professionals*. Geneva: WHO, 2017.

Wiener, Joel H. 'The Nineteenth Century and the Emergence of a Mass Circulation Press'. In *The Routledge Companion to British Media History*, edited by Martin Conboy and John Steel, 206–14. London: Routledge: 2015.

Williams, Carolyn. 'Melodrama'. In *The Cambridge History of Victorian Literature*, edited by Kate Flint, 193–219. The New Cambridge History of English Literature. Cambridge; New York, NY: Cambridge University Press, 2012.

Winslow, Forbes. *The Anatomy of Suicide*. London: Henry Renshaw, 1840.

Winslow, Forbes. 'The Overworked Mind'. *The Journal of Psychological Medicine and Mental Pathology* V (1852).

Wyllie, Clare, Stephen Platt, Julie Brownlie, Amy Chandler, Sheela Connolly, Rhiannon Evans, Brendan Kennelly, et al. 'Men, Suicide and Society: Why Disadvantaged Men in Mid-Life Die by Suicide'. Samaritans, September 2012.

Young, Allan. *The Harmony of Illusions: Inventing Post-Traumatic Stress Disorder.* Princeton, NJ: Princeton University Press, 2001.

Zadorojnyi, Alexei V. 'Cato's Suicide in Plutarch'. *The Classical Quarterly* 57, no. 1 (2007): 216–30.

Index

and identity 119
a symbol of masculinity 96–7, 118
views on 96–7
Weber, Max 16, 63–4, 96–7 (*see also*
    Protestant ethic)
White-collar crime 94–5, 108–11, 114

Winslow, Forbes 25, 28, 33–4, 55 n.89,
    100, 107, 115
work
    changing landscape of 4, 69
    and gender 69–70
workhouses 58–9, 76–9

Lightning Source UK Ltd.
Milton Keynes UK
UKHW021841130522
402981UK00003B/281